MUTUAL FUNDS AND RRSPs ONLINE

ONLINE

Jim Carroll
Rick Broadhead

Prentice Hall Canada Inc.
Scarborough, Ontario

Canadian Cataloguing in Publication Data

Carroll, Jim, 1959-
    Mutual funds and RRSPs online: a financial guide for
    every Canadian

ISBN 0-13-776436-7

1. Finance, Personal - Canada - Computer network resources.
2. Internet (Computer network). 3. World Wide Web
(Information retrieval system).
I. Broadhead, Rick. II. Title.

HG179.C295 1997   332.02400285467   C97-932418-1

 © 1997 J.A. Carroll and Rick Broadhead

Prentice-Hall, Inc., Upper Saddle River, New Jersey
Prentice-Hall International (UK) Limited, London
Prentice-Hall of Australia, Pty. Limited, Sydney
Prentice-Hall Hispanoamericana, S.A., Mexico City
Prentice-Hall of India Private Limited, New Delhi
Prentice-Hall of Japan, Inc., Tokyo
Simon & Schuster Southeast Asia Private Limited, Singapore
Editora Prentice-Hall do Brasil, Ltda., Rio de Janeiro

ISBN 0-13-776436-7

Director, Trade Group: Robert Harris
Copy Editor: Catharine Haggert
Production Editor: Kelly Dickson
Production Coordinator: Julie Preston
Editorial Assistant: Joan Whitman
Art Director: Mary Opper
Cover Design: Sputnik
Cover Photograph: Tony Stone/David Crosier
Page Layout: Jack Steiner

1 2 3 4 5   W   01 00 99 98 97

Printed and bound in Canada

Neither the publisher nor author is rendering professional or
legal advice in this book. If such assistance is required, the
services of a qualified professional should be sought. Every
effort has been made to ensure that the resources listed in
this book were correct at the time of printing. Neither the
author nor the publisher shall be liable for any errors or
omissions in data, nor for any damages that may occur from
the use of any resource contained in this book.

Visit the Prentice Hall Canada Web site! Send us your comments, browse our catalogues, and more. **www.phcanada.com**

TABLE OF CONTENTS

CONVENTIONS USED IN THIS BOOK

To access the resources listed in this book, you will need to have access to the Internet and know how to use basic Internet tools such as the World Wide Web, USENET, and electronic mailing lists. This book does not explain how to use these applications. For general information about the Internet and guidance on how to use it, we suggest that you read the *1998 Canadian Internet New User's Handbook* or the *1998 Canadian Internet Handbook*.

Most chapters in this book make reference to various Web sites, and we have summarized Web site addresses at the end of most chapters. Since many Web sites change the locations of their individual pages on a frequent basis, we have avoided listing exact page references in this book. Instead, the Web site summaries at the end of the chapters will usually provide the main site addresses only.

We have made every effort to ensure that the Internet addresses contained in this book are accurate. All of the addresses were verified at the time of editing. But because the Internet is constantly changing, inevitably some resources will have changed their location or just disappeared. If you find an address that doesn't work, please let us know about it by sending an e-mail to **authors@handbook.com**. We will update the entry in subsequent editions of this book.

OUR BOOKS

This is not our first book. In fact, it is one of almost twenty books about the Internet that we have written for Canadians since 1994. Our extensive list of books for Canadian Internet users is one of the reasons why the Winnipeg Free Press described us as the "Lennon and McCartney of the Canadian Internet!"

Here is a brief rundown of some of our other Internet books. All of them are available at bookstores across Canada.

1998 Canadian Internet Handbook

Our *Canadian Internet Handbook*, updated annually since 1994, has now sold in excess of 300,000 copies in Canada—an absolutely stunning number. If you read this book and want to know more about the Internet in Canada, pick up the *Canadian Internet Handbook*—you'll find it to be an invaluable resource. It focuses on issues that every Canadian should be aware of, from how to protect your privacy as you use the Internet to how to stop your neighbours from peeking at the files on your personal computer. You'll learn how to control the amount of junk e-mail you receive, encrypt your e-mail so that it's secure, analyze who is visiting your Web site, explore the fascinating new world of digital photography, and more! It's full of tricks and tips to help you make the most of your online experience. Whether you're an advanced Internet user or new to the Internet, this is a book that you won't want to miss!

1998 Canadian Internet Directory and Research Guide

The *1998 Canadian Internet Directory and Research Guide* provides details and descriptions of over 3,000 of Canada's best Internet resources. Included in the book is a guide that describes how to do effective research on the Internet. Time and time again, Canadians have told us that their biggest frustration with the Internet is not being able to find what they are looking for! The Research Guide offers tips and techniques that will dramatically improve your online research skills. It's the ultimate book for exploring Canada in cyberspace!

1998 Canadian Internet New User's Handbook

The *1998 Canadian Internet New User's Handbook* is a portable guide for Canadians who are new to the Internet. It explores how to get plugged into the Net; how to use popular Internet tools such as e-mail, the World Wide Web, and discussion groups; and how to locate information online. The book will also take you on a unique virtual voyage from the Yukon Territory to Newfoundland, showing you how Canadians from coast to coast are putting the Internet to work for them. It's a book that no Internet novice should be without!

Canadian Money Management Online: Personal Finance on the Net

Canadian Money Management Online: Personal Finance on the Net describes how Canadians can use the Internet to manage their personal finances. The book covers just about every aspect of personal finance to help you get your financial affairs in order, including mortgages, real estate, retirement planning, banking, insurance, taxation, investments, and mutual funds. Each chapter is packed with fascinating facts and enlightening Canadian statistics. This is the fun way to learn how to manage your money!

Good Health Online : A Wellness Guide for Every Canadian

The amount of health and medical information on the Internet is nothing less than stunning. This book will help you sort the science from the snake oil. It outlines how you can conduct effective online research into health care matters; evaluate the credibility of online health information; avoid the pitfalls of fraudulent, inaccurate, or biased health care information; deal with Internet-illiterate medical professionals; and assess the dramatic changes that the Internet will have on the health care industry. If you're concerned about your own health (and who isn't?), this book will teach you all you need to know to take advantage of the explosion of health information on the Net.

The Canadian Internet Advantage: Opportunities for Business and Other Organizations

Our book on Internet business strategy, *The Canadian Internet Advantage*, identifies and describes over 80 distinct Internet strategies being pursued by government and business organizations across North America.

ACKNOWLEDGMENTS

We would like to thank the entire editorial, sales, market-ing, and production team at Prentice Hall Canada for their effort on this book. Specifically, we would like to acknowledge Judy Bunting, Robert Harris, Hart Hillman, and Joan Whitman on the editorial side; Andrea Aris, Sue Baldaro, Michael Bubna, Trina Milnes, and Linda Voticky for their sales and marketing support; and Jan Coughtrey, Kelly Dickson, David Jolliffe, and Erich Volk for their production assistance. A special thanks to Mary Opper for the beautiful cover!

We are grateful to i*STAR Internet, Internet Light and Power, Rogers WAVE, Sympatico, and NETCOM Canada for the provision of Internet accounts and Web hosting services.

We also owe a big thanks to our families. Rick would like to thank his family for their continuing support. Jim would like to give his heartfelt thanks and appreciation to his wife Christa. Without her massive efforts both in edit-ing and in conceptualizing the content of the books, we would never manage to meet a deadline. And thanks to Thomas and Willie—for understanding the difference between a "daddy work day" and a "daddy play day."

Finally, we appreciate the ongoing support of our read-ers and fans, and the millions of Internet users across Canada. This book would not be possible without you!

ABOUT THE AUTHORS

Jim Carroll, C.A., is a Chartered Accountant who excels at assisting organizations in understanding the future. He is the author of the critically acclaimed *Surviving the Information Age*, a motivational book that encourages people to cope with the future. Mr. Carroll is a prolific writer and contributor to many popular publications, and has written for the *Globe and Mail*, *Computing Canada*, *EnRoute*, *Strategy* and the *Toronto Star*, to name but a few. Mr. Carroll speaks extensively across North America on the topic of the Internet, and is an extremely popular keynote speaker at many annual conferences and meetings for many of the largest associations and corporations in North America. Clients include the Canadian Institute of Mortgage Brokers and Lenders, the Canadian Finance & Leasing Organization, the Canadian Treasury Management Association, the Investment Funds Institute of Canada, CIBC, Montreal Trust, Great-West Life, Scotia McLeod, the Royal Bank of Canada, Credit Union Central Canada, Credit Union Central Ontario, Canada Trust, Ernst & Young, and Yorkton Securities. Mr. Carroll is represented nationally and internationally by the National Speakers Bureau of Vancouver, B.C., an organization that represents Canada's leading speakers and thinkers. Jim can be contacted by e-mail at **jcarroll@jimcarroll.com**, or by visiting his Web site at **www.jimcarroll.com**.

Rick Broadhead, MBA, is a management consultant, industry observer, and leading Internet expert in Canada. A popular speaker, Mr. Broadhead has provided keynote addresses and workshops at conferences, annual meetings, and seminars across North America on the topic of the Internet/information highway and its impact on organizations. He also teaches at York University's Division of Executive Development in Toronto, where he has advised managers from hundreds of leading North American firms and helped them to integrate the Internet into all facets of their businesses. In his consulting practice, Rick has worked with Fortune 500 organizations to assist them with the formulation and implementation of their Internet strategies. His clients have included many government, non-profit, and corporate organizations, including Mackenzie Financial Services, the Financial Management Institute of Canada, Credit Union Central of Canada, the Canadian Institute of Actuaries, Manulife Financial, Microsoft Corporation, VISA International, Imperial Oil, BC TEL, CTV Television, Spectrum United Mutual Funds, and the Canadian Real Estate Association. He can be reached at **rickb@inforamp.net**, or visit his World Wide Web site at **www.intervex.com**.

YOUR EXPERIENCES WITH ONLINE FINANCE

We are always interested in hearing from our readers. We welcome your comments, criticisms, and suggestions and we will use your feedback to improve future editions of this book. We do try to respond to all e-mail sent to us.

We are also very interested in tracking how Canadians are using the Internet to manage their personal finances. How has the Internet helped you with your retirement or financial planning activities? Have you been a victim of online fraud? What financial resources do you find most helpful? What's your favourite investment site on the Web? If you'd like to share your online experiences with us, we'd love to hear from you. We might use your story in a future case study. Similarly, if you are aware of any Canadian organizations that are developing financial products or services for the online marketplace, please let us know so that we can make mention of them in future editions of this book.

Contacting the Authors Directly

To reach	Send e-mail to
Both authors	authors@handbook.com
Jim Carroll	jcarroll@jimcarroll.com
Rick Broadhead	rickb@inforamp.net

Automatic E-mail Information

You can easily obtain current information about this book or any of our other books by sending a message to **info@handbook.com**. You will be sent back a message that will provide details on our books, our online resources, ordering instructions, and other relevant information.

Our World Wide Web Sites

The World Wide Web site for all our books is **www. handbook.com**. There you will find information about all of our publications, including press releases, reviews from the media, and ordering instructions.

Jim Carroll maintains a World Wide Web site at **www.jimcarroll.com**. He posts to this site, on a regular basis, articles that he has written about the Internet and the "information superhighway," including those from the *Globe and Mail*, *Computing Canada*, the *Toronto Star*, *EnRoute*, *Strategy Magazine*, and other publications.

Rick Broadhead maintains a World Wide Web site at **www.intervex.com**, with information about his work, his clients, and pointers to World Wide Web sites from his presentations and speeches about the Internet and the online world.

CHAPTER 1

Investing Online

Twenty years from now you will be more disappointed by the things you didn't do than by the ones you did do. MARK TWAIN

HIGHLIGHTS

- Many Canadians recognize that they will need to take on more responsibility for their financial security during retirement. At the same time, they recognize that they need to improve their knowledge of investment matters.

- The Internet provides Canadians with an unprecedented amount of information on RRSPs, retirement planning, and investments in general. By accessing and using this information, Canadians can take more control over their own financial affairs.

- You don't need to be an Internet-user to read this book. It's a simple, non-technical, and concise guide to the decisions you need to make about your retirement investments. Throughout the book we show you how to use the Internet as an investment and retirement planning tool.

The emergence of the Internet is leading to a very significant and important trend—many people are taking responsibility for their own investment decisions.

That is what this book is all about.

Will the Internet make you an expert when it comes to financial matters?

No—but it will certainly help you with some of the most important financial issues that you are faced with. It can help you to develop a greater understanding of why you should be planning for your retirement today, instead of putting it off to the future. Used wisely, the Internet can also help you make intelligent RRSP and other investment decisions.

> **The Web is nothing more than a universal agreement on a way that one computer can display data from a second and then jump to data from a third, fourth and so on without complex commands. That notion of easily linking data, regardless of a computer's type or location, can change the way people create and organize information. It's leading some businesses and institutions to rethink how they function.**
>
> EVAN RAMSTAD, "ONCE OBSCURE, NOW MAINSTREAM", *THE FINANCIAL POST*, JULY 24, 1996

The Internet can help to demystify what, for many people, is a mystery—the world of finance. The extent of investment and financial information on the Internet is truly amazing. The Internet represents the world's largest collection of financial information from all over the globe.

Spend some time online, and here are some of the things that you can learn:

- you can get a better understanding of what RRSPs are all about, and why they are such an important financial tool

- you can find out how much you need to save for your retirement, or discover if you will have enough for your retirement, based on your current and future RRSP contributions

- you can find out how much tax you can save with your current RRSP contributions

- you can learn more about investing, and discover how to use the Internet to determine what you should be investing in

- you can quickly find out which financial institutions offer the best rates on term deposits and similar investments, or research the risk associated with the new cash-based investment products that so many financial organizations are offering

- you can examine details about hundreds of mutual funds, to help you decide which investments might be best for you

- you can quickly find the top-performing mutual funds in various investment categories

- you can browse through an unprecedented range of information about the stock market, and research tens of thousands of companies that you might invest in

> **Asked about the potential for the sale of mutual funds online, the head of Vanguard Investments, one of the largest mutual fund companies in the US, commented in an article in Investment Dealers Digest, on February 3, 1997, "Two years from now, routine transaction capabilities are going to be a commodity; everyone is going to be doing it."**

- you can monitor the performance of your investments on a day-to-day basis so that you can see how your investments are working for you

- you can buy and sell mutual funds and stocks online and save on commission fees.

Regardless of your financial situation, you will discover the Internet to be an extremely effective and powerful financial tool.

Survey After Survey...

As a financial tool, the Internet couldn't have come at a better time. Open any newspaper or magazine and you will find surveys that show most Canadians agree with two fundamental statements:

- they are concerned that they will have to take on more responsibility for their retirement, since they don't expect that there will be enough money in government and private pension plans to take care of them

- they need to learn more about RRSPs, retirement and investment issues.

Consider a study that was prepared for Scotiabank by the research firm Goldfarb Consultants in December 1996. The study found that:

- Canadians who are 45 and older estimate that 40% of their retirement income will have to come from personal savings and investments

- 58% of Canadians have money set aside in an RRSP

- While half of Canadians expressed a personal interest in investment matters, only two in ten felt they had an expert or high level of investment knowledge.

The bottom line? Canadians need to do a better job at managing their RRSP and investment activities, yet they feel they don't have the knowledge to do so.

That's where the Internet comes in. Never before has there been a tool like the Internet that makes it possible for the average Canadian to effectively deal with these two pressing issues.

Mastering the Internet is a significant and often frustrating challenge for many people. Many people feel overwhelmed by the amount of information online, and are fearful about the possibility of being victimized by an online con artist.

Typically, I got my best ideas on where to look for investment information and trading Web sites from articles and reviews in newspapers and magazines—a sad if inevitable state of affairs for a medium that promises to solve all your information problems.

EDWARD H. BAKER, "ROUNDUP, INTERNET STYLE," *FINANCIAL WORLD*, JAN 21, 1997

We have written this book to help you learn how to use the Internet as an investment and retirement planning tool. You can use this book to:

- learn about fundamental retirement, RRSP, mutual fund, and investment issues; and

- learn how to apply the Internet to your investment and retirement planning needs.

This book is designed for two groups of people:

- those who want a better understanding of issues related to investing in RRSPs; and

- those who want to learn more about investing online— both for general investment purposes and for purposes of retirement.

Throughout this book, we provide plenty of examples that you can use to harness the power of the Internet when it comes to your own RRSP, retirement, mutual fund, and investment decisions. Mastering these capabilities is important. We sincerely believe that you will see dramatic payoffs if you take the time and effort to learn to effectively use the Internet.

Here's a guide to what you will find in the chapters that follow:

- In chapter 2, **Benefits of the Internet for Your Retirement and Investment Activities,** we explain the benefits of using the Internet as an investment and retirement planning aid.

- In chapter 3, **The Risk of Using the Internet as an Investment Tool,** we describe the dangers of using the Internet as a financial resource.

- In chapter 4, **Assessing Investment Information on the Internet**, we describe how to be an "information skeptic" and avoid the risks outlined in the previous chapter.

- In chapter 5, **The Basics of Retirement Planning and RRSPs**, we cover the fundamentals of retirement planning and RRSPs, including why you need to get involved with your own retirement planning, why it is something that you can't postpone until later, and why RRSPs are such an important retirement tool.

- In chapter 6, **Retirement Planning and RRSPs on the Internet**, we outline how you can use the Internet to learn more about the topics covered in the previous chapter.

- In chapter 7, **Using Financial Calculators**, we describe how you can use interactive calculators on the Internet to appreciate the time value of money. Use these calculators, and we are certain that you will be propelled into action!

- In chapter 8, **Basic Investment Concepts**, we review investment fundamentals, summarize the different types of investments that are available to you, and help you to understand key investment concepts such as risk, growth, and income.

- In chapter 9, **Mutual Fund Concepts**, we discuss the basics of mutual funds, and explain why so many people view them as an attractive alternative to other types of investments.

- In chapter 10, **Determining What to Invest In**, we discuss the types of decisions you will face as you try to decide where to invest your money.

- In chapter 11, **Cash and Cash-Equivalent Investments on the Internet**, we explain how the Internet can help you research cash-based and cash-equivalent offerings from financial institutions. These investments include savings accounts, Canada Savings Bonds, guaranteed investment certificates, and term deposits.

- In chapter 12, **Mutual Funds on the Internet**, we describe some of the tools that you can use to research mutual funds on the Internet

- In chapter 13, **Stocks and Bonds on the Internet**, we outline how you can use the Internet to research existing or potential investments in stocks and bonds.

- In chapter 14, **Monitoring Your Performance**, we show you how you can use powerful tools on the Internet to track the value and performance of your investments on a day-to-day basis.

- In chapter 15, **Online Investing**, we describe how you

can use the Internet to buy and sell mutual funds, stocks, bonds, and other financial instruments.

- Finally, in chapter 16, **The Future of Finance on the Internet**, we discuss how the Internet will impact the financial industry in the future, and issue a plea for Canadian regulators to become more active in educating individual investors about the risks of using the Internet as an investment tool.

You Do Not Have to Be a Brilliant Computer Geek to Read This Book

This book has been written with the assumption that readers have a working knowledge of the Internet. This book doesn't describe the fundamentals of sending email and using the World Wide Web. Rather, it describes how you can apply the Internet to your financial needs.

Having said that, you don't need to be an Internet-user to read this book. We have written this book as a simple, non-technical guide to using the Internet as an investment and retirement planning aid. We have deliberately tried to keep the chapters as simple as possible, recognizing that many Canadians are intimidated by the world of finance.

In fact, you might fit into one of the following categories:

- you already use the Internet, and you have dabbled in some of the financial and investment sites on the Web to see if they can help you with your retirement and investment needs

- you might use the Internet, but have not fully capitalized on the wealth of financial information online

- you don't use the Internet, but you are curious about whether it can help you better manage your own personal investments.

We have written this book for all of you. Indeed, this book has been written for the average Canadian—not for computer experts.

For an introduction to the Internet, how it works, and how to use basic Internet tools like email and the Web, we recommend that you consult the *Canadian Internet New User's Handbook*. It's an entry-level guide to the Internet for Canadians. Regardless of your level of experience with the Internet, we also recommend you consult the *1998 Canadian Internet Handbook*. It reviews and discusses important Internet issues and technologies affecting Canadians, such as security, privacy, and junk email. It will enhance your understanding of many of the issues raised in this book. You'll find more information about both of these publications at the front of this book.

Let's move on!

CHAPTER 2

Benefits of the Internet for Your Retirement and Investment Activities

To know, is to know that you know nothing. That is the meaning of true knowledge. CONFUCIUS

HIGHLIGHTS

- The Internet can save you money, keep you up-to-date, expose you to different perspectives on financial matters, and make the whole process of managing your investments a lot more enjoyable. Perhaps most importantly, the Internet is a vital skill that will empower you and give you a competitive edge in the marketplace.

- Financial information on the Internet comes from a variety of different sources, including financial institutions, financial advisors, the media, and investment "supermarkets."

- While the Internet gives you more control over your finan-cial affairs, it should not replace the expert advice of a pro-fessional investment advisor or financial planner.

In this chapter we review the benefits of using the Internet as an investment tool.

Ten Reasons Why You Should Use the Internet as an Investment Tool

1. It is a useful new skill.

There is no doubt that the Internet is here to stay, and that it will forever change the world of finance.

Learning to research the Internet effectively and to take advantage of the information you find online is becoming increasingly important. It is particularly important when it comes to financial decisions concerning your investments, whether they be for your retirement or other personal or business reasons.

2. It can save you money.

Once you are hooked up to the network you can access most information on the Internet for free.

This makes the Internet an unprecedented research tool, providing you with access to very detailed and often "up-to-the-minute" financial information, all for an extremely reasonable cost. With Internet access in most major Canadian cities approaching a flat monthly fee of about $20, (a little more in rural areas) it is probably the most significant information bargain on the planet.

In addition, if you take on more responsibility for your financial affairs, you can save significant sums of money. For example, if you learn how to undertake your own stock trades on a service such as E*Trade Canada, you can save money on stock broker commissions. You can also use the Internet to find the best no-load or commission-free mutual funds, instead of going with "load" funds that involve a commission paid to the financial professional who sells them to you.

Those are but two examples of the direct savings that the Internet can help you to achieve.

3. It can be fun.

Some people find that surfing the Net is fun. It's an entertaining, often hilarious, and amusing way to spend time.

For many people, the Internet is a new form of entertainment—and one that may offer amusement pitched at a higher degree of intelligence than most television shows aim at.

How does this impact your investment decisions? The Internet can turn complex, laborious, or even boring financial tasks into a stimulating experience. After all, anything having to do with finances can be dull, even boring.

Many people find that when they plug into the Internet, their perspective on the world of finance changes. Suddenly, financial matters seem more interesting and more manageable. The Internet can generate enthusiasm for routine tasks, thereby giving people an added incentive to deal with their financial affairs.

4. It can help to change the way you deal with your finances.

Learn about some of the issues we outline in this book, and then visit the sites we recommend. Study the information—and we are willing to bet that your attitude toward certain financial issues will change forever.

Peter Quick, president of Quick & Reilly, a discount broker that operates an Internet trading system, sees the emergence of a do-it-yourself, Home Depot-type of investor who wants "objective advice and information with regard to portfolio and investment allocation." This computer-literate investor is "capable of making investment decisions that would be comparable to the advice that they would get from a broker," adds Quick.

IVY SCHMERKEN, "WIRING CUSTOMERS TO THE STREET," *WALL STREET & TECHNOLOGY*, JULY 12, 1997

We think that once you learn to take advantage of the rich financial information that the Internet offers, you will begin to use it more and, as a result, become more aggressively involved in your own financial affairs. Which is a good thing, since study after study shows two consistent trends in Canada: Canadians feel in the dark when it comes to retirement and financial issues, but they want to become more involved in these areas.

5. It gives you power.

The Internet is slowly tipping the scales of many financial relationships in your favour, since it is helping to introduce new forms of competition into the financial services industry. It helps you, the consumer, by giving you more power.

In the world of finance, this is very significant. You can now:

- make quick comparisons between investment or savings rates at different banks, trust companies, and credit unions

- undertake a quick analysis to find the best-performing mutual funds in a specific category, or research the background of various mutual funds in order to determine which works best for you

- learn more about new financial offerings from banks and other companies, in order to educate yourself about the risks that they don't mention in their advertisements.

The Internet empowers you because you no longer have to rely solely on the information provided to you by stock brokers or other investment advisors.

In effect, you can become a more informed investor. And you will likely develop a new sense of self-satisfaction by mastering your own financial affairs.

6. It keeps you up-to-date.

One of the most powerful aspects of the Internet is that you can use it to keep up-to-date on your investments, or to keep abreast of changes in government policy that might affect your financial position upon retirement.

Think about this—today you might receive or obtain pamphlets and brochures from financial organizations, or read about various financial alternatives in the newspaper. Yet, due to the rapid rate of change in the world of finance, you will often discover that such information is out-of-date as soon as it is printed.

The world of finance changes on an almost daily basis, making it a challenge to obtain up-to-date information when you need it. And the complexity of the world means that you can't afford to be unaware of how you might be impacted by changes in the financial industry.

That is where the Internet comes in. Many Web sites contain the latest, most up-to-date, and most accurate information available, which will enable you to make more informed financial decisions.

Never before has it been so easy for investors to keep themselves current on financial matters, whether it be interest rates, stock prices, investment or business news, or political developments around the world. And with the emergence of online "portfolio tools," which we discuss in chapter 14, you can even track the day-to-day value of your investments.

7. It broadens your perspective to a global view.

Face it—many Canadians tend to get too focused on things like national unity, the deficit, and hockey.

But plug into the Internet, and you suddenly acquire an international perspective. You can now access opinions and expertise from financial professionals all over the world. Access to the world stage might influence your investment or other financial decisions—which can sometimes be a good thing.

8. It provides different perspectives.

There are many different approaches when dealing with investment matters. Journey onto the Internet and you will discover that it provides you with all kinds of different viewpoints and ideas—each of which you can carefully evaluate when making financial decisions. You will learn to appreciate the dictum that there is no right answer.

Financial information is rapidly being commoditized by the Internet—the great democratizer.

IVY SCHMERKEN, "WIRING CUSTOMERS TO THE STREET," *WALL STREET & TECHNOLOGY*, JULY 12, 1997

---

9. It provides access to a full range of financial information.

The more financial organizations get involved with the Internet and establish Web sites, the more information-rich you become.

The quantity—and quality—of information on the Internet is stunning. Since the World Wide Web burst onto the scene in early 1993, the Internet has become the largest depository of financial information on the planet. It provides you with instant access to information on retirement planning, RRSPs, mutual funds, stocks, bonds, GICs, and almost every other conceivable investment topic.

10. It helps you to stay competitive.

Canadians who take the time to learn how to use the Internet as a investment tool will gain a competitive edge in the marketplace. If you want to keep up with the pack, you've got to learn online investment skills. As the saying goes, information is power. And the Internet puts an unprecedented amount of information at your fingertips.

The Financial Industry Online

It is important that you understand how quickly the financial world is evolving when it comes to the Internet.

At the beginning of the decade, if you had suggested that within a few years you would be able to buy and sell shares, do your banking, or conduct research on tens of thousands of organizations on the Internet, most financial professionals would have laughed you out of the room. Yet today, all that and more is possible.

Within the financial industry, the Internet is moving at lightning speed. In fact, it's moving so fast that industry players and regulators can barely keep up.

On the Internet, financial information comes from a myriad of different sources. They include:

Financial Institutions

Banks, credit unions, trust companies, brokerage firms, insurance companies, mutual fund companies—you name

What's the average cost to process a bank transaction?	
In a full-service branch:	$1.07
By telephone:	54 cents
At an ATM machine:	27 cents
On a PC:	1.5 cents
On the Web:	One penny

it, they are all using the Internet to provide information to potential and existing customers.

Financial Advisors

Accountants, lawyers, personal financial planners, life insurance representatives, financial analysts—they are all setting up shop on the Internet, loading their sites with useful (and sometimes not-so-useful) personal financial planning information.

The Media

Many mainstream media organizations in Canada, from newspapers, magazines, and television shows to community newspapers and smaller-scale publications, are establishing their own places on the Internet—and loading them up with tips, advice, strategies, and observations from their experts.

Investment Supermarkets

A newer concept is the "one-stop" online shop where you can browse and purchase the financial services of numerous financial institutions. One of the primary benefits of using these online financial supermarkets is that you can access comparative information from many different financial institutions in one place, without having to visit

> **"Doing business on the Internet is 'orders of magnitude' less expensive compared with providing more traditional services such as toll-free telephone numbers and customer support representatives," said George G. Hathaway III, vice president of strategic planning for Fidelity's retail group.**
>
> JOHANNA AMBROSIO, "FIDELITY POSTS 'NET SERVICES," *COMPUTERWORLD*, AUG 25, 1997

a dozen different sites on the Internet. A Canadian example of this type of service is company called Imoney. On the Imoney Web site, you can shop for a variety of different financial products and services from participating companies such as AGF, Canada Trust, E*Trade Canada, Scotiabank, and Trimark.

Associations

All kinds of financial associations have established Web sites, in order to provide information to their members or to the Internet at large. For example, the American Association of Individual Investors has a Web site that, regardless of its U.S. focus, provides a number of useful information resources for the new or sophisticated investor.

Regulatory Bodies

Government and industry financial regulatory bodies such as the U.S. Securities & Exchange Commission (SEC) and the British Columbia Securities Commission (BCSC) use the Internet as a means of publishing information about their activities. It also serves as a forum by which to notify investors of various regulatory actions and concerns.

> **Online stock trading will account for 60 percent of the discount brokerage industry within four years, according to investment banking firm Piper Jaffray Inc.**

Government

Across Canada and around the world, government departments are using the Internet to publish information with respect to their mandate. This means that you can find information online from such departments as Human Resources Development Canada, where they provide information related to the Canada Pension Plan. Similarly, you can find information about the Canada Deposit Insurance Corporation online.

Financial News Services

Services such as StockHouse and SmartMoney Interactive (sponsored by Dow Jones) provide an organized way to access specialized financial news information, and are among the hundreds of financial news services to be found online.

The Result?

An unparalleled amount of financial information has become available to you, most often at *no charge*.

Becoming More Accountable for Your Own Financial Investments

What it really comes down to is this—the emergence of the Internet is leading to one very significant trend. Canadians are taking on more responsibility for their own RRSP, retirement, and investment decisions.

And that's what this book is all about. It provides you with guidance on how you can learn to master the Internet in all these important areas.

Having said that, we must make one extremely important observation. While it can be tremendously useful to take more control over your financial affairs, there are many drawbacks to doing this.

You must carefully weigh the benefits of deciding to take on more responsibility for your financial affairs against the risks, which we discuss in chapter 3.

It's easy to think that with all the information that's available on the Internet, you can "go it alone," make your own financial decisions, and forgo the added expense of professional advice. But for most people that's not a wise move. Professional investment advisors, personal financial planners, and other professionals in the financial industry usually have the expertise, depth of understanding, investment knowledge, and experience that you do not.

The world of finance can be exceedingly complex. Hence, for the average Canadian, the Internet should not replace the advice you receive from a professional investment advisor. It's important to keep in mind how an investment professional can help you. And this raises another related issue. You need to be vigilant when people are giving you investment advice. You should be aware that in Canada it's illegal for someone to advise you on the purchase or sale of securities unless that person is registered to do so. We discuss this issue further in the next chapter, which explains the risks of using the Internet as a financial tool.

Web Sites Mentioned in This Chapter

AGF Group of Funds	www.agf.ca
American Association of Individual Investors	www.aaii.org
British Columbia Securities Commission	www.bcsc.bc.ca
Canada Deposit Insurance Corporation	www.cdic.ca
Canada Trust	www.canadatrust.com
E*Trade Canada	www.canada.etrade.com
Human Resources Development Canada	www.hrdc-drhc.gc.ca
Imoney	www.imoney.com
Scotiabank	www.scotiabank.ca
SmartMoney Interactive	www.smartmoney.com
StockHouse Online Journal	www.stockhouse.com
Trimark Investment Management	www.trimark.com
U.S. Securities and Exchange Commission	www.sec.gov

CHAPTER 3

The Risk of Using the Internet as an Investment Tool

If a million people believe a foolish thing, it is still a foolish thing. ANATOLE FRANCE

HIGHLIGHTS

- The Internet offers the perfect environment for fraud artists to operate. They can publish any information they want, create their own identities, and reach millions of people with little effort.

- Fraud on the Internet generally falls into one of the following four categories: manipulation of obscure, thinly-traded stocks; unlicensed investment advisors; conflicts of interest; and exotic scams.

- Fraud can originate from several sources on the Internet, including: electronic investment newsletters and Web sites; spam; newsgroups and chat sites; and bogus Web sites.

- Investment information on the Internet can be inaccurate, out-of-date, and/or misleading. In addition, the information you come across may not be applicable to Canada.

- **When using the Internet to manage your investments, you could become the victim of a scam, make a bad decision, have your privacy violated, encounter security problems, or experience a computer glitch.**

- **Other pitfalls of using the Internet for financial advice include getting lost in the details, unsuccessful searches, getting dissatisfied with the Internet, becoming overly confident with your investment abilities, and forgetting about life.**

We're going to cover a lot of useful information in this book. We will examine issues surrounding retirement, RRSPs, cash-based investments, mutual funds, stocks and bonds, and even online trading. But before we plunge into all of those topics, we strongly believe that we must first address one of the most significant issues that surrounds use of the Internet as an investment tool.

There is a tremendous opportunity for you to make bad, invalid, or incorrect retirement and investment decisions based upon the information you might find online. The Internet is proving to be fertile ground for online fraud, misinformation, and rumour. Not only that, but the information you rely upon could be wrong—simply out-of-date or incorrect. And finally, the Internet is not a panacea—while it is a wonderful tool to assist you with your investment decisions, it is but one facet of what you need to properly manage your investments.

Hence, before we begin to examine specific retirement and investment issues, we feel we must first put the risks of using the Internet as an information tool into perspective. In the next chapter we will tell you what you must do to critically appraise the information you find online.

While many of the stories and observations that follow in this chapter and the next apply to stocks, always keep in mind that they can be equally applicable to mutual funds, or can directly affect the value of your mutual fund holdings.

Canadian Horror Stories

Most Canadians are probably familiar with the role that the Internet played in the infamous Bre-X fraud.

If you are not, it is alleged that the Internet played a role in the run-up of the price of the stock, in two ways. First, Bre-X officials used their Web site to disseminate positive information about the company's "gold find," which in the minds of investors helped to provide credibility to the company's value. Second, various online discussion groups played a key role in the hyping of the gold discovery, helping to lead many new investors into the stock. These two factors—which helped to build the perception of a massive gold find—are cited by some in the news media as being partly responsible for the frenzied atmosphere that surrounded the stock.

The Bre-X example illustrates many of our points in this section. Even though the Bre-X situation has been a tragedy for many people, it has had one positive and fortunate impact—it has finally opened the minds of security regulators and the investment industry to the significant problems that the Internet can present when it comes to investing. We hope that these agencies have been stirred into action to try to deal with the problem.

Consider what happened with Bre-X on the Internet:

- Bre-X officials used their Web site to distribute their own press releases, many of which touted the inaccurate and ultimately fraudulent claims of the amount of gold in the company's Indonesian property. Many investors relied on information posted on the Bre-X Web site without questioning the accuracy or independence of what they read.

- It has been reported that Bre-X officials often posted information on their Web site that ultimately contradicted statements made by regulatory officials. People came to rely upon the Bre-X claims, more so than the other statements, often losing sight of the lack of independence of this information.

- Online Internet-based discussion forums such as Silicon Investor became part of the feeding-frenzy mentality which surrounded Bre-X. Individual investors participating in such forums read about and became enamoured by the money being made by those who saw the value of their stock holdings increase at a dramatic clip. Everyone wanted in! In effect, online enthusiasm helped to fuel the gold-rush aura which surrounded the Bre-X stock.

Use common sense. Ask yourself. If this investment is so enticing, why am I being selected for this great opportunity? Common sense is your best protection against fraud.

GRETCHEN MORGENSOM, "DON'T BE A VICTIM," *FORBES*, JUNE 2, 1997 V159 N11 PP: 42-43

Sadly, investment fraud on the Internet hasn't been restricted to the Bre-X situation. It's occurring *right now*, and was occurring long before Bre-X arrived on the scene.

Yet Another Canadian Example

Here's a typical example of how the Internet can be used to manipulate a stock.

This example is based on an article in the August 9, 1997 edition of the *Globe and Mail* called "Hype Artists Spin Stocks on the Web." While some in the investment community debate the accuracy of the article, others indicate that the story it tells is, sadly, all too true.

The story involves a small Vancouver-based company called Ashton Mining. In late April 1997, according to the *Globe and Mail* article, an Internet user reported that the company had pulled a giant diamond from its mine in the Buffalo Hills area of Northern Alberta. Within a matter of hours, online enthusiasm began to reach a feverish pitch, as news of this "find" spread on online discussion forums like Silicon Investor. People began purchasing the stock, which drove up the price enough to get the national media to take notice, which, of course, drove up the price even more.

The result? An increase in the share price from $1.70 in April to $7.65 by mid-May. And even as Ashton Mining denied the report, the buzz on the Internet was that the company was purposefully keeping the huge finding a secret.

What eventually happened? The individual or individuals who started the rumour, which effectively drove up the stock price, probably managed to pocket a great deal of money by selling their stock before the hype died down in June.

It is this type of manipulation which is so very real—and so very easy to do online.

Why Do Scam Artists Love the Internet?

If a fraud artist had been asked a couple of years ago to dream up the perfect tool to help them commit investment fraud, they probably would not have been able to come up with anything as perfect as the Internet. The Internet is made for the fraud artist. For existing and would-be fraud artists, the Internet is almost too good to be true.

Consider this—it is very easy to create your own identity on the Internet, one that might have absolutely nothing to do with the truth. And what is amazing is that all too many people believe what they read online, without taking the time to judge the validity of the information they are accessing.

Online Fraud 101

It is easy enough to use the Internet to take advantage of people. If we wanted to, we could create an elaborate scheme that recommends that people invest in a certain company that makes peanut butter. The basis of our scheme would be this—we would describe that an investment in this company is a good bet, because scientists have just figured out that the ingredients in this particular brand of peanut butter have been shown to result in a dramatic decrease in colon cancer.

How would we go about pulling this off? First of all, we'd create a report from a fictitious "independent" research institute, distribute it to a few key health groups online, and invite people to visit our Web site to learn more. This would help to get a buzz going in some health areas on the Internet. Sadly, a lot of people access medical information on the Internet without questioning its accuracy—a topic we explore in our book, *Good Health Online—A Wellness Guide for Every Canadian.*

We'd create this Web site in a way that clearly authenticated our claims. We would create enthusiastic—but bogus—reports from the medical community as well as fictitious news articles. We'd have a series of press releases describing the research that had been reported worldwide about the link between this particular ingredient in peanut butter and colon cancer.

We would also hit a few online investment discussion forums, and create numerous identities for ourselves. These identities would be used to create an entirely phony "discussion" between three or four "different" people debating the research results. We would even create an identity for a medical doctor who would join the online discussions and comment enthusiastically about the product.

We'd pay a few more people to make their own enthusiastic postings online, recognizing that there are individuals out there who will do this for a fee.

We would try to stimulate the interest of online investment newsletters to help publicize our findings.

We would target, through email, investors whose email addresses we found through online discussion forums. We would send them highly enthusiastic reports that "this investment is a sure bet!" and that "you can't lose on this one!" We would appeal to that most base of human emotions—greed.

And of course, behind the scenes, we would have purchased shares in the company, and would plan to sell them once the price rises, and make some easy money in the process.

Far-fetched? Sadly, no. It happens much too frequently on the Internet.

The Perfect Environment for Fraud

Why is the Internet such a popular target for scam artists? Consider what the Internet provides:

- **The world's largest printing press**

  Anyone can publish information about anything they like on the Internet. And as has been reported over and over, the Internet is difficult, if not impossible to regulate. This means that it's easy for scam artists to spread inaccurate and fraudulent information to an audience of millions of people.

- **A lack of information skepticism**

  The sad fact of the matter is that if we did create the

"peanut butter" story we described earlier, there are some people out there who would believe that what we wrote is true.

There are a lot of people on the Internet who are too willing to believe what they read online without subjecting the information to an adequate degree of what we might call "information skepticism."

These people are lulled into a false sense of security when it comes to information on the Internet. This makes the Net a particularly dangerous tool when it comes to the world of investing, because many scam artists recognize this fact and target investment chat sites such as that found on Silicon Investor on the Internet.

Consider one of the posts that appeared in the Ashton Mining discussion group on Silicon Investor at the start of the stock price rise: *There's only one of two reasons Ashton would stake that much land. 1—They've gone completely mad. 2—They've found diamonds. There's no doubt in my mind that its the latter of the two!!!!"*

Many people would read such a statement online, and act upon it, without questioning its accuracy.

- **A new identity**

It is easy for people to conceal their true identities on the Internet. In fact, you can be anyone you like and thus say anything you like with very little fear of repercussions. This situation will last until regulatory authorities figure out how to deal with the Internet, if they can.

Consider the following. There are a lot of free email services on the Internet that you can sign up with. We went to one, applied for an email address with a

In an article titled "Don't Be a Victim" in the June 2, 1997 issue of *Forbes*, the chief of enforcement of the Securities and Exchange Commission spoke about Comparator Systems, a company that the SEC shut down for fraudulent activity in 1995. The SEC chief noted that the Internet was primarily responsible for "much of the investment" in Comparator Systems, since all kinds of investors were purchasing the stock based on "hot Internet tips" about the company.

user-ID of "Jean Chretien", and received it within a matter of minutes. We were able to send email to friends and relatives, with a return email address that made the messages appear as though they were coming from someone named Jean Chretien.

Next, we assumed the personas of John Felderhof and Bill Gates. We could have easily posted a few messages to investment discussion forums under their names.

Is this legal? Probably not. Is it ethical? Certainly not. Is it easy to do? Most definitely. It is very easy to become whoever you want to be online.

As an investor looking for information online, you have absolutely no assurance as to the identity of the people or organizations with whom you might communicate on the Internet.

In addition to forging email addresses or assuming a false identity in a chat group, fraud artists have been known to set up bogus Web sites that impersonate official ones.

- **Massive reach**
  The Internet presents the scam artist with a global audience, and the ability to reach millions of people with minimal effort.

  Never before has there been a technology that makes it so easy for so few to defraud so many.

- **A technology that is difficult to regulate**
  Scam artists love the Internet because it's so difficult to police. Government and legal authorities as well as securities regulators are having a tough time curtailing investment fraud on the Internet.

  Consider what has been said by the North American Securities Administrators Association (NASAA), which bills itself as "the oldest international organization devoted to investor protection." *"Even if the several thousand people in the United States who work at the Securities and Exchange Commission (SEC), state securities agencies, National Association of Securities Dealers (NASD), and the stock exchanges, were somehow able to put aside all other tasks in a massive bid to shut down online investment scams, it is doubtful that this problem could be stamped out altogether."*

- **Ease of execution**

Finally, scams are easy to perpetrate.

Think about the peanut butter scam we described earlier in the chapter. It would be very easy for us to expand upon those thoughts, and write a step-by-step book called *How to Conduct an Effective Investment Fraud on the Internet.*

It wouldn't be a difficult book to write—we could describe the techniques in just a few short pages. Sad to say, it would probably be a bestseller.

We're joking of course, but we are also quite serious about the prevalence of fraud—it is very easy for *anyone* to come up with an effective Internet investment scam. That is perhaps the scariest thing about the Internet when it comes to the world of finance.

Considering the facts we've enumerated above, it's important to develop a good sense of "information skepticism" as you use the Internet for investment purposes. This is a concept that we discuss in the next chapter.

Types of Online Fraud

In addition to understanding why fraud is so easy to perpetrate on the Internet, it's important that you become familiar with the different ways that an online fraud can occur.

The North American Securities Administrators Association (NASAA) has identified the four most common types of fraud that occur on the Internet. Each type is described below.

Manipulation of Obscure, Thinly-Traded Stocks

Some fraud artists attempt to inflate the value of little-known stocks, taking advantage of their low profile to make a quick profit.

They do this by making claims about "awesome new discoveries" or "significant new developments" relating to these companies. This often results in a flurry of buying activity, which in turn raises the stock price. As the stock price rises, other people begin to take notice of the company, causing even more stock purchases, and an even higher stock price. A feeding frenzy begins with a sudden and sharp increase in the stock price. Everyone wants in!

Fraud artists profit from this type of activity by buying their shares at a low price and then cashing them in once the stock price reaches a certain level. Everyone else is left holding the bag, losing money when the price of the stock eventually collapses upon discovery of the bogus information.

Unlicensed Investment Advisors

You must be licensed by an appropriate provincial or state authority in order to provide advice on the buying or selling of securities. In Canada, provincial and territorial securities commissions regulate the licensing of investment advisors. Many of the people who offer investment advice on the Internet aren't qualified to be dispensing such advice and they are doing so illegally because they aren't licensed.

The Ontario Securities Commission (OSC) is aware of the problem. In 1997, they shut down a Web site called the Federal Bureau of Investments because the person operating the site was offering investment advice without being registered with the Commission.

Yet think about this—the Internet doesn't know about provincial or national borders. How does the OSC deal with someone based in Utah offering advice about a Canadian stock?

Conflicts of Interest

It is a common practice for companies to pay promoters to hype their stocks on the Internet. The fact that the promoters are being paid to say positive things about the company and its stock is often not disclosed to investors who are reading the information.

For example, in 1997, a Florida stock promoter by the name of George Chelekis was charged by the U.S. Securities and Exchange Commission after it was discovered that he had accepted at least $1.1 million from more than 150 companies, as well as 275,500 shares of stock from 10 companies, in exchange for recommending their stock on his Web site. Chelekis, who distributed a newsletter on the Internet called "Hot Stocks Review," was charged by the Commission for "materially false and misleading statements" concerning six publicly-traded companies as well as for failing to disclose the fact that he was receiving money from the companies he was promoting.

Think about what can happen on the Internet. Someone establishes an online newsletter full of investment tips and advice. Yet behind the scenes, the person writing the publication is receiving money from the very companies that he promotes in his newsletter.

Exotic Scams

Exotic scams are schemes where investors are promised big returns in exchange for making large investments in a venture.

A popular type of exotic scam is the "pyramid scheme." Typical pyramid schemes sign up people to be distributors for certain products and/or services and then promise to pay those people commissions if they recruit even more distributors.

You should be cautious of any venture that claims you will make money by recruiting new members instead of by selling products or services yourself.

How serious is this problem? In just *one day* of searching the Web in late 1996, the U.S. Federal Trade Commission and other law enforcement agencies found over 500 Web sites that may have been involved in illegal pyramid schemes. Don't fall for these scams!

> **Tempted to invest in a Hawaiian inventor's vibrating condom? How about a Russian immigrant's eel farm? Or a Costa Rican coconut plantation? Those get-rich-quick schemes may sound harmless. But they're offered on the Internet and that's making securities regulators nervous. Purveyors of everything from penny stocks to pyramid schemes are taking advantage of the computer network's low cost, broad reach and anonymity.**
>
> PATRICK MCGEEHAN, "CYBER-SWINDLES TAKING ROOT BUSINESS DEALS ON THE INTERNET HARD TO REGULATE," *USA TODAY*, JANUARY 31, 1996

Common Sources of Fraud

Having discussed the most popular types of online fraud, you may be wondering where fraud is most likely to occur on the Internet. There are four primary sources. Each is described below.

Electronic Investment Newsletters and Web Sites

There are countless numbers of investment newsletters on the Internet, and massive numbers of investment-oriented Web sites. Any one of these could be a scam. As we pointed out earlier, anyone can publish on the Internet.

Spam

No doubt, if you have an Internet email address, you will have received electronic junk mail, which is often referred to as "spam" or "junk email."

An increasing number of junk email messages promote investment opportunities, many of them fraudulent. Fraud artists are discovering that they can use the Internet to send a message to millions of people for a very low cost. Inevitably, they will draw some people in.

Newsgroups and Chat Sites

If you want to see how the Internet can influence what people do with their investments, spend some time browsing an Internet newsgroup (discussion group) or an investment chat site such as Silicon Investor.

In their StockTalk section, you can join any number of discussion areas about particular stocks and companies. Read some of the messages in the forums, and you'll see all kinds of claims about the future potential of certain stocks.

As you read this information, keep in mind the risks that we described earlier. How do you know that any of these people are real investors? How do you know that the people making enthusiastic comments about specific stocks aren't being paid to do so? How do you know that two different people posting messages under different identities aren't really the same person?

Online discussion forums can be useful and powerful tools, but they are also one of the primary methods used by scam artists. To use them effectively, you must have a level head and a very strong sense of information skepticism. Otherwise, you are the perfect target for a scam artist. Be vigilant at all times.

Bogus Web Sites

Finally, the Financial Services Auithority (formerly known as the Securities and Investments Board) in the United Kingdom has warned that "copycat" Web sites are being set up by "unscrupulous operators who copy the Web pages of legitimate firms and then set up bogus ones of their own, passing themselves off as the real thing."

In other words, fraud artists are creating forgeries of investment sites on the Internet, with the intent of tricking Internet users into thinking they're looking at the real thing. Scary indeed.

Quality of Information Issues

The risk of fraud isn't the only problem you should be conscious of as you use the Internet. Even information that is placed online by reputable, established organizations often suffers from problems that affect its reliability.

Many of the issues above are specific to stocks, or might not occur as frequently with other types of investments as they do with stocks. Yet the issues that follow are applicable to any type of investment, including mutual funds.

1. The information you access might be incorrect.

Always keep this in mind—there is no guarantee that anything you read online is accurate or true. Mistakes happen. Consider what happened in the United Kingdom in mid-1997. Following crucial talks between the finance minister and the Bank of England governor, Britain's Treasury Department reported on the Internet that the governor had asked for a half-point rise in interest rates, when in fact he had asked for a quarter point rise. Fortunately, the error was quickly identified, but only after the incorrect news had reached Britain's financial markets.

2. Information might be out-of-date.

When accessing financial information on the Internet, you might rely on information that is out-of-date, and hence, technically incorrect.

Many organizations on the Internet are still experimenting with the Internet, and have yet to commit the necessary funds to ensure that their sites are kept up-to-date at all times.

When you visit a financial Web site on the Internet, always try and ascertain when the site was last updated. Sometimes Web sites don't provide this information, and it's difficult to tell if the information you are reading was created yesterday or twelve months ago. Needless to say, its dangerous to rely on outdated information for the purpose of making important investment decisions.

It's important to realize that this problem isn't restricted to small Web sites. For example, in early 1997, the Toronto Dominion Bank's Web site was still indicating that the age limit for RRSP contributions is December 31st of the year you turn 71, when in fact the age limit had recently been changed to 69. This type of situation underscores the need to double-check the accuracy of information you obtain off the Internet.

3. Information might not be applicable to Canada.

When visiting a financial Web site, always try to ascertain what country the site is in. Why is this important? If you're accessing advice on a Web site that is based in the United States, the advice being offered might not be applicable to Canada. In addition, the products or services being advertised might not be available in this country.

The global nature of the Internet means that you could find yourself using irrelevant information—and making an incorrect decision as a result.

4. The online tools you rely on might be wrong.

In this book, we recommend a number of online calculators that can help you with your investment decisions as well as assist you in understanding the financial implications of retirement.

Who is to say that such calculators are correct? How do you know they have been programmed properly? How do you know that they have been updated to reflect recent tax or interest rate changes? How do you know that the assumptions used in these calculators are valid for your particular financial circumstances?

The answer is—you don't.

> **Con artists have found that if the technology is exciting enough, people will buy anything. "Whenever a new technology comes over the horizon, we see the same types of scams," says Paul Huey-Burns, assistant enforcement director at the SEC.**
>
> JOHN WAGGONER, "JOKE'S ON INVESTORS AS SCAMS ABOUND," *USA TODAY*, MAY 23, 1996

5. The information might be misleading.

The Internet can thus make a complex financial decision seem all too easy. For example, there are sites that we describe in this book that will help you to "choose" what types of investments are appropriate for you. These sites simplify what are really complex decisions.

Avoid blind reliance on these Web sites; use the information they provide only as guidance.

How Can the Internet Harm You?

Finally, in addition to fraud and misinformation, you might find that the Internet will harm you in other ways if you rely on it as a tool for investment purposes.

As you use the Internet to manage your money, here are some of the pitfalls you should be aware of.

1. You might get ripped off.

There are all kinds of scams and fraudulent activities on the Internet. If you are not careful about what you do, you are likely to be "taken."

Be cautious at all times, and don't trust anyone!

We really think that this point needs stressing. Given that the Internet is such a new territory to explore, and with many people fascinated with what they can find online, the truth is that it is all too easy for the scam artist to take advantage of people—particularly when many people have not yet started to question the validity of the information they find online.

2. You might make bad decisions.

Just because the Internet presents you with a lot of information, it doesn't make you an expert. Information is useful only if you learn to analyze it. The Internet is not a substitute for your own judgment, nor it is a substitute for the advice of a professional financial advisor.

3. Your privacy might be violated.

You should be aware that your personal privacy is at risk when you use the Internet.

For example, many Web sites ask you to register or answer a series of questions before you are allowed to access the information or tools the site makes available. The information you provide might be sold to a telemarketing/direct mail firm or added to a database without your consent or knowledge.

For example, in chapter 14 we describe how you can use an online mutual fund/stock tracking service at various sites belonging to the Southam newspaper group. What we didn't discuss in that chapter is the fact that Southam wants you to fill out a form and provide them your name, income, net worth, occupation, and other personal information.

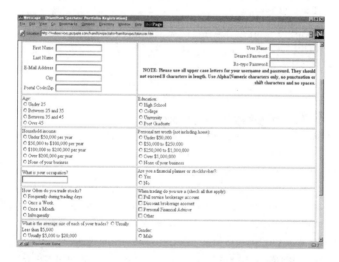

Now think about this—if you go ahead and fill out the form, there is no legislation in Canada (except in the province of Quebec) to prevent this company from doing whatever they might like with the information that you've just willingly provided to them.

There are plenty of other examples on the Internet. Recognizing that this practice worries a lot of Internet users, some companies have published privacy policies on their Web sites, which explain how they intend to use the information they are collecting from you.

4. Your communications might be monitored.

Some investment firms routinely monitor correspondence between their financial advisors and their clients. They do this to ensure that their employees are operating within the law when advising clients about the purchase or sale of securities. Not surprisingly, given the fact that so many investment advisors now communicate with their clients through email, some investment firms now monitor email communications as well. In the United States, some firms have gone so far as to install special programs that examine all outgoing messages for certain words that might indicate the broker is doing something illegal or unethical.

While this obviously makes some investors feel uncomfortable, keep in mind that this type of monitoring is being conducted for your protection and security.

Last November, the SEC filed the first lawsuit to halt securities manipulation over the Net against Charles Huttoe, chair of Systems of Excellence, a video tele-conferencing equipment manufacturer in McLean, Virginia, and Theodore Melcher and Shannon Terry, the operators of an electronic newsletter, SGA Goldstar Research.

"CLICK BUY, CLICK SELL," *WORKING WOMAN*, FEBRUARY 1997

---

5. You might suffer from a security problem.

Banks build physical bank branches, and spend enormous sums of money on elaborate security measures to protect their buildings. Yet, regardless of how much money they spend on security, hold-ups still occur, and bank vaults still get broken into.

So it is with the Internet. Hundreds of major financial institutions are providing financial services online—everything from online banking to stock trading—in a very secure environment. Financial organizations have gone to great lengths to ensure that their Web sites are secure for financial transactions. Having said that, you should also recognize that when it comes to an issue such as security, you are placing a certain degree of faith in the financial institution you are dealing with, and in the computer industry in general.

Sometimes, the complexity of the Internet can exceed even the preparations of the most security-conscious organization. Consider the following.

In mid-1997, a security hole was discovered in a programming language called JavaScript that is used in the two most popular Web browsers—Netscape and Microsoft's Internet Explorer. The security hole meant that someone with a bit of programming knowledge could copy any information that you entered into Web sites, such as credit card numbers, banking IDs, passwords, and more.

In another case, reported in the *Globe and Mail*, an employee at Ontario Hydro who tried to access his bank account over the Internet found that he was looking at the bank records of a colleague instead. Why? Because the other employee had just accessed his bank account over the Internet. Because of the way that Ontario Hydro's computer network was configured (it caches, or saves, pages from a site to speed up their retrieval the next time someone visits the same site) the second employee saw the first employee's account information.

While they are quite rare, security problems like the ones described above can happen at any time.

6. You might experience technical problems.

Imagine this—you sign up for an online stock trading service, and use it for a few months. Then one day, you need to sell the shares that you own in a particular company. You want to get rid of them urgently, since you are quite convinced that their price is going to drop dramatically.

You try to connect to the Internet, but you can't get through, and all you get is a busy signal. You keep trying and trying, and finally you manage to connect. Then you go to the Web site of your online trading service, only to find it intolerably slow. Finally, you get to the screen where you can sell your shares, and you begin entering the necessary details. Wham! Your Web browser crashes, you're disconnected from the Internet, and you get that nasty little "This Program Has Terminated Abnormally" message.

You re-dial your Internet provider, and you get a busy signal again...

By the time you manage to sell your shares, they've dropped 30% in price. Or to put it another way, the time you lost trying to connect to the online brokerage cost you an extra $3,000.

Is our story unrealistic? Not at all. Technical problems can occur at any time. In one widely reported case in the United States in 1997, a computer glitch at discount brokerage firm Charles Schwab meant that many of its customers were unable to determine whether their mutual-fund and stock trades had been carried out.

The Impact of the Internet On You

As you use the Internet for your own financial transactions, keep the following issues in mind.

1. You might become lost in the details.

The Internet is too big—and this poses a problem. You might set out to find a solution for a particular personal financial planning issue—and hours later may still find yourself surfing aimlessly through the Web, having accomplished nothing.

We think that the "Internet intimidation factor" is a very real and significant problem for any Internet user. Successfully mastering the financial capabilities of the Internet requires time and patience.

2. You might not find what you are looking for.

It can be tremendously challenging and frustrating to search the Internet. You will find information on the Internet only if it exists, can be easily located, and if your search skills are good enough to find it.

If you want to learn how to effectively search for information online, consult our *1998 Canadian Internet Directory and Research Guide*. It provides tips and techniques to help you learn how to search the Internet faster and more efficiently.

3. You might become dissatisfied with the Internet.

You might decide that the "old ways" of managing your

money worked better. While the Internet offers a lot of information and valuable tools, it isn't for everyone.

4. You might become overly confident in your investment abilities.

The Internet provides the average consumer and investor with a lot of power, in the form of information and research capabilities.

Too much power can be a terribly negative thing. It's easy for people to get carried away with the Internet and think that they can do a better job than their professional investment advisor. This line of thinking can be very dangerous. As we've already pointed out, the Internet doesn't replace sound financial advice from a professional advisor.

5. You might forget about simple pleasures.

Lastly, the Internet is wonderful, it's fun, and it's useful. Yet it can never compare to real-life experiences. Going to an open house will always be more fun than looking at a house on a Web page. Visiting a stock exchange will be more fun than watching a ticker scroll by on the screen. As you learn to use the Internet, don't lose your humanity.

Web Sites Mentioned in This Chapter

North American Securities Administrators Association (NASAA)	www.nasaa.org
Silicon Investor	www.techstocks.com
Toronto Dominion Bank	www.tdbank.ca
U.K. Financial Services Authority	www.sib.co.uk
U.S. Securities and Exchange Commission	www.sec.gov

CHAPTER 4

Assessing Investment Information on the Internet

My sources are unreliable, but their information is fascinating. ASHLEIGH BRILLIANT

HIGHLIGHTS

- It's important that you learn to question the validity and credibility of any investment information that you access on the Internet.

- Always check the credentials of the people you are dealing with online; use caution when receiving investment advice from strangers, anonymous individuals, and people who claim to have inside information; don't buy thinly-traded stocks on the basis of hype; and be aware that people may be getting paid to promote a stock on the Internet.

- The Investment Dealers Association of Canada has strict by-laws and regulations governing advertising by member firms and their employees. These rules also apply to the Internet.

- When evaluating the credibility of online information, you need to consider the background and credentials of the site's creators; the source of the information; the overall look and feel of the site; as well as independent news coverage of the site or its creators.

While there are definite advantages to using the Internet as a financial tool, it is possible that you might make a poor decision based on information that you obtain online, particularly in light of the risks that have been described in the previous chapter.

Does this mean that you should shy away from using the Internet? Not at all. But it does mean that you should use caution when accessing investment information from this source. In particular, you should always question the *validity* and *credibility* of information you access online.

It's possible for information to be credible, but not valid. How so? When accessing investment information on the Internet, you need to consider factors such as:

- Is the information applicable to your own financial circumstances?

- Is the information applicable in Canada?

- Is the information accurate? and

- Is the information up-to-date?

In other words, just because information is coming from a credible source doesn't mean that it is accurate or applicable to your specific financial situation. There is a lot of out-of-date information on the Internet. By the same token, there is a lot of information on the Web that contains mistakes, even though it comes from highly respectable sources. Don't take anything you read on the Internet for granted. Before acting on any information that you received online, consult a financial advisor or other trusted professional or colleague.

A more serious problem on the Internet is the information that is neither credible nor valid. This type of information usually manifests itself in the form of a scam or fraud. One way to protect yourself from these illegal schemes is to understand how fraud is perpetrated on the Internet. In this chapter, we describe some of the warning signs that you should watch out for.

Many of our comments in this chapter have to do with investment fraud involving stocks. This is because the stock market is subject to a greater degree of risk and manipulation than the mutual fund industry. While fraud *does* occur in the mutual fund industry, it is less common than stock fraud. Even so, the following tips should be kept in mind for any investment information that you might access on the Internet.

10 Tips for Avoiding Fraud on the Internet

Regulatory authorities recognize that fraud is a serious problem on the Internet. Part of their response to the problem involves educating the public about the risks of obtaining investment advice off the Internet.

The North American Securities Administration Association (NASAA) has published a document on its Web site called "Cyberspace Fraud and Abuse." It describes the most common methods for fraud to be perpetrated on the Internet. We highly recommend that you read it.

HOW A TYPICAL CYBER-SCHEME WORKS

"Is anyone out there following Company X?"

"I heard that Company X is about to make a major announcement. Email me or call this toll-free number to get an information package."

"I spoke to Company X's CEO, who confirmed details of next month's big news. I've bought 10,000 shares. Look for share price to double in the next month! Get it now!"

"Big news is just around the corner. We hear from a friend who has visited Company X that it is going to be even bigger than we thought. There's still time to get in."

"Short sellers are in the market! Keep the faith… This will bounce back. The smart money will use the price as an opportunity to buy more and dollar average."

FROM THE NORTH AMERICAN SECURITY ADMINISTRATORS ASSOCIATION WEB SITE IN THE "INVESTORS EDUCATION" SECTION. "CYBERSPACE FRAUD AND ABUSE" (www.nasaa.org)

In the pages that follow, we outline some of the basic assumptions and attitudes that you should carry with you as you use the Internet for investment purposes.

1. Don't expect to get rich quickly.

If the information you find on the Internet sounds too good to be true, it probably is.

People have an amazing capacity to suspend their disbelief when it comes to money and investments, and they often end up doing something that they later regret. Don't let this happen to you.

Some of the claims that you will see on Web sites, in investment newsletters, and on discussion groups on the Internet are so obviously false it is hard to believe that people fall for the claims that are made. Suggestions that you can "double your money in six months," or that an investment is a "guaranteed sure thing" or that "you, too can share in the wealth explosion" should immediately set off alarm bells in your head.

Unbelievably, many people fall for such pitches. The fraud artists wouldn't be working the Internet as hard as they do if the public wasn't so easy to victimize. Fortunately, investor education programs such as those undertaken by the NASAA are helping to combat the problem.

2. Question the validity of any information you read online.

In the previous chapter, we talked about the fact that you must develop a degree of "information skepticism" as you use the Internet.

If you plan on using the Internet to assist you with your financial decisions, it is important that you learn to judge the validity of what you read. This is such an important topic, we discuss it in more depth later in the chapter.

3. Don't rely on securities regulators to police the Internet.

Securities administrators, stock exchanges, financial institutions, governments, and the rest of the financial industry are still coming to grips with the problem of investment fraud on the Internet. The Bre-X scandal has had the effect of waking up the investment and regulato-

It's not easy being a financial regulator these days.

"CHALLENGES OF THE FINANCIAL CYBERCOP," *INSTITUTIONAL INVESTOR*, APRIL 1997, V31 N4 PP: 99

ry community and raising awareness of the seriousness of the problem.

Some stock exchanges and provincial securities commissions do employ staff who monitor the Internet for illegal activity, but given the sheer size of the Internet, the fact that it's borderless, and the ease with which fraud artists can conceal their identities, these efforts aren't always successful.

Recognizing how massive the problem is, some regulatory bodies are looking for ways to automate surveillance on the Internet. In the United States, the National Association of Securities Dealers (NASD) has developed a program that will automatically search Web sites on the Internet for evidence of fraud.

Yet many of these activities are in their early stages, and are by no means comprehensive. You are very much on your own.

4. Don't buy thinly-traded stocks on the basis of online hype.

Many of the most common investment scams involve small, relatively unknown stocks that aren't traded very frequently. These are called "thinly-traded stocks" because they aren't traded very often. On the Internet, outrageous claims are often made about these stocks, leading to a frenzy of trading activity and a sudden increase in the share price.

Consider the stock price of a company called Ashton Mining. Prior to April 1997 there was very little trading activity in this stock, except for a brief burst in January 1997. Then, all of a sudden, shares started to trade hands at an alarming pace, and the stock price shot up. You can see what happened in the graph on page 44 from the Canada Stockwatch Web site.

It is possible that such bursts of activity are legitimate, but they should make you suspicious. Our advice? Be cautious.

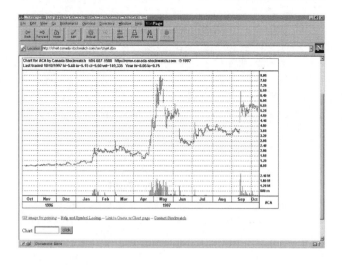

You should be aware that certain stock exchanges have a less-than-savoury reputation, and represent many of the thinly-traded stocks that are often used for scams. For example, the Vancouver Stock Exchange (VSE) has been referred to in such publications as *Forbes* magazine as the scam capital of the world, and the Alberta Stock Exchange (ASE) has suffered from its share of problems with the manipulation of small, relatively unknown stocks.

Both exchanges indicate they are working hard to clean up their reputation, but there is no doubt that extra caution is in order when dealing with VSE- or ASE-listed stocks.

That's not to say that the other major Canadian exchanges in Montreal and Toronto have entirely clean reputations. The TSE, for example, has had its reputation battered and bruised by the Bre-X scandal.

5. Don't make any investment decisions based on the advice of someone who conceals their identity.

Why would you? How could you?

There are many places on the Internet where you can participate in online discussions about specific companies. Two of the most popular sites for investment discussions are The Motley Fool and Silicon Investor. Silicon Investor seems to be the most popular, with the company claiming that 70% of all online financial discussions take place on its Web site. Both of these sites allow users to remain anonymous and use other identities instead of their real names.

Take a look at the following posting from Silicon Investor which occurred in the midst of the Ashton Mining affair we described earlier.

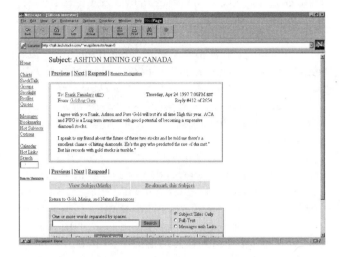

What could possibly possess you to make an investment decision based upon the posting of someone who has given themselves the online name of *"Goldbug Guru"*?

You need to exercise caution when obtaining investment information from any online discussion group. Even if a person reveals his true identity, how do you know he is who he says he is?

6. Don't trust strangers.

Not only should you not trust people who post information to the Internet under a false identity, you should be wary of strangers in general.

Some people are very good at winning your confidence online. They will tell you that they have personally checked out an investment opportunity, and that there is nothing you should be worried about.

Are you prepared to risk your hard-earned money on promises made by someone you don't even know? Because it's difficult to judge the character of anyone you meet online, you need to be careful.

7. Treat any claims about "insider information" with suspicion.

At one point during the Ashton Mining affair, one individual challenged another on the Silicon Investor Web site, and questioned the source of the other person's claims about a massive diamond find. The person doing the challenging asked the other individual where he was getting his information from. The individual responded, "from people in the know in and around the business."

In another posting in the same forum, *GoldBug Guru* noted, "*I speak to my friend about the future of these two stocks and he told me there's a excellent chance of hitting diamonds. He's the guy who predicted the rise of dia met.*" (You will notice that we haven't corrected the spelling mistakes.)

Let's explain what is being said here. *GoldBug Guru* says that his "friend" believes there's an excellent chance that the companies in question will strike diamonds. Furthermore, *GoldBug Guru* claims that his friend is the same person who predicted the rise of "dia met." *GoldBug Guru* is referring to DiaMet, another mining company that had a spectacular price rise during 1997.

This type of statement is typical of what you might find in an investment forum on the Internet. It might be made with an intent to commit fraud, or simply by someone who is bragging about their investment prowess. Whatever the case may be, caution is in order.

If you browse investment discussion groups and financial Web sites, you'll find all kinds of people who purport to be "in the know." They say they know someone inside the company, or someone in the industry, or someone close to the boyfriend of the daughter of the CEO. They're "in the loop." Or so they say.

Always treat such claims with extreme suspicion.

8. Be aware that people may be getting paid to hype an investment.

It is sad but true that sometimes companies pay people to "talk up" their stock online—either on Web sites or in investment discussion forums. In most cases, the people doing the promoting do not disclose the fact that they're being paid to publicize the stock. These paid promoters sometimes pose as investors in investment discussion forums and plant positive rumours designed to drive up the price of a company's stock.

9. Check the credentials of those you deal with.

The law in Canada and the U.S. is clear—only registered securities dealers/investment advisors may provide advice to people regarding the purchase of securities. And they can only advise people in the province where they are registered. This means that someone who is registered with the British Columbia Securities Commission to sell stocks in British Columbia should not be advising people in Ontario. And someone who is registered with the Ontario Securities Commission (but not with the British Columbia Securities Commission) should not be advising residents of British Columbia. Of course, it is next to impossible to enforce these rules on the Internet.

Mutual funds can be sold by all kinds of groups—such as the sales force for mutual fund companies, banks, trust companies, as well as personal financial planners and brokers. These sales take place with little regulation. For several years, the Ontario Securities Commission has been trying to proclaim that it has the right to regulate the mutual funds industry in Ontario, but has had no success to date. Hence, the industry is not regulated to the same extent as securities as described above. As a result, it is critical that you check out the qualifications and credibility of whomever you might be buying your mutual funds from.

On the Internet there is obviously a challenge with credibility—tens of thousands of people provide investment advice and counsel on the Internet each and every day, by way of investment newsletters, Web sites, comments in discussion forums, electronic mail, and other electronic means. Many people don't have the credentials to provide such advice—and hence are providing it illegally.

Provincial securities commissions in Canada are beginning to crack down on unlicensed individuals who are dispensing investment advice on the Internet. For example, in 1997 the Ontario Securities Commission (OSC) shut down the Web site of one individual who was providing investment advice without being licensed. However, we can just imagine how many other individuals remain

TIPS ON NOT FALLING PREY TO A CON ARTIST

Avoiding being hurt by a con artist is as easy as doing your homework—before you invest.

Contact your provincial securities regulator (The British Columbia Securities Commission) to see if the investment vehicle and the person selling it are registered.

Your provincial securities regulator will also be able to tell you if the salesperson has a disciplinary history, that is, whether any civil, criminal or administrative proceedings have been brought against him or her.

Contact your local Better Business Bureau to see if any complaints have been filed against the venture's promoters or principals.

Deal only with dealers or advisers having a proven track record.

Ask for written information on the investment product and the business. Such information, including financial data on the company and the risks involved in the investment, is contained in a prospectus. Read it carefully. Don't take everything you hear or read at face value. Ask questions if you don't understand, and do some sleuthing for yourself. If you need help in evaluating the investment, go to someone independent whom you can trust such as an attorney or an accountant.

Steer clear of investments touted with no down-side or risk.

FROM THE B.C. SECURITIES COMMISSION WEB SITE, IN THE SECTION "BE AN INFORMED INVESTOR" (**www.bcsc.bc.ca**)

online, far beyond the reach of the OSC, in jurisdictions beyond the reach of Ontario and Canadian law.

If in doubt about someone's credentials, you should check with the appropriate securities regulator to find out if the person is licensed to provide advice on buying or selling securities. In Canada, this means checking with your provincial or territorial securities commission. In the

United States, check with the state securities agency. We provide addresses and contact information for Canadian securities commissions in appendix A.

10. Recognize that there are rules to protect you.

Some of the large investment firms in Canada have policies governing what their financial advisors can and cannot do on the Internet. For example, Midland Walwyn is developing a policy that would require all of the financial advisors employed by Midland Walwyn to locate their Web sites on the official Midland Walwyn site.

In addition, there are strict by-laws and regulations governing advertising by investment firms that are members of the Investment Dealers Association of Canada (IDA). The IDA is a self-regulating body within the Canadian securities industry that ensures that its members operate accordingly to certain rules. IDA member firms and their employees who wish to advertise on the Internet *must* have their Web materials approved by a designated official within the firm who is responsible for advertising. As well, advertising must meet other criteria. For example, it must not:

- contain any untrue statement or omission of a material fact

- be false or misleading

- contain an unjustified promise of results

- contain any opinion or forecast of future events which is not clearly labeled as such

- fail to fairly present the potential risks to the client

- use unrepresentative statistics to suggest unwarranted or exaggerated conclusions; or fail to identify the material assumptions made in arriving at these conclusions.

Canada's stock exchanges also have their own by-laws and rules concerning promotional activities and disclosure of pertinent company information by their member firms.

These rules are designed to protect you, the investor, and it's important for you to know that they *do* extend to the Internet. For purposes of enforcement, most regulatory bodies treat the Internet just like any other advertising medium.

BE ALERT FOR TELLTALE SIGNS OF ONLINE INVESTMENT FRAUD

Be wary of promises of quick profits, offers to share "inside" information and pressure to invest before you have an opportunity to investigate.

Be careful of promoters who use "aliases." Pseudonyms are common online, and some salespeople will to try to hide their true identity. Look for other promotions by the same person.

Words like "guarantee," "high return," "limited offer," or "as safe as a C.D." may be a red flag. No financial investment is "risk free" and a high rate of return means greater risk.

Watch out for offshore scams and investment opportunities in other countries. When you send your money abroad, and something goes wrong, it's more difficult to find out what happened and to locate your money.

FROM THE U.S. SECURITIES AND EXCHANGE COMMISSION WEB SITE IN THE "INVESTOR ASSISTANCE & COMPLAINTS" SECTION. "INVESTOR ALERTS" (www.sec.gov/consumer/b-alert.htm)

Evaluating the Credibility and Validity of Online Information

Earlier in the chapter, we discussed the importance of assessing the credibility and validity of information you access on the Internet. Over the next few pages, we give some tips on how to do this.

10 Steps for Evaluating the Credibility and Validity of Online Information

1. Does the person or organization who created the site have a reputable track record?
2. Do the site creators list their credentials?
3. Is the information on the site subject to some type of review process?
4. Does the information seem to be professionally maintained, or does it seem "thrown together"?
5. What is the nature of the information?

6. Does the information seem to be too good to be true?
7. Can you back up the information with other independent sources?
8. Is the site updated frequently?
9. Does the site simply seem to want your money?
10. Are independent news reports available about the initiative?

1. Does the person or organization who created the site have a reputable track record?

When traveling through the Internet, keep in mind that Web sites are prepared by many different people and organizations. You need to think about whether you can trust information from certain sources. Understanding the source of the information will help you to judge the credibility and validity of what you read online. For example, when looking at a Web site, it's important to determine whether the site is being funded or financed by a particular organization. If this is the case, this might mean that the information in the site is biased toward the products or services of the sponsoring firm.

More than likely, sites created by banks, credit unions, trust companies, mutual fund companies, newspapers, and others will be more credible than those established by a layperson who just has an interest in a specific investment topic.

LEARNING CENTRE

Be sure to spend time in the Investor Learning Centre at the Canada Trust Web site (www.ctsecurities.com/ilc/). It features some very good information on investing and an excellent overview of "Investor Protection" issues.

Initiatives by major organizations such as GLOBEfund from the *Globe and Mail* and The Fund Library, both of which are obviously well-financed and quite serious, are generally more credible than those initiatives that are done on a shoestring budget by small, relatively unknown companies. And initiatives that have been endorsed or sanctioned by a professional association bear more credence than sites that are not.

All kinds of factors such as these must weigh into your assessment as to the validity and credibility of the information you are reading.

That's not to say that a page of information prepared by an investment professional or small company will be unreliable or incorrect. There are many excellent, reputable sources of information from smaller, lesser-known organizations.

2. Do the site creators list their credentials?

You can sometimes judge the validity of the information on a site by examining the background of the individuals or organizations who have put the site together.

Browse through the site, and see if it includes details on the background of the site's creators. Determine if investment professionals have assisted in the preparation and review of materials on the site. Find out what type of review process information on the Web site is subject to.

You should clearly understand that in the investment industry there is a difference between those people who are licensed to advise on securities and those that can provide general financial advice. This is a real source of confusion for novice investors. Provincial securities commissions do not regulate financial planners, bank employees, or mutual fund salespeople, but they do regulate brokers. This difference is really important when evaluating the credentials of people who provide information on the Internet—remember, there is no licensing process for mutual fund salespeople in Canada.

Finally, be on the lookout for bogus credentials— sometimes people will list qualifications that they don't really have.

3. Is the information on the site subject to some type of review process?

Sometimes you will find a site that not only clearly and unequivocally indicates the background of the people involved with the site, but also indicates that the information contained on it has been subject to some form of approval process. This information can be helpful when evaluating the credibility of financial information you find on the Internet.

Although it is usually not mentioned on Web sites, remember that any online advertising by investment firms that are members of the Investment Dealers Association of Canada must be approved by an official of the firm.

> We don't need more information about investment
> matters. We need less information that's more relevant.
> There's a ton of investment information on the
> Internet and much of it is junk. But you can find useful
> information from quality providers if you know how to
> harness the power of the Internet.
>
> JIM KERSHAW, "NET BENEFITS: UNWARY SURFERS MAY END UP
> SWIRLING IN WHIRLPOOLS OF CONFUSION, BUT FOR THOSE WHO
> KNOW WHERE TO LOOK, THE INTERNET IS RICH WITH INVESTMENT
> TOOLS AND KNOWLEDGE," *BC BUSINESS*, JANUARY 1996

4. Does the information seem to be professionally maintained, or does it seem "thrown together"?

Sometimes a quick tour of a site can give you a "gut feeling" for the quality of the information that you may find there.

If you browse a Web site and discover a lot of broken links, pages that don't work, and evidence that the site isn't being maintained properly, this should diminish your confidence in the information the site provides. The same holds true if the site is poorly organized, shows poor use of grammar, or has a lot of spelling mistakes—all the things that would generate in you a lack of confidence in the information found on the site. The quality of the site is often related to the quality of the information found there.

5. What is the nature of the information?

There is obviously a big difference in the information supplied on the Web site of the Royal Bank of Canada and a posting made by an individual in an online discussion forum. And obviously the Web site of the Montreal Stock Exchange provides more reliable information than you might find in a small investment newsletter that is emailed to everyone on a mailing list.

Hence, you should consider the nature of the information you are dealing with. Corporate information sites from established organizations would rank as more reliable than a newsletter put out by a small group of amateur investors, and a news report would bear more credence than a posting in a chat room.

6. Does the information seem too good to be true?

If so, it probably is.

7. Can you back up the information with other independent sources?

Information that you find online should always be verified with additional, independent sources that suggest the same thing.

> ...the SEC's point man on the Internet is uncertain of how much longer traditional regulation can ride this whirlwind. "Is it moving so quickly, with so many different influences, that for the first time, you're in a qualitatively different ball game?" asks SEC commissioner Steven Wallman.
>
> "CHALLENGES OF THE FINANCIAL CYBERCOP," *INSTITUTIONAL INVESTOR*, APRIL 1997 V31 N4 PP: 99

Never, never, never take something for granted that you read online without confirming it with other sources. How can you check out details about a particular company or person you might read about online? There are many information sources—both online and offline—that you can consult. For example, you should check with an investment or financial professional, such as an investment advisor or accountant, before acting on information you retrieve off the Internet. In addition, check the information you obtain online against what is being reported in newspapers, magazines, and on radio and television. Also check out company annual reports and prospectuses.

8. Is the site updated frequently?

If you encounter a site that has not been updated for some time, you should probably be leery of using the information found there. After all, the world of finance changes at a regular rate. How can you rely on information from a site where the owners don't take the time to ensure that the information they provide is kept up-to-date?

9. Does the site simply seem to want your money?

If you visit many sites you will inevitably come across some that want your credit card number as quickly as possible. Be suspicious of any sites that seem overly interested in your money.

10. Are independent news reports available about the initiative?

Finally, doing a search for news articles about a particular site, the site's creators, or on a specific investment topic may often reveal information that helps you to determine the validity of the information you are reading online. Sites that have been reviewed positively in the media often feature copies of these articles on their sites. Articles from independent news sources can help judge whether the information sources you are using are credible.

Keep in mind that positive media reports don't guarantee that the information you are reading is credible or valid. But it is another item in your checklist that may help you decide on the overall reliability of an online information resource.

Where to Get Help

If you're suspicious about an online investment opportunity, you want to report a scam, or you simply want to verify whether a certain person is licensed to sell securities in your province or territory, you should contact your provincial or territorial securities commission. The North American Securities Administrators Association (NASAA) has a search engine on its site that you can use to find the mailing addresses and email addresses of securities regulators across Canada and the United States. We provide contact information for provincial and territorial securities commissions in appendix A.

If you're interested in reading more about how you can protect yourself against fraud on the Internet, and investment fraud in general, you can contact the NASAA in Washington, D.C. at 1-8888-4-NASAA.

Web Sites Mentioned in This Chapter

British Columbia Securities Commission	www.bcsc.bc.ca
Canada Stockwatch	www.canada-stockwatch.com
GLOBEfund	www.globefund.com
Midland Walwyn	www.midwal.ca
Montreal Stock Exchange	www.me.org
National Association of Securities Dealers	www.nasd.com
North American Securities Administrators Association (NASAA)	www.nasaa.org
Royal Bank of Canada	www.royalbank.com
Silicon Investor	www.techstocks.com
The Fund Library	www.fundlibrary.com
The Motley Fool	www.fool.com
Vancouver Stock Exchange	www.vse.ca

CHAPTER 5

The Basics of Retirement Planning and RRSPs

To me—old age is always ten years older than I am.
ANDRE BERNARD

HIGHLIGHTS

- Like most Canadians, you will need to take responsibility for your financial affairs during your retirement. You can't rely on the government or your employer for support. Income from the government and your corporate pension plan, if any, will likely be inadequate.

- To properly understand retirement planning issues, you should be prepared to answer a fundamental question: how much money will you need when you retire?

- An integral part of the retirement planning process involves determining how much money you need to save each year in order to retire with a predetermined income in the future.

- An RRSP is the most important retirement vehicle available to Canadians. RRSPs are attractive because most contributions to an RRSP are tax-deductible. In addition, the investment income produced by an RRSP is tax-free until you begin to withdraw it.

> • Once you retire, you can convert your RRSP into an annuity, a registered retirement income fund, or a life income fund. This allows you to begin to use the money upon retirement while minimizing the tax payable on that money.

"Retirement planning."

For most people, the phrase conjures up the image of running out to the local bank on February 28 to deposit their annual RRSP contribution—and figuring out while they're standing in line what type of investment they will place their money into.

But retirement planning is about much more than this—indeed it is a crucial component of one's financial life. Only by confronting the financial issues of retirement—and understanding why you need to begin saving right away—can you get a full appreciation of the retirement planning process.

There are many questions that you need to ask yourself when you start to plan for your retirement, such as how much am I going to need?, how am I going to save that much?, and what happens to the money when I actually do retire? The fact of the matter is that sometimes there are so many questions that the process can be overwhelming, and indeed, almost frightening. But by breaking the process down into several phases you will find that it can become very manageable. The key things you need to think about are:

- Do I really need to save for my retirement?

- How much am I going to need when I retire?

- How much money do I have now for my retirement, and how much more do I need to save?

- What can I invest in?

- Where do RRSPs fit in? What are some of the key things that I should know about RRSPs?

- What happens to the money I have in my RRSP when I retire?

In this chapter, we cover the general aspects of these issues, while in the next chapter we put into perspective how you can use the Internet to learn more about many of the specifics related to retirement and RRSPs.

Do I Need to Save for My Retirement?

The basic answer is yes, you do.

If you have a job, you can't expect that your company's pension plan or the Canada Pension Plan will necessarily provide you with enough income upon retirement. In fact, these sources might very well be inadequate to give you the income necessary to meet your retirement expectations. Further, given some estimates that many people will find themselves working in as many as six to eight different jobs in their lifetime, it is likely that many people won't have one good, long-term corporate pension plan to take care of them in the future.

> For small business owners, the biggest hurdle to retirement planning is getting started. Like most Canadians, owner-managers tend to procrastinate in making their registered retirement savings plan contribution. Unlike many Canadians, they haven't a company pension to fall back on.
>
> SUSAN NOAKES, "SAVING FOR RETIREMENT REQUIRES DISCIPLINE," *FINANCIAL POST*, FEBRUARY 20, 1997

If you are self-employed, as many Canadians are, the situation is even more dramatic—you are solely responsible for taking care of yourself in retirement, since there isn't any company pension plan whatsoever.

Let's look at these challenges in greater detail and put them into perspective.

The "Social Safety Net" Will Not Be Adequate for Many Canadians

Many Canadians who are used to a fairly affluent lifestyle will find that Canada's social programs will not allow them to maintain such a lifestyle in their retirement.

For a long time, Canada has lived with the philosophy that the government should provide monies to all Canadians to ensure they have an income upon retirement. The Canada Pension Plan was established in 1966, and its founding principles still stand—every employed and self-employed person working in Canada contributes to the plan, and both they and their family members are eligible to receive payment from the plan in case of retirement, disability, or death.

In March of last year, Finance Minister Paul Martin presented a deficit-reduction budget. Martin's message was clear: Don't expect much help from Ottawa in funding your retirement.

BRIAN QUINLAN, "A DO-IT-PRETTY-MUCH-BY-YOURSELF RETIREMENT PLAN," *FINANCIAL POST MAGAZINE*, JANUARY 1997

Yet the government's "social safety net" doesn't provide much money—the Canada Pension Plan provides payments of less than $15,000 per annum to those who were gainfully employed. Another plan, the government Old Age Security system, provides less than $5,000 per annum to most Canadian citizens over the age of 65.

That is not a lot of money to maintain the type of lifestyle that you may be enjoying today. Clearly, you must take responsibility for your future financial circumstances.

There Is Widespread Concern Over the Health of the Government Social Safety Net

The financial press is full of stories of the problems anticipated with the Canada Pension Plan (CPP).

Quite simply, the CPP is not adequately funded—the total payments due to all potential retirees today and in the future far exceeds the funds that will be available if contributions by the existing labour force in Canada don't change.

The net effect is that if politicians don't deal with the Plan's fundamental structural problems, it is expected to run out of money sometime early in the next century. That's why there was much talk of reform of the CPP system in late 1997, with a suggestion that CPP contributions

> **"The first beneficiaries of the CPP will receive retire-
> ment benefits averaging over 11 times greater than
> their contributions,"** she says, **"while those entering the
> plan today will receive a return equal to one-half of
> their contributions. Why should young Canadians will-
> ingly support such an unfair scheme?"**
>
> DIANE ABLONCZY, A MEMBER OF THE REFORM PARTY, COMMENTING
> ON SCHEMES ANNOUNCED IN LATE 1997 TO REVAMP THE CANADA
> PENSION PLAN SYSTEM. JONATHAN CHEVREAU, "CPP REFORMS
> LEAVE THE YOUNG LIVID," *FINANCIAL POST*, SEPTEMBER 25, 1997

by employees be doubled. Given the highly politicized
atmosphere surrounding the Plan, it will probably take
quite some time for the government to deal with the
issue.

The result? Many baby boomers and Generation X-ers
wonder—rightly so—if there will even be a Canada
Pension Plan when they retire, and are beginning to realize that they will have to take care of themselves. In particular, the younger generation has come to realize that
the funds they are paying into the CPP today aren't being
put away for their own retirement, but are being partly
used to pay the benefits of current retirees. Further, the
rest of their contributions will be fully used up when massive numbers of baby boomers begin to retire in the next
few decades. If nothing is done, there will be nothing left
by the time they retire.

Company Pension Plans Might Not Be Adequate

Many Canadians think that their company pension plan
will be sufficient for their retirement years. Yet, once they
really look into these pension plans they often discover
that the payments upon retirement might not be what
they had thought.

Not only that, but there is some risk attached to corporate pension plans—there have been a few situations
involving the failure of a corporate plan, or situations in
which a plan had insufficient funds to pay what had been
promised. What guarantee do you have that a company
pension plan will be able to meet all of its obligations in
the future?

With the Loss of Job Stability Comes a Need for Self-reliance

Clearly we have entered an era in which the "job-for-life" is no longer guaranteed.

Many people realize that even if their employer offers a company pension plan, chances are that their jobs won't last long enough for them to contribute an amount that will provide them with adequate retirement income. The result is that they will have to take care of themselves!

The Loss of a Job Can Mean Sudden Pension Planning

Those who have quit or been laid off from their jobs often find themselves with a lump sum pay out from the corporate pension plan.

They must learn—and learn fast—about retirement planning in order to figure out what to do with the money and how to avoid undue tax penalties. In these situations many people become their own pension plan managers—whether they want to or not!

Canada isn't the only country in which the government pension plan will be inadequate. In the article "Boomers: A Population Time Bomb," *Newsday*, September 18, 1997, it was noted that baby boomers will cause immense stress on the U.S. retirement system as they age. The article stated, "Their expectations for retirement will affect not only themselves, but also the course of the nation. If they demand and receive the same Social Security, Medicare and Medicaid benefits as their parents, these entitlements will consume the entire federal budget (less interest payments) by 2030."

There Might Not Be Enough for Early Retirement

More and more Canadians want to retire early, yet discover that if they do, their pension plans will hit them with substantial financial penalties.

That is because the amount provided under many pension plans assumes that an individual will work to the age of 65. If you retire early these financial assumptions are thrown out of whack, often resulting in a lower regular pension payment.

How Much Am I Going to Need When I Retire?

All of the reasons above should indicate to you that you must begin to figure out how to take care of yourself upon retirement.

Obviously, once you retire, you will no longer have a salary, but you will still need money to pay for your day-to-day living expenses. In addition to that, you might need money to travel, to help out your family members, or even to purchase a retirement home in Florida or elsewhere if you are so inclined.

How do you go about figuring out how much money you will need to save to retire? The place to start is by understanding what it is you spend your money on today, and then deciding if that is something that you will spend money on when you retire. You should think about what you might spend each month, for example:

- **Mortgage/Rent payments.** Do you make these payments now? Do you think you will have to make them when you retire, or will you be self-sufficient in terms of home ownership? How much money might you need to cover any future potential nursing home expenses?

- **Living expenses.** What do you spend today on clothing, food, utilities, automobiles, and other necessities? What might you expect to spend upon retirement?

- **Family expenses.** Do you support any children? Will the children be finished their education by the time you retire, or might you be supporting them? Do you think you will have to support any other family member when you retire?

- **Entertainment and travel expenses.** Do you plan on traveling when you retire? If so, how much do you want to have available to you for such discretionary expenses in the future?

These are only a few examples of what you will need to consider when you go about determining how much money you will need on a yearly basis when you retire. You have to give a lot of thought to where you might be spending money some twenty, thirty, or forty years from now, to get a rough idea of the annual income that you will need.

And just to add a bit of complexity to the matter, the yearly income amount that you will be calculating is based on today's dollar. To properly figure out your required annual income on retirement, you will need to consider inflation in all of your calculations.

What should you do? We'd suggest sitting down with pen and paper—or a spreadsheet—and work out some math to get a rough idea as to the annual income you will need upon retirement, based on what you are spending today and what you might spend in the future.

As we will see in chapter 7 there are a few tools online that can help you to do this.

How Much Money Do I Have Now for My Retirement, and How Much More Do I Need to Save?

Having figured out how much you will need to retire, the next question is knowing how much you will need to save in order to achieve that goal.

No matter what the amount, you have to begin saving today. To have a secure financial future upon retirement, you will have to have put away a sum of money now, and in every other year leading up to your retirement, in order to supplement any funds that might be available from your pension plan and from the Canada Pension Plan. The money that you save will then be used to provide you with your desired retirement "salary" for the remaining years of your life.

Of course, to figure out how much you need to save every year, you must spend a bit of time figuring out the answers to two of the hardest questions when it comes to retirement planning.

- What annual income will you need throughout your retirement?

A Royal Trust survey released in 1996 indicated that most people start saving for their retirement at the age of 34. If they put aside $4,000 per year, they'd have a little more than $532,000 set aside when they retire at the age of 65. But if they started saving at the age of 20, they would have had $1.7 million set aside. That's why it makes sense to start saving sooner rather than later.

SOURCE: ROYAL BANK WEB SITE, **www.royalbank.com**

- How long do you expect to live after you retire?

The complexity doesn't stop there—there are other factors that will affect how much you need to save as well. For example, at what age do you plan to retire? There can be a big difference between the amount you must save each year if you plan to retire at the age of 55 instead of 65.

Let's put all of this into perspective using a very simplified—and financially inaccurate—example. Let's say you plan on retiring early, at the age of 60, and figure you will live to the ripe old age of 80. You'd like to have an annual income each year of $50,000, figuring that will be enough to take care of your needs, based on the work that you did as we described above. Today, you are thirty five years old. This means that you have 25 years to save a million dollars—or in other words, you must save $40,000 each and every year leading up to your retirement.

That's the basic way that retirement planning works—however, the calculations above are grossly inaccurate, since they ignore what financial people call the "time value of money." The actual amount we would have to save every year, assuming we earn about 10% on our investments and with inflation estimated to run consistently at 3%, is only $12,236.80 each year, not $40,000.

The Need to Save Today—Due to the Time Value of Money

Where did we come up with this figure of $12,236.80? We used the Internet—given the tools that are becoming available online, it is not too difficult to calculate how much you need to save today in order to retire with a certain income level in the future.

But before we take a look at such online tools, you should have an understanding of how the "saving equation" works. The key point that you need to understand is that the sooner you start saving for your retirement, the better.

That is directly due to the "time value of money"— which is a complex way of saying that money that is invested today earns money on itself each and every day up until you retire. The earlier you invest it, the longer the period of time that it can earn money on itself—and the larger it will grow. Hence, the need to put away only $12,236.80 each year, instead of $40,000.

What happens if you do put away $40,000 each year? You might think that if you put this away each year for the next twenty five years, you'll have your million dollars. But not quite—you will have much more than that. To be precise, you will have $2,529,961.51, according to one financial calculator that we found on the Internet. This is because each year's savings will earn interest or other income, depending on what you invest it in. Hence, the value of your savings will "compound."

The time value of money makes your retirement planning rather complex. Let's take a look at how compounding works. Say you invest your $40,000 each year, on your birthday, in an investment that earns ten percent interest per year. At the end of the first year you will have $44,000: your original $40,000, plus $4,000 in interest. At the end of year two, you will have not just $80,000 but $92,400.00: $40,000 from each of years one and two, for a total of $80,000, plus $4,000 in interest from year one, and $8,400 (($80,000 + $4,000) × 10%) in interest from year two.

What do you have by the time you are 60? Do the math, and you'll see that it is somewhere around $2.5 million. What happens is that the money you save each year earns *compound interest*, that is, you earn interest on the interest.

Since you have to take this compounding factor into account, calculating how much you need to save each year is not as simple as adding up $40,000 for each of 25 years. This makes it a little complex for you to figure out exactly how much money you need to save each year to retire comfortably in the future.

Fortunately, as we will see in chapter 7, there are a number of online calculators that take into account this time value of money in their estimate of what you must save each year. Many of these calculators also take into consideration any income that you may receive from a company pension plan if you have one, or the Canada Pension Plan, helping you to come up with a more accurate calculation.

Understanding Your Current Coverage

Don't forget where your company pension plan fits into this whole situation. Money that is invested in a pension plan of which you are a member is also compounding—and your company pension representatives can give you a good idea of what type of payment you can expect during your retirement as a result.

A key point is that if you are employed and your company has a pension plan, you should definitely consider taking part! Second, ask your company pension representative for a clear calculation of the benefits you will receive upon retirement. Make sure you understand what the benefits would be if you decided to retire early. Third, ask them if you are taking advantage of maximum contributions—you might not be contributing the maximum allowable amount each year. If not, find out how to do so, and whether you can make "prior-year catch-up payments" in order to ensure that you have contributed the maximum amount for all prior years.

You should also determine what you will get from the Canada Pension Plan, keeping in mind that you might not even see some of this money since it could be "clawed back" through your income tax return. There is a lot of talk that as the Canadian Pension Plan system is restructured, those in a high income bracket upon retirement will have to "pay back" the CPP payments they have received—which is often referred to as a "claw back."

Take some time to understand what monthly or annual payment you might get from these two sources upon retirement, because we will use them in some of the retirement calculators that we'll look at in chapter 7.

What Can I Invest In?

After you complete these calculations, you will likely be shocked at the amount you need to save to fund your retirement expectations. For many people it might not be easy to save $12,000 or so per year for their retirement.

In order to work out a plan to accomplish your objectives there are some issues that you must address. Two of the key issues are:

- how you will save the money necessary for your retirement, and

- what kind of investments will provide a suitable return to help to ensure that your money grows.

The first issue can be a pretty serious challenge for many people, and there is not much advice we can give on what to do. If you don't have any extra money that you can save and things are pretty tight, you must simply decide that saving for your retirement is something that you really want to do, and that you will work hard to accomplish it. This means cutting back current expenses and rejuggling your current financial situation—it can mean that you have a lot of work to do to improve your current financial circumstances. If you need some help with financial planning, we would suggest that you take a look at our book, *Canadian Money Management Online—Personal Finance on the Net.*

The investment issue is more straightforward—the types of things you can invest in are endless. Everything from bonds, Guaranteed Investment Certificates (GICs), Canada Savings Bonds (CSBs), common and preferred shares, real estate, mutual funds, etc. For many people, their primary retirement investment consists of the value of their home—given the likelihood that it will be mortgage-free upon retirement, and can be sold for a profit (assuming that there is someplace else to move to!)

The whole issue of investing is a complex topic, and hence we have devoted several chapters to this issue.

Where Do RRSPs Fit In? What Are Some of the Key things I Should Know About RRSPs?

Some time ago, the federal government established the Registered Retirement Savings Plan (RRSP) when it realized that it would be in its best interest to encourage Canadians to save for their retirement.

> **Your RRSP is still "the single most important piece in your retirement planning," says Neil Russell, director of financial counselling for Royal Trust. That's why it is so disturbing to find that Canadians are not taking full advantage of this opportunity to save for retirement, he says.**
>
> MONICA TOWNSON, "COLD COMFORT," *FINANCIAL POST*, JANUARY 11, 1997

An RRSP is essentially a retirement investment—made under very stringent rules—that provides you with a tax deduction equal to the amount you invest. The amount that you can invest depends on your particular situation. Making the maximum RRSP contribution that you can each year is probably one of the smartest financial activities that you can undertake, for reasons that we will see below.

What Types of RRSPs Are There?

There are essentially two types of RRSPs, non-directed and self-directed.

Non-directed

Non-directed RRSPs are investments offered by banks, trust companies, insurance companies, credit unions, etc. In this case, you simply decide what type of investment you want—generally, a savings account, guaranteed investment certificate (GIC), term deposit, or mutual fund. Once you have established the RRSP, it is managed for you by the financial institution. You will occasionally get involved to figure out what to do with the money when a GIC matures, or if you wish to switch it to another type of investment. Such RRSPs are very simple and straightforward, in that you invest your money, and receive a tax receipt that you can use to claim your RRSP deduction.

Self-directed
In this case, you take on more responsibility for managing your own RRSP and choosing what to invest in, much as you would manage your non-RRSP retirement investments. You set up a self-directed plan with a financial institution, and from that point, figure out what types of investments you would like to include in the plan. You can invest in a wider range of financial instruments than in a non-directed plan, such as stocks and bonds. There are some restrictions on the types of transactions that can be undertaken in a self-directed RRSP.

What Are the Advantages of Having an RRSP?
There are two key tax advantages to investing in an RRSP:

- The amount you contribute is usually deductible on your tax return, making the RRSP one of the last remaining "tax loopholes" with which to reduce your income tax.

In the past five years, the numbers of investors turning to self-directed plans rose 85 per cent and assets in such plans have more than doubled, according to Colin Deane, a principal with Ernst & Young Management Consultants.

KRISTIN GOFF, "SELF-DIRECTED RRSPS FASTEST-GROWING TREND," OTTAWA CITIZEN, FEBRUARY 7, 1996

- The income earned in an RRSP is tax-free until you withdraw the funds, meaning that it is not taxed until you begin to withdraw the money on a regular or lump sum basis upon retirement.

What an RRSP lets you do, in essence, is obtain "free money" from the government. What do you do to get this free money? You promise to put away your own money and not touch it until your retirement.

The amount of tax that you can save by investing money in an RRSP can be dramatic, depending upon your level of income, and hence, the tax bracket or "marginal tax rate" that you fall into.

Let's say you take $5,000 of your savings and put it into an RRSP. That $5,000 counts as a deduction on your tax return, and if your marginal tax rate is 27 percent, you will have a tax savings of $1,350.

Result? A $5,000 investment that really cost you only $3,650! Right now in the tax system there is no better bargain.

Understanding Your Marginal Tax Rate

The only significant number to understand when it comes to tax planning and things like RRSPs is the *marginal tax rate*—that is, the amount of tax that will be paid on each additional dollar of income, or the tax that will be saved on each additional dollar of tax deduction, at your current level of income. It is a concept that you will have to become comfortable with, as complex as it might seem.

Many people fall into the trap of thinking about averages when it comes to tax rates. For example, if you have a net income of $80,000 and you paid $35,000 in tax, you might assume that your tax rate is about 43.75% percent ($35,000 divided by $80,000).

But the way the Canadian tax system works, that isn't really a useful number—and in fact, it is quite meaningless.

After all, think about what happens if your income increases by $1,000 to $81,000. How much additional tax might you owe on that extra money? Thinking your tax rate is 43.75%, you might guess $437.50.

But that's not the right answer—if you are resident in the province of Nova Scotia in 1997, you'll face an additional $500 in tax on that extra $1,000, not $437.50. That's because the marginal tax rate for every extra dollar earned in Nova Scotia at that level of income is 50%.

Why do they make things so complex? Because the tax system in Canada is tiered—you pay a low amount of tax on the first bit of income that you earn, a higher rate on the next bit, and an even higher rate on the remainder. This tiering has been done so that those with a lower income pay a lower rate of tax.

It is the rate that you pay on that last bit of income that is important—that is what is known as your marginal tax rate. And if you are only at the second tier of income, you have a lower marginal tax rate than if you have an income at the higher tier.

Marginal tax rates in Canada vary as a result of the different provincial tax rates. The maximum marginal tax rates, and the income levels at which those marginal tax rates come into effect, are seen in the table below.

Top 1997 Marginal Tax Rates

B.C.	$70,400	54.2%
Alberta	$63,400	46.1%
Saskatchewan	$63,400	52.0%
Manitoba	$63,400	50.4%
Ontario	$65,000	51.6%
Quebec	$63,400	52.9%
N.B.	$93,000	51.1%
P.E.I.	$63,400	50.3%
Nova Scotia	$79,200	50.0%
Newfoundland	$63,400	53.3%
Yukon	$63,400	46.6%
N.W.T.	$63,400	44.4%

COURTESY KPMG, www.kpmg.ca

Marginal Tax Rates and Your RRSP

What is the impact of the marginal tax rate when it comes to RRSPs? Knowing the marginal tax rate is critical to figuring out how much of a savings you might get from your RRSP contribution.

Let's say you live in Ontario, you want to contribute $10,000 to an RRSP, and your income is $80,000. By contributing the $10,000 you will be reducing your taxable income to $70,000, thereby saving tax dollars at the highest tax rate, i.e., you will save $10,000 $\times$ (1 − 0.516), or $4,840.

That calculation is why the marginal tax rate is so important.

Not only that, but any income earned on the $10,000 RRSP investment is shielded from the taxman until you begin to withdraw that money, usually after you retire. If you are thirty-five years old and plan to retire when you are sixty-five, your investment will earn income, tax free, for thirty years before you have to begin to pay tax on it. Add in the effect of compounding that we have described above, and your RRSP will grow even faster.

What Type of Investments Can I Hold in My RRSP?

The type of investments that you will choose to hold in your RRSP will depend very much on what type of investor you are, and whether you go with a non-directed or self-directed plan.

You can hold many different types of investments in your non-directed RRSP, including mutual funds, guaranteed investment certificates (GICs) and term deposits, savings accounts, or Canada Savings Bonds. You can also hold foreign investments, but they must not exceed 20 percent of the total value of your overall RRSP.

Self-directed RRSPs can include these investments, as well as stocks and bonds and other forms of investments.

Is an RRSP Protected If the Organization in Which the Investment Is Held Collapses?

It depends on the type of investment:

- Your RRSP is protected (up to $60,000) if it is in a savings account, GIC, or term deposit (being held for less than five years) at a financial institution covered by the Canada Deposit Insurance Corporation (CDIC).

- If your RRSP is at a credit union and is in a savings account, GIC, or term deposit, it might be covered up to a certain amount by a provincial credit union insurance fund. For example, RRSPs in credit unions in British Columbia are covered for up to $100,000.

- If your RRSP is held in a mutual fund, it is not covered by the CDIC but might be covered by the Canadian Investor Protection Fund (CIPF), an initiative established by the Toronto, Montreal, Vancouver, and Alberta Stock Exchanges, The Toronto Futures Exchange, and the Investment Dealers Association of Canada. The fund provides coverage of up to $500,000 should a member financial institution in which you have an RRSP fail. Many brokerages such as Nesbitt Burns and Midland Walwyn are members of the CIPF.

An important point is that this fund only applies to the failure of a member financial institution—there is no coverage if the value of a particular mutual fund decreases because of the decrease in value of the investments which are held in it.

- If you have a self-directed RRSP and hence invest your RRSP in stocks, bonds, or other similar financial instruments, you are not covered if an organization in which you had bought a stock, bond, or other eligible investment collapses. You undertake the same risk as you normally would if you have these investments outside of an RRSP.

What we would suggest is that you always check into the insured status of any RRSP investment that you make. Fortunately, the Internet can assist you in this regard.

How Much Should/Could I Put into an RRSP?

If you have a job but are not a member of a pension plan at the company where you work, or if you are self-employed, your maximum RRSP contribution will be equal to 18 percent of your previous year's "earned income," up to a maximum of $13,500. You can contribute any amount you like up to this maximum. If your earned income is $43,000, the maximum you can contribute to your RRSP is $7,740 ($43,000 × 18%).

If you are a member of company pension plan, your allowable RRSP contribution amount may be adjusted downward by a "pension adjustment" or "p.a.". In short, you can contribute the same amount described above, less your "p.a," which appears on your T4. If you would like to know this number immediately, contact the pension department of your company.

Earned income is broadly defined as salary, bonuses, commission, net business income, and other sources of income that exclude investment income, employment insurance, etc.

LOTS OF ROOM FOR IMPROVEMENT!

According to Industry Canada statistics, in 1995 Canadians were eligible to contribute $153 billion to their RRSP, but actually contributed only $23 billion.

If you are not sure of the amount you can contribute to your RRSP, call the Tax Information Phone System (TIPS) at Revenue Canada. They will be able to give you the information you need. You can find the number for TIPS at the Revenue Canada Web site, since there is a different number for each region of the country.

Should I Put Money into an RRSP or Pay Down My Mortgage?

The only two significant financial decisions that many Canadians have had to make are:

- taking out a mortgage to buy a home
- investing in an RRSP.

If they have the money available, some people wonder if it makes more sense to pay down their mortgage or if they should invest the money in an RRSP.

Because of the tax benefits of RRSPs, if you have not used up your full contribution limit you should always invest in your RRSP before paying down your mortgage. We will take a look at a calculator on the Internet in chapter 7 that puts this into perspective.

Somewhat related to this topic is the fact that you can use a portion of your RRSP investment to purchase a home. This is done through the Home Buyers' Plan. There are various restrictions to this program, but essentially it allows first-time buyers to borrow up to $20,000 from each of their RRSPs to buy a home, at no interest and with no withholding taxes.

Does It Make Sense to Borrow to Make My RRSP Contribution?

Every year financial institutions and investment advisers urge Canadians to consider taking out a loan in order to maximize their RRSP contributions.

The idea behind this is simple—you take out a loan to invest in an RRSP. The result will be a reduction in the tax you owe or a tax refund. If you get a refund you can take the resulting tax refund cheque and use it to pay off part of the loan. You then work on paying off the balance of the loan over time.

Does it make sense to do this? Yes, because as you will see, it lets you add money to your RRSP for a rather low cost.

But first and foremost, you would do this only if you can't afford to make the full RRSP contribution with your own funds, and only if you can afford to pay off the balance of the loan in a reasonable length of time.

How do you calculate the savings from making an RRSP contribution that is financed by a loan?

- Figure out how much you can save on your own and deduct this from the amount that you are permitted to contribute to your RRSP, up to the $13,500 yearly limit. The difference is what you have to borrow.

- Calculate the tax savings on that borrowed portion. Do this by taking the amount that you borrowed and multiplying it by your "marginal tax rate." This is the amount of tax savings you will achieve.

- The amount of the loan that you will have to pay back can be reduced by any tax refund that you may receive from the government.

Let's look at an example. Assuming you can contribute the full $13,500 and that you have saved $3,500 to contribute on your own, you can borrow an additional $10,000 to reach your maximum RRSP contribution. If you are at a 45 percent tax rate you will have a tax savings of $6,075. Assuming that your circumstances are such that the $6,075 tax savings results in a full tax refund of $6,075, you can immediately use the refund to pay down your loan.

That means you will have $13,500 in the bank paid for with $3,500 of your own money and a loan that only cost you, in effect, $3,925 ($10,000 less the $6,075 refund). You will have obtained a $13,500 investment for only $7,425 ($3,500 + $3,925)—not a bad deal at all. Now you can start working on paying off the $3,925 loan balance.

What if you would like to take out a loan, contribute it to your RRSP, and get a refund back that exactly matches the amount of the loan that you took out? Doing this would let you pay the loan off immediately with your tax refund.

You can do this if you have some money to contribute to the RRSP on your own. A simple calculation will show you how much of a loan you should take out.

- Take the amount you have to contribute ($3,500).

- Divide this by 1 minus your marginal tax rate, assuming a marginal tax rate of 45 percent $(1 - 0.45)$, i.e., $\$3,500 \div (1 - 0.45)$.

- This equals $6,363. From this amount subtract the amount you can contribute on your own ($3,500) to get the balance to borrow: $2,863.

- You will have a $6,363 deduction on your tax return. At the 45 percent marginal tax rate this will equal a refund of $2,863—the exact amount needed to pay off your loan.

There will be a tiny bit of interest to pay—given that it might take a month or two for your refund to come back.

As you can see, it is definitely in your best interest to take out a loan to invest in your RRSP—in effect, you have contributed just $3,500 but have $6,363 in the bank.

An important point to keep in mind is that the interest that you pay on the loan is not deductible on your tax return.

What Is a Spousal RRSP?

As you get into the world of RRSPs, you will keep encountering the phrase, "spousal RRSP." Spousal RRSPs are a good idea, because they can help to lower the overall tax burden of a couple.

How do they work? The spouse with the higher income contributes to the RRSP of the spouse with the lower income. The benefit comes in two ways:

- The spouse with the higher income takes the tax deduction now, which results in getting the maximum tax deduction possible. Because that spouse probably pays tax at a higher rate, this helps to reduce the overall amount of tax paid by the couple.

- The spouse with the lower income now has an RRSP investment. Upon retirement that spouse will earn the income from this investment.

Note that at the time of writing the Revenue Canada definition of spouse was:

- *a legally married spouse and a common-law spouse. A common-law spouse is a person of the opposite sex who, at that particular time, is living with you in a common-law relationship, and:*

- *is your child's natural or adoptive parent (legal or in fact); or*

- *had been living with you in such a relationship for at least 12 continuous months, or had previously lived with you in such a relationship for at least 12 continuous months (when you calculate the 12 continuous months, include any period of separation of less than 90 days).*

- *Once either of these two situations applies, we consider you to have a common-law spouse, except for any period that you were separated for 90 days or more because of a breakdown in the relationship.*

The key to making a spousal plan work for you in the future is to make sure that both of you will be in about the same tax bracket when you retire. This means making sure that not all of the retirement income is in one person's name.

What Happens If I Need Money?

You might be asking yourself if you can withdraw funds from your RRSP, and wondering what the consequences would be.

If you take money out of your RRSP you will be taxed on the amount that you withdraw, in essence making it a bad idea. It might also serve to move you into a higher tax bracket, making the penalty that much worse.

If you need to withdraw funds from a spousal RRSP, be careful of what Revenue Canada calls "attribution rules." What this means is that if the funds are withdrawn within three years of making a contribution, then the withdrawn amount will be included on your tax return, not that of your spouse's—and since you are likely at a higher tax rate, you end up paying more in tax.

If you need money you may be better off getting a regular loan from your financial institution.

What Happens to the Money I Have in My RRSP When I Retire?

You have three choices, any one of which you must carry out by December 31 on the year you turn 69:

- You can withdraw all the money from the RRSP and pay tax on it immediately—not a terribly good idea, since much of the money will be taxed at the highest possible tax rate, which could mean that you could immediately lose one half of your total RRSP investment!

- Move the money into an "annuity" (which you can actually do before the age of 69) so that you withdraw the monies gradually throughout your retirement. This helps to ensure that much of the money in your RRSP is taxed at the lowest possible tax rates—after all, you will remember from our discussion of marginal tax rates that with the tiered tax rate system in Canada, you want to ensure that you get as much income as you can taxed at the lowest possible rate. This can be accomplished by spreading your RRSP money out over a number of years.

- Move the money into a Registered Retirement Income Fund (RRIF), which is like an annuity, but which has some special features that make it more attractive.

Clearly, you have to decide between choosing an annuity and a RRIF.

Annuities are most often sold by insurance and trust companies. An annuity is an investment that pays you a sum of money on a regular basis, usually every month, over a fixed period of time, such as ten years. This allows you to receive the money from your RRSP investment over a period of time, spreading out the tax bill on those moneys. Income earned on the money in the annuity is

---

RRSPs have been called the most powerful wealth-building tool that Canadians can use. An RRSP contribution not only reduces your tax bill, thus giving you more money to invest, it also allows you to earn income in your RRSP on a tax-deferred basis. The combination of the tax deduction and tax-sheltered growth will make your investment grow up to three times as fast as a similar investment outside an RRSP

ROBERT KERR, "YOUNG INVESTOR SEEKS RISK-FREE GROWTH," *THE MONTREAL GAZETTE*, SEPTEMBER 16,1996

subject to tax as it is earned. Once you purchase an annuity your control of how the money is invested ends—it is left up to the company that you purchased the annuity from to decide how to invest it. Also, unless you buy an indexed annuity, the amount of your monthly payment will be the same year after year, regardless of inflation or any changes in your financial needs.

A *RRIF* is like an annuity in that you are provided a regular stream of payments, thereby spreading the tax bill over several years. However, unlike an annuity, the income earned on the money in the RRIF is accumulated tax-free. As some have said, a RRIF is like an RRSP in reverse, since the money earned in the RRIF is tax-free, and instead of contributing over time you are withdrawing over time. Another key difference from an annuity is with a RRIF you determine what you wish to invest in, much as you do with your RRSP. One other important aspect of a RRIF is that you must withdraw a certain amount each year, ranging from seven to nine percent depending on your age.

Obviously, a RRIF will make sense for most people given that the income in it accumulates tax free.

The Internet and RRSPs

This chapter has provided a bit of a whirlwind tour of RRSP concepts, and has touched briefly on what are some fairly complex topics.

Fortunately, the Internet can be an extremely useful tool to help you understand how to learn more about RRSPs and retirement issues. We will devote the next chapter to providing you with an overview of how you can best use it in that regard.

Web Sites Mentioned in This Chapter

Canada Deposit Insurance Corporation	www.cdic.ca
Canadian Investor Protection Fund	www.cipf.ca
Revenue Canada	www.rc.gc.ca

CHAPTER 6

Retirement Planning and RRSPs on the Internet

Research is what I'm doing when I don't know what I'm doing. WERNHER VON BRAUN

HIGHLIGHTS

- The Internet is an extremely useful resource for educating yourself about the fundamentals of retirement planning and RRSPs.

- There are five popular sources of RRSP and retirement information on the Web. These include sites with general retirement information; sites developed by financial organizations; newspaper and magazine Web sites; sites produced by accounting firms; and information provided by financial planners, advisors, authors, and journalists.

- Use caution when accessing RRSP and retirement information on the Internet. Many of the sites you will visit are clever sales pitches. We recommend you favour those sites that educate you rather than ask for your money.

The world of retirement planning and RRSPs might seem excessively complex and, dare we say, even dull. After looking at the issues described in the previous chapter, one might find little enthusiasm for the task at hand.

Fortunately, the Internet has emerged as a tool to help you make your way through the morass of complex RRSP and retirement issues—and bring a little bit of excitement to your efforts. It's a veritable gold mine of useful background information that can help you learn more about retirement issues and help you understand RRSPs.

Sales Pitches Online

Of course, there is a double-edged sword at work with the Internet—useful as this technology might be to help you to learn about retirement planning and RRSPs, you will also discover it to be a cesspool of sales pitches.

Voyage online and you will discover a wealth of advertising, marketing, and sales-oriented material. Each and every investment site seems to offer its own definitive theory about how Canadians should invest for their retirement. All too often, a company will suggest that the magical solution to your retirement planning needs is simply to buy a particular mutual fund that they happen to sell.

It is estimated that 60 percent of mutual fund interaction with investors will be done through the Internet in 10 years.

AMERICAN CENTURY INVESTMENTS

Your challenge in using the Internet is to sift through the vast amounts of sales-oriented information and find the useful stuff.

That is where this chapter will come in handy. We offer some guidance on what you should be looking for, and where you should be looking, in order to get useful retirement- and RRSP-related information.

Learning About Retirement Planning and RRSPs

The previous chapter provided an overview of some of the important issues relating to retirement planning and RRSPs, yet the topic itself can be infinitely more complex than the topics we covered.

One of the first things you can do with the Internet in this area of personal finance is use it to learn more about retirement planning and RRSPs. Whether you're investing in an RRSP for the first time or looking for a better understanding of your existing RRSP and retirement situation, the Internet is an invaluable resource.

There may also be times when you will have an urgent or pressing need to get an answer to a question about these topics. For example, you might be a member of a company pension plan, and have suddenly lost your job. With the termination has come a lump-sum payout of your pension plan—and you wonder what your alternatives are. If you take the time to search online, you can probably locate an answer to your question.

The chart below indicates the types of sites that provide useful background information about retirement planning and RRSPs.

Where To Look for RRSP/Retirement Planning Information

Type of Site	Example	Description
General Retirement Web Sites	RetireWeb	Online guides that provide general information about retirement and RRSP issues. Their advice is usually objective because they aren't affiliated with a financial organization.
Financial Organizations	Scotiabank	Many banks, trust companies, credit unions, brokerage firms, insurance companies, and mutual fund companies have retirement information on their Web sites. Watch out for sales pitches—we find that many such sites seem too eager to sell you their product and ignore the need to educate the Web visitor first.
Newspapers and Magazines	*Ottawa Citizen*	Some newspapers in Canada have accumulated archives of financial articles on their Web sites. These are a good source of unbiased information. Some Canadian financial magazines have Web sites as well.

Type of Site	Example	Description
Accounting Firms	Ernst & Young Canada	Many accounting firms provide specialized retirement information on their Web sites, often in the form of tax tips or online tax newsletters.
Financial Planners, Advisors, Authors, and Journalists	Canadian Association of Financial Planners (CAFP)	Many financial planners/advisors have established their own Web sites as a service to existing and potential clients, and sometimes these sites contain useful retirement-related information. The Canadian Association of Financial Planners also maintains its own Web site, which can be a useful starting point. However, beware of the sales pitch—the income of many financial advisors is commission-based, and therefore their advice is not always independent. Also consider Web sites established by financial authors, journalists, and writers.

General Retirement Sites

There are some Web sites that provide information about retirement or financial planning concepts, yet aren't affiliated with any particular financial organization. This makes them a good source for independent information.

One of the best examples is RetireWeb, a resource that provides a good, concise overview of the retirement planning process. The authors of the site suggest that you could spend a good five hours reading the information and using the tools they make available.

The site provides useful background information about what you can expect from the government upon retirement, as well as pointers to documents that describe the crisis within the Canadian pension system. It also includes a glossary if you run into retirement or financial terms you don't understand.

We do have concerns with how frequently the site is updated—when we visited, it hadn't been updated for over six months, so you should take care to ensure that any information that it provides is up-to-date.

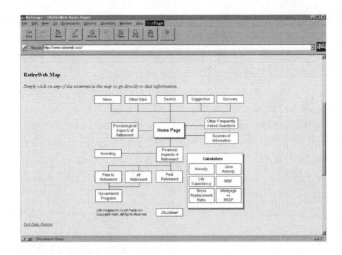

A Royal Trust survey conducted by Environic Research Group in September 1997 found that 51% of Canadians intended to contribute to an RRSP in the 1997 tax year—an increase of 34% from 1996.

ROYAL BANK WEB SITE **www.royalbank.com**

What if you have retired already or are about to, and need specific retirement information such as what payments you can expect from the government?

Take a look at the Seniors Computer Information Project. This is an initiative set up to help senior citizens access online information resources, and it features the *Manitoba Senior Citizens Handbook*, which includes a

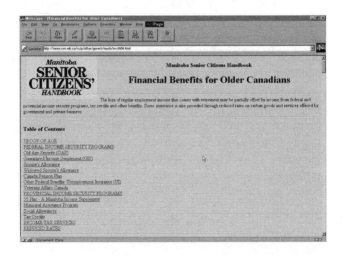

lengthy overview of the financial benefits that can be expected upon retirement. It is one of the best online sources for basic information about the Canada Pension Plan and other government income sources.

With so much focus on the CPP and its ability to make payments in the future, you might expect the Canadian government to offer a useful online guide about retirement planning. But at the time this book went to press, we couldn't find one—any information seems to be scattered here and there. You can find snippets of information at the following sites.

Revenue Canada maintains a Web site with answers to questions about retirement/RRSP issues as they relate to taxes, but it's not an easy site to use, nor does it contain a lot of useful information.

You can visit the official Canada Pension Plan site, but it seems more oriented towards informing you about how the Canadian pension system might be overhauled.

And finally, if you go to the Human Resources Development Canada Web site, and look at the section "Income Security Programs," way down at the bottom of the screen, you can find a useful site with the specifics of what you can expect from the Canada Pension Plan and Old Age Security programs upon retirement.

Yet why do you have to look in three different places? We wonder why they can't just have a simple, big button on their Web site labeled "Retirement/RRSPs" that will lead you to a site full of useful, friendly, and easy-to-read information about the topic.

"The state has been signaling frantically for years that you have to save and look after yourself," says Peter Campbell, manager of technical support for RRSPs at the TD Bank. **"That's what RRSPs are all about."**

DIANE FOREST, "NAVIGATING THROUGH THE WORLD OF RRSPS," *MACLEAN'S*, JANUARY 16, 1995, V108 N3 PS1(5)

The government of Canada seems prepared to spend billions of dollars to encourage Canadians to save for their retirement, but it can't seem to scrape up a few bucks to build a truly useful education site about the topic. If it weren't so sad, it would be shameful.

Financial Organizations

The second source of retirement planning information are the Web sites run by Canada's banks, trust companies, mutual fund companies, insurance companies, and other investment organizations.

Many of these sites offer information about retirement planning, given that they are actively involved in the RRSP business, but the quality and depth of information varies from organization to organization. Some organizations offer pages and pages of information that is nicely organized and easily accessible, while others offer only a couple of paragraphs.

> **Canadian mutual fund assets currently stand at $273 billion, according to recent Investment Funds Institute of Canada figures—a tenfold increase over the past decade. And, with $30 billion in net sales in the first half of 1997, the industry is well on its way to another banner year.**
>
> GORDON POWERS, "FUNDS UNAPPEALING TO GIC HOLDER," *THE GLOBE AND MAIL*, SEPTEMBER 18, 1997

In addition, some of the advice you will come across is nothing more than a thinly-disguised sales pitch. It is all too typical for a site to provide just a little bit of basic background information about RRSPs while at the same time suggesting their own products as the best solution to your retirement needs. We find the approach of many financial organizations to using the Internet to be extremely shallow as a result.

For example, the Web site belonging to First Canadian Mutual Funds, the mutual funds arm of the Bank of Montreal, features an "Education Supplement" called "Retire Right."

We were amused to discover that all of the solutions to the questions posed on the site seem to suggest that you buy First Canadian Mutual Funds.

This is the type of thinly disguised, shallow sales pitch that you should be cautious of as you use the Internet. Sadly, such sites all seem to follow a similar pattern that works somewhat like this:

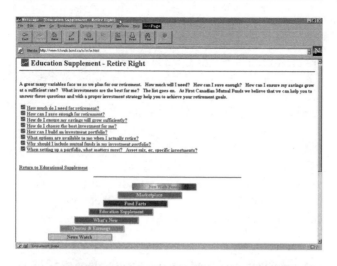

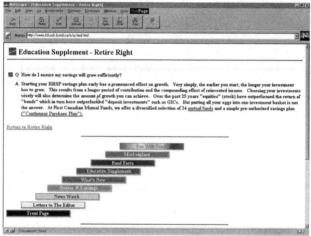

- you need money to retire

- hence you need an RRSP

- you should put mutual funds in your RRSP

- buy ours!

As you use the Internet, you will quickly learn to take an immediate right turn at such sites—leave them quickly. If they haven't taken the time to try to educate you, the information they offer is generally of little use.

That's not to say that the investments they offer are not any good. But if your objective in visiting the site is simply to learn about retirement issues in general, the last thing you want is a sales pitch.

You need to develop the skill to separate useful, education-oriented information from the biased sales pitch. You need to seek out the sites that offer good, concrete, unbiased advice. Look for financial sites that devote their time and effort to educating you about RRSP and retirement issues, rather than those that simply want your money.

Where can you find such sites? The Toronto Dominion Bank has one of the best sites we've seen with *useful* retirement information—without a built-in sales pitch. TD's site contains a fairly comprehensive document with answers to frequently asked questions about RRSPs.

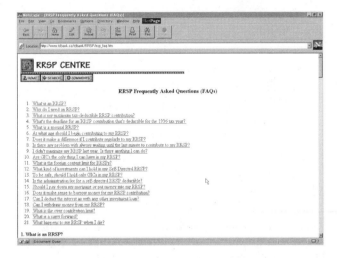

Similarly, Scotiabank offers a fairly good RRSP/retirement centre.

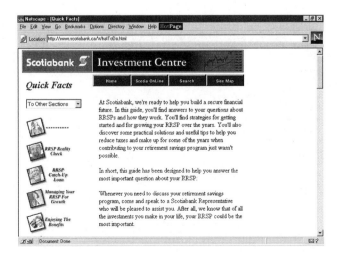

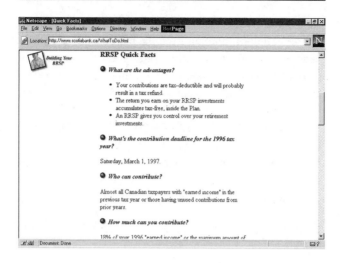

You should also take a look at "RetireNet"—CIBC's online retirement guide. While it's a little heavy on the sales side, you could end up spending several hours browsing through it. It provides an excellent point-by-point analysis of the retirement and RRSP issues you need to be familiar with.

Finally, you can also find helpful advice on some of the Web sites belonging to Canadian mutual fund companies. Altamira's Web site has an RRSP center that provides answers to some of the more esoteric retirement questions you might encounter, such as what to do if you receive a lump sum payout or a retiring allowance upon losing your job.

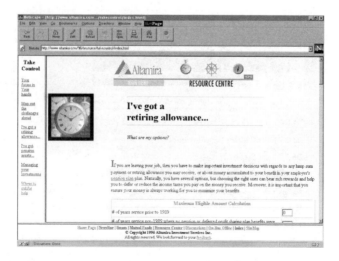

The Mackenzie Financial Web site features a helpful guide called "Planning for Retirement", and Fidelity Investments Canada features an easy-to-understand "Guide to RRSP Planning"—both of which are also useful in terms of their educational value.

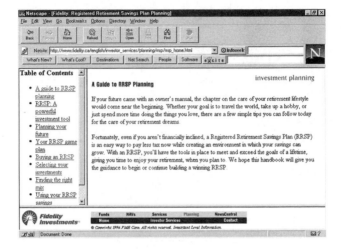

Newspapers and Magazines

A third source of RRSP and retirement information is Web sites that are run by major newspapers and magazines.

These sites are particularly useful during "RRSP season" in January and February, when most publications generate a flood of material devoted to the topic. Fortunately, many publications do not remove their RRSP articles once the season has ended, recognizing that they are of benefit to people long after the primary RRSP season is finished.

A number of publications have taken previously-published articles and used them to create special financial

Stumped by a mutual fund term? Turn to the site of most Southam newspapers (www.southam.com)—such as the *Montreal Gazette* or *Hamilton Spectator*—and you'll find a Mutual Fund Glossary. You'll find it in their "stocks/mutuals" section in the money news, or business section. Once there, look under the "more" category of the mutual fund item.

sections on their Web sites. These article collections are an excellent source of independent financial advice.

For example, the *Ottawa Citizen* Web site features articles and commentary about RRSPs in the "Your Money" section. It is an excellent starting point.

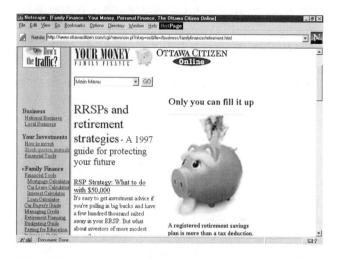

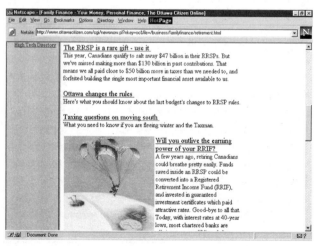

And you can check out a site such as GLOBEfund, from the *Globe and Mail*. Although oriented towards mutual funds, its education centre does feature some retirement information.

There are several Canadian financial magazines with Web sites, but we have found them sadly lacking in terms of online content. Two notable examples that cover retirement/RRSP issues in print are the *All-Canadian Mutual Fund Guide* and *IE:Money*, but you won't find much useful information online.

Contrast what they have done with the Internet activities of large U.S. magazines such as *Money* or *SmartMoney*. Both of these magazines feature massive retirement information sections. However, use caution when browsing these sites since much of the information they provide doesn't apply to Canadians. Nonetheless, they offer a wealth of information about retirement planning in general, and a number of useful columns and pointers that can help you understand many of the issues you are faced with.

Accounting Firms

You will find that many small, regional accounting firms and some of the "big six" accounting firms (Arthur Andersen, KPMG, Deloitte & Touche, Ernst & Young, Price Waterhouse, and Coopers & Lybrand (at the time of writing the mergers of Price Waterhouse with Coopers & Lybrand and KPMG with Ernst & Young were announced. Both are to be effective in 1998)) offer tax information on their Web sites, which sometimes includes details about RRSPs and retirement.

Statistics Canada shows that of $20,883,715,000 contributed to RRSPs in 1994, 14.1% was contributed by [the] 40–44 age group. This was only exceeded by the 45–49 age group at 14.2% and, no surprise here, the 55+ age group accounted for 27% of the 1994 total. The average contributor's age was 43, and the 1994 median contribution $2400.

KELVIN BROWNE, "WILL YOU EVER BE ABLE TO AFFORD RETIREMENT?" *SATURDAY NIGHT*, FEBRUARY 1997, V112 N1 P67(2)

This information is often available in the newsletters which these organizations publish online, or in specially designed "RRSP centres." Because such firms are not actively involved in the sale of financial products, but limit their activities to the provision of financial advice, the information they offer is very independent.

One of the best online services offered by one of the big accounting firms in Canada is the "tax mailbag" feature offered by Ernst & Young Canada. On the Ernst & Young Canada Web site, tax professionals respond to questions submitted by Internet users, and the answers are published publicly so that everyone can benefit from the responses. Since many of the questions pertain to RRSPs and retirement planning, it is an excellent source of free, yet valuable information.

However, despite the foregoing, as with newspapers and magazines, you will find many of the accounting firm sites to be lacking in terms of useful content.

Financial Planners, Advisors, Authors, and Journalists

You can also find retirement information on the Web sites of many professional financial planners and advisors.

Since many of these operations are small, one-person organizations, you will find that their Web sites are often limited in the scope of information they offer. Indeed, it seems that the number of such planners and professional advisors who provide truly useful retirement information online is rather limited—we haven't found many that have good, compelling, useful background information with respect to retirement/RRSP issues.

When you do find a site that provides some information, you should keep in mind that many financial planners represent particular mutual fund or other financial organizations, and are directly involved in the sale of such products. Given that their income is most often generated on a commission or similar basis, the advice they offer is not necessarily always independent or unbiased.

Having said that, for a rather humorous take on the time value of money as we discussed in the previous chapter, take a look at the Screaming Capitalist Web site—and in particular, take a look at the "Why Save?" fable.

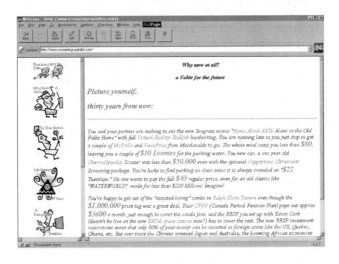

Where else should you look? Keep in mind that many financial authors and journalists have set up their own Web sites to disseminate investment information. For example, Gordon Pape, a well-known Canadian financial expert, has his own Web site. You can often find useful retirement/RRSP related information there and in other similar sites.

Summary

When using the Internet to learn about RRSP and retirement issues, we suggest you use those sites that educate rather than those sites that focus on the hard sell. It is hard enough to try to get a good understanding of retirement and RRSP issues without trying to figure out what retirement products are the best suited to your particular circumstances.

Here are five tips to help you when you are looking for retirement and/or RRSP information on the Internet:

- **Constantly Revisit Sites**

  Web sites change constantly. Revisit sites on a regular basis to see what's new.

- **Learn to Distinguish Useful Content from a Sales Pitch**

  Look for those sites that take the time to answer your questions, rather than those that simply seem to want to sell you something. As you use the Internet, you'll come to recognize the difference between the two approaches.

> What if one mutual fund company were to try and edu-
> cate investors, rather than stop at creating warm fuzzy
> feelings? They could teach the unsophisticated the dif-
> ference between a fund and an RRSP, preach to the
> initiated on how high management expense ratios eat
> into long-term performance, and show the knowledge-
> able do-it-yourself types how top foreign fund man-
> agers use currency swaps to hedge risk. Empowered
> with this knowledge, investors would probably reward
> their teacher with their business.
>
> ANDREW WILLIS, "FORGET THE HYPE, WHAT'S AN RRSP?" *THE
> GLOBE AND MAIL*, FEBRUARY 4, 1997

- **Look for a FAQ**

  Many sites with useful content will provide a retirement or RRSP "FAQ." This is a summary of answers to
  "frequently asked questions," and is an excellent place
  to start.

- **Enhance the Information**

  The information you might obtain from the Web sites
  of banks, mutual fund companies, and insurance companies should be enhanced with independent sources of
  information such as articles and reports from newspapers, magazines, and accounting/consulting organizations.

- **Question the Independence**

  Check any information you obtain off the Internet.
  Many publications and newsletters that you might read
  online are sponsored by companies or individuals with
  a direct involvement in the sales of products mentioned
  in the publication.

Web Sites Mentioned in This Chapter

All-Canadian Mutual Fund Guide	www.mutualfundguide-ca.com
Altamira Investment Services	www.altamira.com

Arthur Andersen Canada	www.arthurandersen.com/offices/CANADA
Canada Pension Plan	www.cpp-rpc.gc.ca/
Canadian Association of Financial Planners	www.cafp.org
CIBC	www.cibc.com
Coopers & Lybrand	www.ca.coopers.com
Deloitte & Touche Canada	www.deloitte.ca
Ernst & Young Canada	www.eycan.com
Fidelity Investments Canada	www.fidelity.ca
First Canadian Mutual Funds (Bank of Montreal)	www.bmo.com/fcfunds
GLOBEfund	www.globefund.com
Gordon Pape	www.gordonpape.com
Human Resources Development Canada	www.hrdc-drhc.gc.ca
IE:Money	www.iemoney.com
KPMG Canada	www.kpmg.ca
Mackenzie Financial	www.mackenziefinancial.ca
Money	www.pathfinder.com/money
Ottawa Citizen	www.ottawacitizen.com
Price Waterhouse	www.pw.com/ca
RetireWeb	www.retireweb.com
Revenue Canada	www.rc.gc.ca
Scotiabank	www.scotiabank.ca
Screaming Capitalist	www. screamingcapitalist.com
Seniors Computer Information Project	www.crm.mb.ca/scip/
SmartMoney Interactive	www.smartmoney.com
Toronto Dominion Bank	www.tdbank.ca

CHAPTER 7

Using Financial Calculators

If something is so complicated that you can't explain it in 10 seconds, then it's probably not worth knowing anyway. CALVIN AND HOBBES

HIGHLIGHTS

- Many Web sites feature financial calculators that will help you manage your RRSPs and plan for your retirement.

- These financial calculators can be used to answer five fundamental questions:

  How much money will I need to retire comfortably?

  How much money will I need to save each year to meet my retirement goals?

  What tax savings will my RRSP contribution generate?

  Should I borrow to contribute to my RRSP?

  Should I contribute to my RRSP or pay down my mortgage?

- Exercise caution when using financial calculators. They work under a certain set of assumptions that may or may not be valid for your particular financial situation.

Perhaps the most useful aspect of the Internet when it comes to retirement planning is the many retirement and RRSP "calculators" available on the Web.

These tools put into perspective, often dramatically, some of the important concepts related to saving for your retirement. Many of these calculators will serve as a wake-up call, helping you to quickly determine that retirement planning is not something that you should put off.

Play around with these calculators and you will quickly discover how much money you should be putting away today to retire comfortably in the future, or how much tax you will save by contributing to an RRSP this year. Some online calculators will also let you assess aspects of your expected financial position upon retirement.

Five Important Financial Questions

We tried to emphasize in chapter 5 that you shouldn't delay in saving for your retirement. Showing you why you shouldn't delay is the one area where the Internet can really be a great help.

Many financial institutions and other organizations are providing "financial calculators" on their Web sites. These calculators help you to understand how much you will need to save to retire, what level of income you might expect upon retirement, or how much money you will save with a certain RRSP contribution.

Using such calculators will, more than anything else, hammer home the importance of starting to save for your retirement as soon as possible.

How Much Money Will I Need to Retire Comfortably?

Many financial sites provide you with online calculators that help you to understand how much money you will need upon retirement.

For example, the First Canadian Mutual Funds Web site provides a "retirement planner" that helps you prepare a cash flow projection. This will help you figure out how much money you might have coming in and going out during your retirement. It is a good starting point for determining how much income you will need to retire comfortably.

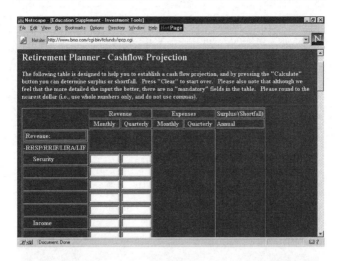

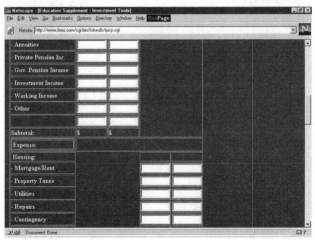

LOOKING FOR OTHER FINANCIAL CALCULATORS?

Strangely enough, you should check out the site for The Institute of Biological Engineering (www.ibeweb. org). Under the category IBE Web Resources, and then IBE Tools, you'll find an entry for "Online calculators." From there, you can discover all kinds of tools, including many financial calculators, some of which are specifically Canadian. In addition, do a search for the phrase "RRSP calculators" on a search engine such as AltaVista, and you'll be rewarded with an extensive list.

While not an online calculator, AGF Group of Funds has a handy worksheet on its Web site that you can use to figure out how much of an income you will need when you retire. You'll need a calculator or spreadsheet to use it.

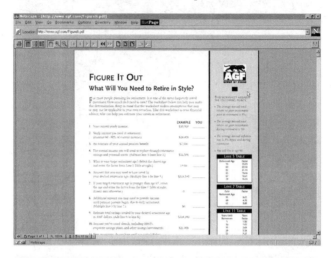

Obviously, such tools are not definitive, but they will get you thinking about the types of expenses that you will be faced with upon retirement, and the level of income you will require to meet those expenses.

Knowing what level of income you need is critical to determining the answer to the next question—how much you need to save this year, and each and every other year that follows.

How Much Money Will I Need to Save Each Year to Meet My Retirement Goals?

Not only will the Web help you to understand how much you need to save now to retire comfortably in the future, it will help you appreciate the time value of money.

For example, Altamira Investment Services has an RRSP calculator on its Web site that you can use to determine how much you will have to save each year in order to retire with a certain income in the future. Using such a tool will help you to realize what you need to be doing today in order to adequately plan for your retirement.

To use the calculator, you need to answer a number of questions, such as the value of your current RRSP holdings, your desired retirement income, the rate of return you expect to earn annually on your RRSP investments,

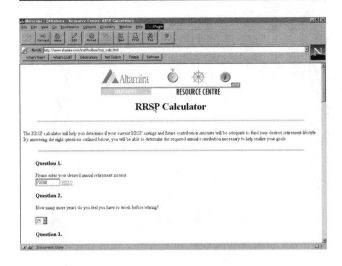

and other information. If you need assistance while filling out the form, you can access an online help screen.

Once you've filled in all the required information, you are provided with a simple and straightforward report that describes how much you will have to contribute to your RRSP each year in order to meet your goals.

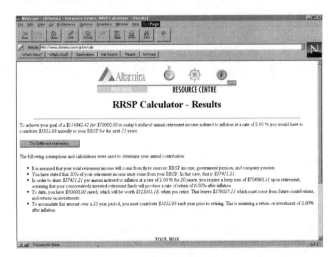

Dynamic Mutual Funds provides a similar calculator on its Web site (see following page). It helps you understand what you need to contribute to an RRSP, and how much you need to invest in non-RRSP savings, in order to retire with a certain level of income in the future.

One of the most important fundamentals of saving for your retirement is recognizing the importance of starting

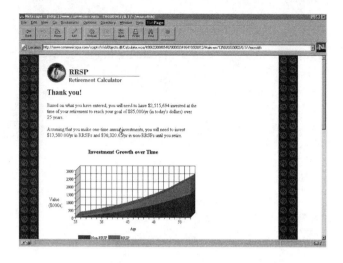

to save earlier rather than later. This concept is best illustrated by using an Internet calculator that helps you to understand the importance of time when contributing to an RRSP.

The Mutual Group provides just such a calculator. Provide the calculator with information on your current salary, age, and amount you'd like to contribute monthly to an RRSP, and it will calculate the retirement income that will be available to you at the age of sixty-five. It tells you how your situation would differ should you decide to wait five or ten years before starting to invest in your RRSP.

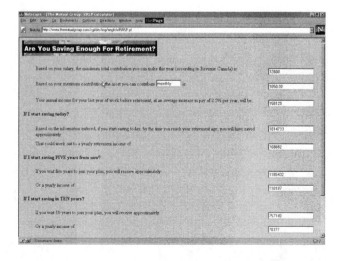

What Tax Savings Will My RRSP Contribution Generate?

Another important issue is knowing how much tax you will save by making a contribution to your RRSP.

Ernst & Young Canada has a calculator on its Web site that tells you how much of a tax saving you can expect from your RRSP contribution. Simply provide the form with your taxable income and RRSP contribution, and the site will calculate the tax savings you can expect to receive in each Canadian province and territory.

> **This year, Canadians qualify to salt away $47 billion in their RRSPs. But we've missed making more than $130 billion in past contributions. That means we all paid close to $50 billion more in taxes than we needed to, and forfeited building the single most important financial asset available to us.**
>
> GARTH TURNER, "THE RRSP IS A RARE GIFT—USE IT," FOR SOUTHAM NEWSPAPERS, FEBRUARY 6, 1997

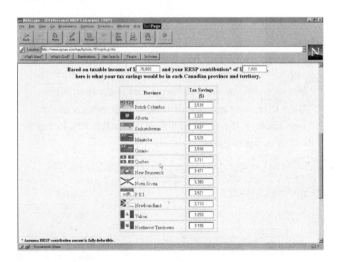

Should I Borrow to Contribute to My RRSP?

In chapter 5 we told you that it sometimes makes sense to borrow money to invest in an RRSP. The tax implications of doing so are generally in your favour.

The Scotiabank Web site (see following page) includes a calculator that you can use to see the benefits of taking out a loan to contribute to your RRSP.

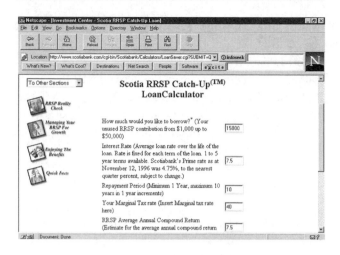

Should I Contribute to My RRSP or Pay Down My Mortgage?

In chapter 5 we looked at a dilemma facing many Canadians—whether to invest any extra money they might have in an RRSP, or whether it should be used to pay down their mortgage.

> ....(Talbot) Stevens also asserts that "mathematically, most people should maximize their RRSP before paying down a personal debt like a mortgage, unless the interest rate on the debt is at least 3 per cent higher than their average RRSP return...this means that paying down credit cards ranks ahead of RRSPs, but generally not mortgages."
>
> MICHAEL B. DAVIE, "INVEST IN AN RRSP - OR PAY DOWN YOUR MORTGAGE? WHY NOT BOTH?" *THE HAMILTON SPECTATOR,* FEBRUARY 7, 1996

RetireWeb includes a calculator that can help you make this important decision. First, provide the calculator with information about the extra money you have, your tax rate, your mortgage rate, and other factors.

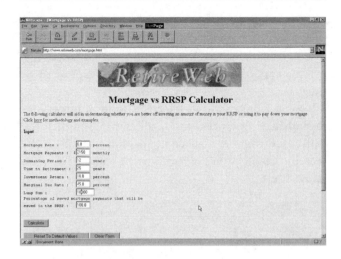

Based on the information you have supplied, the calculator will present its recommendation. An example is seen on the screen below. If you need more information about the recommendation, read the information screen that the Web site provides.

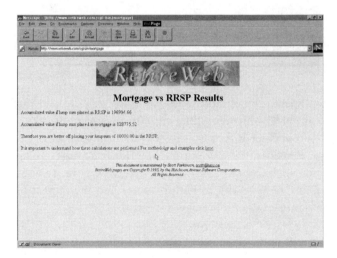

The Emergence of Sophisticated Planning Tools

Finally, as you use many of these calculators, you will find some that are more sophisticated than others. Many calculators are starting to give you a lot of flexibility in the way that you can analyze your retirement options.

Scotiabank's Web site, for instance, features an interactive tool called the Scotiabank Reality Check. It can be used to determine whether you will be able to meet your retirement goals based on your current level of RRSP savings.

As an example, the screen below shows a report for a hypothetical Internet user. It indicates the shortfall that will result from an inadequate investment in an RRSP, based on the person's current income and RRSP investment levels.

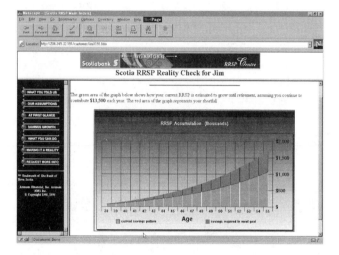

Spend a bit of time in this particular Web site, and you can "play" with many different retirement scenarios—and truly appreciate the necessity for action on your part!

Similarly, Canada Trust's Web site lets you examine multiple scenarios that might affect your retirement plans, helping you to better understand the impact of varying levels of retirement savings.

The key point is this: using the Internet to help you understand RRSP and retirement issues can be extremely beneficial, for it can help to bring some realism to the questions that you are struggling with.

Two Final Hints

As you use the calculators described in this chapter, we suggest that you take the time to double check their math. If you find calculators on different Web sites that perform the same function, it wouldn't hurt to check your numbers in each of them to see if they match. After all, these are computers that we are dealing with, and computer calculations aren't necessarily always 100% reliable.

In addition, most financial calculators operate under a certain set of assumptions. These assumptions may or may not be applicable to your particular financial situation.

The bottom line is to always question the information you obtain from the Internet, even if it is a tool such as those described in this chapter. Financial calculators aren't a substitute for sound financial advice. Check with a financial advisor or financial professional before acting on any of the results provided by a financial calculator.

Web Sites Mentioned in This Chapter

AGF Group of Funds	www.agf.ca
Altamira Investment Services	www.altamira.com
AltaVista	www.altavista.digital.com
Canada Trust	www.canadatrust.com
Dynamic Mutual Funds	www.dynamic.ca
Ernst & Young Canada	www.eycan.com
First Canadian Mutual Funds	www.bmo.com/fcfunds
RetireWeb	www.retireweb.com
Scotiabank	www.scotiabank.ca
The Mutual Group	www.themutualgroup.com

CHAPTER 8

Basic Invest-
ment Concepts

The safest way to double your money is to fold it over once and put it in your pocket. KEN HUBBARD

HIGHLIGHTS

- In order to determine what types of investments you want to place your money in, you need to understand your financial objectives, your risk tolerance level, and whether you are an active or passive investor.

- Assessing a financial investment involves examining its income, growth, and risk characteristics. Every investment can be evaluated on these three important criteria.

- Most investments fall into one of three basic categories: cash-based (e.g., savings accounts), debt (e.g., bonds), and equity (e.g., stocks).

The Internet will present you with both opportunities and challenges if you decide to use it as a tool to assist you with your investment decisions. But before we plunge into an overview of exactly how you might use the Internet as a financial tool, we want to review some basic investment concepts.

Whether you intend to place your RRSP money into an investment such as a mutual fund that is managed by someone else, or decide to establish a self-directed RRSP so that you can more closely and directly manage your own investments, you will need to have an understanding of the type of financial investments that are available and appropriate for you. One of the first steps is determining your financial goals and considering the type of risk that you are willing to accept with your investments.

This isn't an easy thing to do. Determining what kind of investments to make can be quite a challenge. The Internet can aid you greatly in this regard. If you learn to use it properly, it will help you with your investment decisions. But by the same token, if you don't fully comprehend what you are trying to accomplish before getting online, the Internet can confuse you greatly or cause you to make poor financial decisions.

That's why we've written this chapter. The purpose of this chapter is to review basic investment concepts so that you have a solid grounding in these issues *before* you plunge into the vast array of financial resources that are available online. This chapter discusses two important concepts:

- do you know what type of investor you are; and

- the types of investments that are available.

In the next chapter we discuss mutual funds and where they may fit in with your investment decisions.

Do You Know What Type of Investor You Are?

Many Canadians do not invest in anything other than savings accounts, Canada Savings Bonds, or mutual funds. Even when they place their money in these types of investments, they often haven't taken the time to consider why they chose a particular investment, or the type of return that they might earn on such an investment. In addition, many Canadians give little thought to the risk associated with the investments they've chosen.

What is the reason for this? From our research we get the feeling that many people have an overwhelming sense that the world of finance is too complex for them to comprehend. And there is no doubt that there is inertia at work here. Many people simply don't take the time to learn about investing, and as a result, seek the easy way out by choosing an investment that offers the least

> **Puts. Calls. Strip bonds. Warrants. Equity investments.
> DRIPs. Bulls and bears. Even without the jargon,
> investing in the stock market often intimidates people.
> After all, it is about money and risk.**
>
> ANDREW POON, "GROUPS SHARE INFORMATION IN A SOCIABLE ENVIRONMENT,"
> *INVESTING: A BEGINNER'S GUIDE*, FOUND AT *THE LONDON FREE PRESS* WEB SITE,
> **paddle4.canoe.ca/InvestingGuide**. THE GUIDE INCLUDES SEVEN VERY GOOD
> ARTICLES ABOUT INVESTMENT BASICS.

amount of complexity. Hence, every year around February 28th, Canadians rush to buy mutual funds without really thinking about what they are doing.

Intelligent RRSP decisions involve more than simply grabbing the first uncomplicated financial investment that's put in front of you. To really know what you are doing, you have to understand the types of investments that are available to you. But even before you consider specific types of investments, you need to know what type of investor you are.

Income, Growth, and Risk

When it comes to making an investment, the trick to deciding where to place your money is to determine the types of investments that you feel the most comfortable with. To figure this out, you need to consider the growth and income potential of your investments, as well as the risk of the various investments you place your money into.

Any investment that you make will offer a potential return. You will see the value of the investment grow (such as increase in the stock price), and you might earn income on the investment (such as interest on a bond). Some investments will offer both growth potential and income (such as dividend paying stocks), others will offer only income (as with a term deposit), and yet others will offer only the potential for growth (gold, for example).

But investments are characterized not only by their growth potential or the income they might generate. They also carry a certain degree of risk.

When it comes to risk, there is a general rule of thumb that applies to investing. Low risk investments usually offer fairly low returns. Investments which are riskier generally offer high returns. Hence, if you want high returns, you usually have to be willing to accept high risk.

Figuring out what types of investments you are most comfortable with requires an understanding of your risk tolerance level—simply, how much risk you are willing to put up with when it comes to your investments. The higher your risk tolerance level, the more risk you are willing to take.

For some people, the thought of holding an investment where they might see significant growth but where they have an equal chance of losing 30% or more of their money causes many sleepless nights. But for other people, this is quite an acceptable level of risk, and necessary to obtain a higher return on their investment. You need to find what level of risk you are comfortable with before you start investing.

There are many articles and newsletters in financial magazines and newspapers that discuss the concept of risk. In addition, many financial organizations have designed questionnaires that you can fill out to help you to understand where you fall on the "risk scale." Determining the extent of risk that you are willing to tolerate really comes down to doing some creative thinking on your part, as well as thoroughly examining your own particular financial circumstances and investment attitudes.

Ultimately, when you assess a particular investment you need to think about its growth, income, and risk characteristics, and whether these factors fit your investment goals.

Diversify!

Once you have determined the level of risk that you are willing to tolerate, the next step is to put together a long-term investment strategy.

It is important to keep in mind that when it comes to investing for your retirement, your strategy is for the long term. After all, you will be putting money away for ten, twenty, or thirty years or more.

It may sound complicated to put together an investment strategy, but it really isn't. If you decide that you are at the low end of the risk scale, that is, you don't want to tolerate a high amount of risk, then your strategy for

> **Diversification: The investment in a number of different securities. This reduces the risks inherent in investing. Diversification may be among types of securities, companies, industries or geographic locations.**
>
> TERM FROM GLOSSARY FOUND AT IFIC WEB SITE, **www.mutfunds.com/ific/glossary.html**

investing should be to find very stable, guaranteed types of investments. These investments offer little risk, but steady income and/or growth. If you find you are at the high end of the risk scale, and you are willing to take a chance on losing some of your investment money, your strategy should be to find investments that have high growth and income potential.

Regardless of where you are on the risk scale, you should always invest in more than one type of investment. This is what many call diversifying your portfolio— you might consider placing some of your money in a high risk investment to achieve some growth, and part of it in low risk investments to ensure stability in the value of your investment.

Putting all your money into low risk investments may let you sleep at night, but your investment may not grow enough over the long term to give you the level of income that you will need to retire with. Conversely, investing in only high risk items may give you high growth and income potential, but you may lose a substantial amount of your investment if a few investments fail. This is another way of saying "don't put all your eggs in one basket." You want to be able to spread your money over different types of investments so that you can achieve the growth you need and the retirement income you desire.

Once you have decided on a long-term strategy, (i.e., what percentage of your investments will be low, medium, and high risk), stick to it!

Remember that your strategy is for the *long term*. You might not see results with a particular investment right away. And given the constant fluctuation in such areas as the stock market or the price of gold, there will be ups and downs along the way. But it is the cumulative effect that you need to pay attention to. For example, over the long term, the value of investments on the stock market have risen, even though there were substantial decreases in 1987 and in the early 1990s.

Understand What You Are Investing In

One final thing before we go into detail about the types of investments that you might consider. Make sure you understand what you are investing in *before* you invest.

This may sound like a silly statement, but a lot of people are guilty of not doing this. How many times have you gone to the bank on February 28th to make your RRSP contribution, only to have the bank manager inform you of some new investment opportunities? Then she asks you why you're not taking advantage of the foreign content rules.

There you sit, stumped! Here you had thought you had figured out what you were going to invest in, but suddenly you find yourself grabbing the first RRSP investment she pushes at you.

It will do you a lot of good to do some research beforehand to understand the types of investments you should be considering. For one thing, you will be able to assess the new financial products that come onto the market every year, and determine if they are right for you. Second, you will be able to ask the right questions about these new products when talking to your bank manager or financial professional. Questions such as:

- what is the risk of that investment?

- what is its growth potential?

- is there any type of guarantee on the value of the investment? Is it covered by any type of deposit or other form of insurance?

- what is the growth and income history of the investment?

What Type of Investor Are You?

One important outcome of this preparatory work is that you will begin to understand whether you are an active or passive investor.

An active investor is an individual who takes great delight in tracking the value and activity of their investment portfolio on a daily basis, and enjoys tracking stock markets, financial news, and other information.

A passive investor, on the other hand, is an individual who doesn't have the time or inclination to track each and every investment on a day-by-day basis, and takes little joy in the whole activity of investing and finance.

It is fair to say that your investment decisions with respect to growth, income, and risk will probably be reflected in the type of investor you are. If you have the time, interest, and passion to track your investments on a regular basis, you will probably also be more interested in investments that offer a little more growth yet bear more risk. In comparison, investors who can't afford the time to track their own investments will usually be interested in investments that are more conservative.

Types of Financial Investments

Once you have put together your long-term investment strategy, assessed your risk level, and determined what type of investor you are, it is time for you to find the investments that are right for you.

According to Statistics Canada, 487,500 Canadians were employed in the financial services sector in 1996.

When it comes right down to it, there are essentially three types of investments that you might make:

- **Cash-based**
  Your investment is a form of cash, such as a savings account or GIC.

- **Debt**
  You invest in the debt issued by an organization, such as a bond. Your income is derived from the interest that the organization pays on that debt, as well as any gain or loss in the underlying value of the debt. It is important to keep in mind that the overall value of a bond fluctuates on financial markets just as stock prices do— even though a bond might be issued for $1,000, its value on the market can range above or below this amount before its due date (also referred to as "maturity"). On its due date it will be worth exactly $1,000.

- **Equity**
  You invest in some type of ownership in the organization. Your return is derived from any increase in the overall worth of the organization, as well as from any payment of income (usually in the form of a dividend) on the investment.

  The financial world has dreamed up all kinds of hybrids of these three basic options, but for simplicity's sake, anything you invest in fits into one of these three basic categories.

  Every investment has three basic characteristics that we described earlier in the chapter:

- **Income**
  The amount of income produced by the investment. Income is often in the form of interest or dividends.

- **Growth Potential**
  This is the amount that the investment increases or decreases in overall value in addition to any income earned. The growth potential might range from low, to high, to aggressive. The larger the growth potential, the higher the potential risk of the investment.

- **Risk**
  Some investments are riskier than others by being more prone to loss. This loss may occur in several ways. For example, the investment may decrease in value (such as might happen with a stock). Alternatively, you could lose the full value of the investment (such as might happen with your shares in a company that goes bankrupt or collapses in value).

  The table below can be used as a rough guide to the income, growth potential, and risk associated with the various types of investments that we discuss in this book.

  One type of popular financial instrument that we don't include in this table is the mutual fund. Where do mutual funds fit into the following list of investments? As we will see in chapter 9, they are simply a type of investment that includes one or more of the investments described in the chart below. Since mutual funds are made up of any or all of the following investments, they carry with them the underlying characteristics of those investments. For example, a mutual fund that invested in term deposits and

SOME FACTS FROM THE STATS CANADA NEWS RELEASE "SAVERS, INVESTORS AND INVESTMENT INCOME—1995", OCTOBER 24, 1996:

- Canadians earned $28.3 billion in interest and dividend income in 1995, up 18% from 1994.
- Fifty-two percent of the individuals reporting some investment income on their tax return were women.
- Taxpayers aged 55 and over earned 66% of investment income, while accounting for only 42% of savers and investors.
- In 1995, 1.7 million investors reported $14.9 billion from Canadian corporation dividend payments and other investment income. This was a 13% increase from 1994.

STATS CANADA WEB SITE **www.statcan.ca**

Investment	Income	Growth Potential	Risk
Savings account	Low	Low	Low
Canada Savings Bonds (CSBs)	Medium	Low	Low
Term Deposits/ Guaranteed Investment Certificates (GICs)	Medium	Low	Low/Medium
Preferred Shares	Medium	Low	Medium
Common Shares	Low/Medium	High	Medium/High
Bonds	Medium/High	Low	Low/Medium/High

GICs would carry the inherent income, growth, and risk characteristics of those investments.

The table above is a general guideline and does not represent hard and fast rules. For example, you can have a GIC investment that has high risk if it is obtained from a financial organization that is not insured by the Canada Deposit Insurance Corporation (CDIC) or by one of the various other organizations that provide insurance coverage of such investments. Even in Canada, in the past we have seen circumstances in which people thought a particular type of investment was low risk and was insured, only to discover that it was not. Just ask anyone who invested in GICs at the Principal Group of companies in Alberta in the 1980s. This was a large, supposedly stable group of investment companies. However, to the chagrin of many investors, their investments were found to be worthless when that financial organization collapsed amid reports of potential fraud, mismanagement, and other shenanigans.

It is always in your best interest to find out if your investment is insured and by whom. This should be one of the things you consider before you decide to make an investment.

Savings Accounts and Canada Savings Bonds

The safest and most straightforward investment that you can make is to place your money in a simple bank account, or in a Canada Savings Bond (CSB).

Keep in mind that many "branchless banks" that are setting up shop in Canada, such as mbanx and Ing Bank, offer a rate of interest on savings accounts higher than most other financial institutions. Even so, in these days of low interest rates and low inflation, the returns on savings accounts are minimal.

You can purchase CSBs at most banks, earn interest income on them, and cash them in at any time. It is almost like having your money in a savings account that pays a better rate of interest.

Canadians have flocked to CSBs for 50 years, partly from habit, partly because of the patriotic glow the government tries to impart to them, and partly because employer-sponsored monthly purchase plans offer a discipline many investors otherwise lack. Add to that a $5-million advertising campaign and it is little wonder $5.7 billion worth of CSBs were sold last autumn.

JONATHAN CHEVREAU, "CSB BUYERS TRADE YIELD FOR LIQUIDITY," *THE FINANCIAL POST*, OCTOBER 4, 1997

There is not much more to discuss in terms of analysis or education when it comes to a savings account or a Canada Savings Bond.

There is relatively little risk with such an investment, since most bank accounts are insured by the Canada Deposit Insurance Corporation for up to $60,000, and the federal government guarantees the value of the Canada Savings Bond. Since there is little risk, the income earned is rather low. Given the current low rate of inflation in Canada, you can expect an interest rate of less than 2% on a savings account, and with CSBs, rates of 3% increasing to 6.5% in later years, based on 1997 rates.

The growth potential? None, since there is no other increase in the value of the investment other than the interest that you will earn.

GICs and Term Deposits

The next types of investment are GICs (guaranteed investment certificates) and term deposits.

These are usually offered by banks, credit unions, and trust companies. You invest your money (usually a minimum amount from $500 to $1,000) in a term deposit (also known as a certificate of deposit) or a GIC for a fixed period of time, ranging from thirty days to five years or more.

You are paid a guaranteed rate of interest on your investment at the end of the investment period on a term deposit, and on a monthly, quarterly, or yearly basis on a GIC.

Buying non-redeemable GICs or term deposits means you cannot cash them in during the fixed term. Redeemable GICs or term deposits can be redeemed during their term, although there is sometimes a penalty. You generally get a lower rate of interest on the latter type of investment.

GICs and term deposits are attractive alternatives to savings accounts and CSBs, since they often offer a higher rate of interest. The risk is low if the GIC or term deposit is taken out in Canadian dollars and has a term of less than five years, since it will likely be insured by the CDIC or similar deposit insurance corporation. The CDIC does not insure term deposits if the investment period is longer than five years.

Stocks

If your objectives and risk profile suggest that you would like to enhance your opportunity for growth, you might want to think about investing in the stock market.

Stocks are the primary means by which you can "grow your money." As anyone has seen in the last several years, the stock market in Canada, the U.S., and elsewhere has been roaring, with the result that some people are seeing average increases in the overall value of their stock investment of 20% to 30% or more.

Yet by the same token, any particular stock investment can turn out to be disastrous when the price falls. Just ask anyone who still held shares in Bre-X when it collapsed, or in the Ottawa-based telecommunications company Gandalf when it went out of business in 1997.

You can invest in either common or preferred shares, in which case your return comes from any dividend declared on the shares as well as any increase (or decrease) in the stock's value on a stock exchange. Common shares normally give you voting rights within the organization, while preferred shares do not. But this is probably a moot point, since your vote will have little influence on what the company does.

So what is the difference between common and preferred shares? Typically, the value of a common stock will fluctuate more on the stock market compared to a preferred stock, thus providing greater opportunity for growth, or more of a risk of a loss. Preferred shares offer a stated dividend, making them a good investment for a regular stream of income when compared to common stocks.

There are various terms used to describe particular "categories" of stocks based upon the risk, income, and

As the population ages and more Canadians begin to save for retirement, the demand for investment advice continues to grow. Many people find the information they need in books, magazines, newsletters and seminars. But an increasing number of amateur investors are taking it a step further by enrolling in courses designed for investment professionals.

"LEARNING WITH THE PROFESSIONALS," *MACLEAN'S*, MARCH 4 1996, V109 N10 P63(1)

growth profile of the investment. Although there is no definitive list, here are some of the categories you are likely to hear about:

- **Blue Chip Stocks**

  A term used to describe large, solid, stable and reliable companies whose stock price is not expected to fluctuate much over time. Examples include Bell Canada, General Motors, and other companies. Such stocks usually offer regular income in the form of dividends, low risk due to the stability of the company, and regular growth in the value of the stock due to a steady stream of growth in the underlying value of the company.

- **Large Cap Stocks**

  Large cap stocks are stocks that aren't considered to be blue chip because they have a bit more risk, don't have a consistent history of dividend income, and might be a bit more risky—but that have a market value of billions of dollars. There is a ready market in various stock exchanges for such stocks, making them fairly low risk, reliable investments.

> **Did you find an old stock certificate in the attic?**
> **Capital Asset Recognition & Recovery is an organization that will track down for you, for a fee, whether the stock is worth anything. You can find them on the Internet at www.capitalasset.com**

- **Small Caps**

  The term "small caps" is used to describe the stock of small, startup companies or large-scale new ventures. Such stocks might or might not be traded on major stock exchanges. The risk is higher, yet they offer more opportunity for growth in the stock value. The income stream from dividends is usually non-existent or inconsistent.

- **Emerging Growth Stocks**

  Emerging growth stocks are stocks that have a good chance of growing faster than the stock market in general. Often found in hi-tech computer or biotechnology sectors.

- **Speculative Stocks**
  Stocks that are rather risky are called speculative stocks.

Bonds

Bonds are investments in the debt of a company or government body. You derive a regular stream of interest income on the debt, as well as on any fluctuation in the market value of the debt instrument itself, should you sell it prior to its maturity.

In essence, a company or government issues a bond to borrow money—and they promise to pay regular interest on the bond, as well as pay off the amount owing on the bond after a fixed period of time.

Government bonds issued by the Canadian, and most provincial, or municipal governments are very low risk, whereas bonds issued by corporations will often match the risk profile of the stock of those companies.

Mutual Funds

As we mentioned earlier, mutual funds are just a combination of various investments. But since they are such a specialized topic, we will address them separately in chapter 9.

Other Financial Investments

Of course, the investments we've described on the last few pages are only a sample of what's available. Venture into the world of finance, and you can discover many other financial investments, ranging from commodities to gold bars to futures contracts. Clearly, the scope of these other investments is beyond the scope of this book.

That isn't to say that these other alternatives aren't available to you—they are. And certainly you can learn to use the Internet to learn about other types of investment. If you do, keep in mind the key caveat of investing. For any investment, assess its income, growth, and risk characteristics in light of your own financial objectives and investor profile.

The Role of the Internet In Investing

The Internet can help you choose which investments you should be considering, but you shouldn't become overly reliant on the technology.

Your personal judgment and analysis of potential investments is the key to deciding what best suits your particular financial situation and investment objectives.

Having said that, there are a number of organizations that are providing online information and interactive tools to help you determine the types of investments that might be best for you. These tools will teach you about some of the financial implications and risk factors we mentioned in this chapter, and how those factors should guide your investment decisions.

When it comes to your investments, the Internet can help you in several ways:

- **learning** more about investing

- **deciding** what to invest in

- **buying and selling** the investments you are interested in

- **monitoring** the value of your RRSP and/or other investments.

In subsequent chapters we'll look at each of these topics in greater depth. We'll also review some Web sites and tools that will help you to manage your financial decisions.

Mutual Fund Concepts

Science says we must live and seeks the means to pro-long life
Wisdom says we must die and seeks how to make us die well... UNKNOWN

HIGHLIGHTS

- A mutual fund is a pooled investment that carries certain growth, income, and risk characteristics.

- In order to assess whether a mutual fund fits your investment objectives, you need to examine the types of investments that make up the fund as well as its associated growth, income, and risk profile.

- Common types of mutual funds include equity funds, bond/income funds, money market funds, mortgage funds, dividend funds, resource funds, specialty funds, and balanced funds.

- Mutual funds are attractive to Canadians for several reasons, including their flexible risk, low cost, and the management talent that oversees the performance of the fund.

- When evaluating a mutual fund, consider the fund's portfolio and its risk factor, its management fees and commissions, the reputation of the organization where you are purchasing the fund, and the reputation of the fund management team.

Many Canadians who choose not to invest directly in the stock or bond market, and who wish to invest in something other than CSBs, GICs, or term deposits have turned to mutual funds instead, fuelling what has become an explosive industry.

Of course, many invest in mutual funds without having an understanding of exactly what these investments are.

Mutual Fund Basics

If, like many Canadians, you plan to invest your money in mutual funds, you should have a good understanding of what mutual funds are, and of the risk, income, and growth characteristics of the various funds available to you.

Mutual funds are, quite simply, "pooled investments." Rather than buying your own stocks, bonds, or even gold, you and many other people buy into a fund that is managed by a professional investor. The investor places this pool of money into investments that match the particular objective of the fund. You trust the good judgement and reputation of this investor to invest in things that will give you a good return for your money.

> **Every game has its rules. That includes the mutual fund game. Few people would try to play tennis, baseball or gin rummy without knowing the rules. Yet people invest in mutual funds every day without fully understanding what they're doing.**
>
> STAN HINDEN, "KNOWING INVESTMENT RULES HELPS THE PLAYERS," *NEWSDAY*, JANUARY 7 1996

It's as if you and a bunch of friends got together, pooled your money, and decided to use the funds to buy a few stocks, bonds, GICs, or bars of gold. You then hire a good buddy who has some great experience in the investment world to oversee your investments, and to continually assess whether they should be shifted to something else.

There are over 1,600 mutual funds available in Canada. Every mutual fund has a specific objective with respect to risk, income, and growth, all of which is detailed in a formal "prospectus," a document that summarizes everything about the fund. Your task as an individual investor is to ensure that you invest in mutual funds that match your own investment objectives.

But even before covering those topics, it is probably useful for you to understand the Canadian mutual fund industry.

Canadian Mutual Fund Companies

There are several distinct types of mutual fund companies in Canada. They include:

- **Subsidiaries of large banks and trust companies**
  All of the big banks and trust companies in Canada sell their own mutual funds directly to their customers. You can purchase a mutual fund from them simply by walking into your local bank branch.

  However, it is important that you recognize that you are not dealing directly with the banks, but with special mutual fund investment companies that they have set up. This is an important point, for it directly impacts the type of protection that you might have on your investment. More about that later.

  You should read the fine print when dealing with one of these companies. For example, at their Web site you can read about the mutual funds offered by the Royal Bank of Canada. But it is only by reading the fine print that you are told that "*Royal Mutual Funds are sold by Royal Mutual Funds Inc., a member of Royal Bank Financial Group....*" Similarly, visit the Canada Trust Web site, and you will discover in the fine print that "*Investments in Canada Trust Funds are made through CT Investment Management Group Inc., a separate corporate entity and wholly owned subsidiary of Canada Trust.*"

- **Mutual fund companies**
  There are other companies not affiliated or owned by major banks and trust companies, but which are independent firms or subsidiaries of other Canadian or U.S. financial organizations.

  Names you will encounter include MacKenzie Financial, Trimark, Altamira, AGF, Talvest, and many others. These are companies solely in the business of establishing mutual funds and offering these funds for sale to the public.

- **Insurance companies**
  Some insurance companies offer mutual funds directly for sale through subsidiaries, similar to what banks and trust companies have done. Others offer a special form of mutual fund called "segregated funds," which are often sold by their life insurance agents. These mutual funds differ from other mutual funds in that they have a "guarantee clause" that limits your risk. You can buy segregated funds directly, but some are tied to life insurance policies or retirement plans.

THE TOP FIVE:

Canada's largest mutual fund companies ranked by assets, in billions

1. **Investors Group $19.8**
2. **Trimark Investment Management $13.8**
3. **Royal Mutual Funds Inc. $12.3**
4. **Mackenzie Financial Corp. $11.7**
5. **AGF Management Ltd. $7.7**

SHIRLEY WON, "PLAYING IN THE BIG LEAGUES (CANADIAN MUTUAL FUNDS CONSOLIDATE)," *MACLEAN'S*, FEBRUARY 12, 1996 V109 N7 P48(1)

Where Can You Buy Mutual Funds?

This might seem like a silly question, but it isn't. There are some very real distinctions in terms of where you can go to buy particular mutual funds.

If you are interested in a particular fund, one of the first things you must do is determine whether you can purchase it directly from the fund company, or whether you must go through some third party, such as a financial planner, broker, or agent.

Let's put things into perspective:

- Banks and trust companies sell their mutual funds directly through their bank branches or through 1-800 numbers.

- Many mutual fund companies will sell their funds only through the agents, independent financial planners, and brokers who represent them. Companies that fall into this category include AGF, Dynamic, and Trimark.

- Other mutual fund companies, such as Altamira, Caldwell, Phillips, Hager & North, Saxon Funds, Sceptre Mutual Funds, and Scudder Funds of Canada sell their funds directly through 1-800 numbers, in addition to selling them through agents, financial planners, and brokers. They have become known as discount fund companies.

- Finally, there are a few fund companies, such as Investors Group, which sell their funds only through their own direct-sales representatives.

Do You Need Financial Advice?

Why is there a difference in the way that funds are sold? Why can you purchase some directly, and not others? Why should you have to deal with a financial planner or broker to purchase some funds, and not with others? Does this impact on the quality of the investment?

The answer to these questions has to do with the way the mutual fund industry has evolved.

Originally, most, if not all mutual funds were sold directly through brokers, financial planners, or agents of the companies that established the funds. The role of these people was to ensure that the investor had adequate information to assist them in selecting funds appropriate to their financial objectives. To fund this "middleman," a commission (referred to as a "load") was charged on the sale of the fund.

This structure began to change with the arrival of discount fund companies—organizations that sold their funds directly through their own representatives, often through a local office or via a 1-800 number. By doing so, they often eliminated the commission paid to the financial advisers. Thus the "no-load" fund was born.

This distinction is still evident today—you can choose to use the financial advice offered by particular fund companies if you are interested in their product, or you can choose to go the no-load route.

But you should also note that the emergence of the Internet in the world of finance is blurring this distinction even further. One example is E*Trade Canada, a company that offers online stock trading and mutual fund sales directly through the Internet. At their Web site you can purchase mutual funds from AGF, an organization that has historically only sold its funds through financial planners and brokers.

What Does a Mutual Fund Company Do?

The best way to understand this question is to consider what happens when a new mutual fund is created.

In 1997, Altamira announced two new funds, the Altamira T-Bill Fund, and the Altamira Short Term Canadian Income Fund. Let's look at the former.

When creating the T-Bill Fund, Altamira established several objectives for the fund. As they note in the description of the fund on their Web site, the fund would be for "conservative investors who can sustain only minimum risk" and who might need "emergency cash reserves" or who are "saving for short-term goals."

In effect, the specified fund objective is to minimize the risk of any loss in the value of the investment, provide the ability for the investor to obtain their money from the fund as quickly as possible should they need it, while providing more income on the investment than if the investor had placed their money in a savings account or other type of cash investment.

The specific investment strategy established was for the fund to "invest exclusively in Government of Canada Treasury Bills or other short-term debt instruments of, or guaranteed as to the principal and interest by, Canadian federal or provincial governments denominated in Canadian dollars."

A professional investor named Frances Connelly, a Vice President at Altamira, was assigned as the fund manager. With 17 years investment experience, three of those years at Altamira, she had previously managed other mutual funds at the organization such as the Altamira Short Term Government Bond Fund, and the Altamira Dividend Fund.

What did she invest the money in? A look at the Web site for the fund indicated that it held a mix of Canadian government treasury bills (a form of government bond), which offered various levels of interest.

What is her role? To oversee the strategy of the fund and manage its activities, in order to achieve the stated goals of the fund. And, if you invest in the fund, you are deciding that you will place your faith in her ability to do that.

What does the mutual fund company Altamira do? In effect, it establishes and then manages many mutual funds in addition to this T-Bill fund, each of which has a manager that oversees that fund. The manager of each fund, together with his or her investment team, oversees their fund on a day-to-day basis, deciding what new investments they might purchase for the fund to improve its performance, and selling or "divesting" other investments that are performing poorly.

What Mutual Funds Invest In

Most mutual funds are established in order to fit a particular investment profile, and have specific objectives. In effect, your money is placed in investments that have particular growth, income, and risk characteristics that match the objectives of the fund as much as possible.

Clearly, any mutual fund bears the very characteristics of the investments it holds. The Altamira T-Bill fund described above would be very low risk, given its investments in T-Bills, but would offer little in the way of growth potential, since such investments don't grow in value over time.

When trying to determine what type of mutual fund to purchase, you should examine the type of assets that make up the fund you are considering. For example, does it invest in common stock, debt, or mortgages? Other types of investments? What are the characteristics of those investments, in terms of risk, growth, and income?

It isn't an easy decision to figure out where to place your money, given that there are hundreds of mutual funds available for sale in Canada, each of which is based on a different mix of assets, promises a different rate of return, and has a different risk profile.

Nonetheless you will discover that mutual funds can be grouped into several basic categories, as seen in the table on pages 134–135.

Within these categories you can find several subcategories, based on whether the fund is based in Canadian, U.S., or international investments.

Type of fund	What they invest in....	Your return comes from....	Risk profile
Equity	Stocks of publicly traded or privately held companies.	Growth in the value of the stocks held, plus any income from dividends declared on those stocks.	Medium to high, depending on type of stocks invested in.
Bond/income	Bonds of publicly traded or privately held companies.	Primarily interest income on the bonds held, plus any growth in the underlying value of the bond.	Low to medium, depending on the types of companies that have issued the bonds.
Money market	Government or corporate debt i.e., treasury bills or other forms of debt.	Interest paid on the debt, plus any growth in the underlying value of the investment.	Low to medium. Most government-based money market funds are extremely low risk. The risk can be a bit higher if invested in commercial paper offered by the corporate sector.
Mortgage	Commercial or residential mortgages.	Income earned on the mortgages in the form of interest paid on the mortgage, plus any growth in the underlying value of the mortgages.	Medium to high, depending upon the type of mortgage held, and the types of companies involved. For example, a mortgage fund that holds mortgages on speculative commercial properties is more risky than one that holds straightforward personal real estate mortgages.

Type of fund	What they invest in…	Your return comes from…	Risk profile
Dividend	Preferred or common shares of public or private companies which have a consistent dividend payment record.	Income earned on dividends on these shares, plus any growth of the underlying value of the shares.	Low to medium, depending on the type and background of the companies that make up the portfolio.
Resource	Gold, silver, or other resources.	Income primarily from fluctuations in market value of particular resources.	High.
Specialty	Investments in a particular sector i.e., resource stocks and bonds of a particular industry such as oil and gas.	Income from stocks, revenue from bonds/debt instruments, plus growth in underlying asset value.	Varies depending on industry and asset mix.
Balanced Funds	A mix of stocks and bonds.	Income from stocks, revenue from bonds/debt instruments, plus growth in underlying asset value.	Varies.

> **Have you shopped around for a mutual fund lately? If so, you probably needed a crystal ball to help you sort through the dizzying array of choices.**
>
> CHRISTINE DUGAS, "FUND JUNGLE. IT TAKES LOTS OF WORK, AND POSSIBLY A GUIDE, TO CUT THROUGH THE THICKET OF INVESTMENT CHOICES," *NEWSDAY*, FEBRUARY 26, 1995

Net Asset Values

When you start to deal with mutual funds, you will have to become familiar with the term "NAV" ("net asset value"). If you turn to the financial pages of a newspaper, you will discover that they often print the previous day's NAV for various mutual funds.

When you invest in a fund, you buy a certain number of units. If you invest $10,000 in a fund, and the current net asset value is $2.00, you will own 5,000 units in the fund.

The NAV is the current value of one "unit" in a mutual fund, the value of which is based upon its underlying assets. So if your mutual fund invests in gold, your net asset value goes up and down as the price of gold rises and falls. If the mutual fund invests in a wide variety of stocks, the NAV will go up and down with the market value of those stocks.

The NAV can go up or down for two other reasons. First, income earned on the investments held in a mutual fund is often reinvested back into the mutual fund, rather than being distributed to each mutual fund owner. This increases the NAV of the fund. Second, as we will see below, most mutual funds carry some type of management fee, and are often charged other expenses which must be paid either by the income earned within the fund or by the sale of some assets, which decreases the NAV.

What Makes Up the Income, Growth, and Risk Profile of a Mutual Fund?

Key to your selection of a particular mutual fund is determining whether it fits the income, growth, and risk characteristics that you seek in an investment. The type of underlying investment held in a fund—stocks, bonds, debt, etc.—will have a definite impact on the type of income, growth, and risk associated with the fund.

Consider three extremes: a mutual fund that invests in debt issued by the government of Canada, one that invests in precious metals such as gold, silver, and platinum, and one that invests in the shares of new, small Canadian companies.

Obviously, the value of the first fund will remain steady since the value of debt—say, a government bond—issued by the government of Canada does not fluctuate greatly. Such a fund would offer a steady stream of income from the interest payments on the debt, very low risk, and little prospect for growth, and would be chosen by someone who simply wants a secure investment that promises a steady stream of income.

The value of the precious metals mutual fund will fluctuate according to the market values of these precious metals. It would offer good potential for growth, should the value of precious metals increase on worldwide markets—yet would obviously carry a fair degree of risk, due to the large fluctuations that can occur in the metals markets. The potential for regular income is very small, since the only income that would be derived on the fund would be from an increase in the market value of the precious metals in the fund.

Finally, a mutual fund that invested in the stocks of small Canadian startup companies would have high risk, due to the potential for significant fluctuations in the stock price of those companies. It would likely offer a low level of regular income since such companies would not be regularly distributing and declaring dividends. Yet the opportunity for growth in the value of the fund is high, since the inherent value of the fund is directly linked to the potential of these small companies to grow larger over time.

Clearly, the assessment of the income, growth, and risk characteristics of any particular mutual fund is dependent upon the underlying investments which make up that fund.

Are Mutual Funds Insured?

Investments in mutual funds are *not* insured in the same way that bank deposits are. This means that if a mutual fund company fails, you could lose all or some of the value of your investment.

This is true regardless of where you bought the fund. Many people mistakenly believe that mutual funds they purchase from a bank are safer than those from a mutual fund company—in the belief that the regular deposit insurance at their bank applies to their mutual funds.

But this is not true. As we noted previously, even if you are buying a mutual fund *at* a bank, it doesn't mean you've bought it *from* a bank. Once again, read the fine print at the bank or trust company Web site—you will note that you've bought the fund from a subsidiary of the bank, and that it is not insured. For example, consider what is posted at the Royal Bank of Canada and Canada Trust Web sites respectively:

"Royal Mutual Funds are available only to residents of Canada. Royal Mutual Funds are sold by Royal Mutual Funds Inc., a member of Royal Bank Financial Group, and are not insured by the Canada Deposit Insurance Corporation, the Régie de l'assurance dépôts du Québec or any other deposit insurer nor guaranteed by Royal Bank or Royal Trust."

"Investments in Canada Trust Funds are made through CT Investment Management Group Inc., a separate corporate entity and wholly owned subsidiary of Canada Trust. CT Investment Management Group Inc. is the manager and principal distributor of the Funds. Mutual funds are not insured by the Canada Deposit Insurance Corporation, The Régie d'assurance-dépôt du Québec, or any other government deposit insurer, and are not guaranteed by The Canada Trust Company or CT Investment Management Group Inc."

Mutual funds certainly carry a higher risk profile than bank deposits, GICs, term deposits, and other monetary investments that are directly insured, even if the assets that exist in a mutual fund consist of those particular types of investments.

What is the nature of the risk? The risk is twofold:

- each mutual fund invests in certain things—stocks, bonds, precious metals, etc. You have a risk in the decrease of the value of your investment in the fund, should the value of the investments held in the fund decrease

- second, there is the potential risk, however small, of the failure of the mutual fund company.

There is not much you can do with the first type of risk, other than to carefully think through the risk characteristics of a particular mutual fund that you might be interested in.

For the second type of issue, you should be aware that the Canadian Investor Protection Fund (CIPF) might apply to your fund—always check!

The CIPF is managed by the Canadian investment industry, and provides coverage for individuals making investments through members of the CIPF. The CIPF covers customers' losses of securities and cash balances, including mutual funds, up to $500,000. However, the amount of cash losses that you can claim as part of the $500,000 limit may not exceed $60,000. Visit their Web site for more detailed information.

Note that coverage only applies if a particular institution becomes insolvent. Once again, we must stress that coverage doesn't apply to the normal fluctuations in the value of your fund. If you invest in a fund that invests in stocks, and the stock market crashes, the value of your mutual fund goes down accordingly. You aren't covered for this risk.

Sometimes, when a mutual fund company fails, other mutual fund companies step in to take over the assets of the fund—resulting in little risk to the holder of those funds. Fortunately, it is rare for a mutual fund company to fail.

Remember the importance of not only diversifying your investment monies among multiple types of investments, but also of diversifying among different mutual fund companies to get maximum insurance coverage.

The Pros and Cons of Mutual Funds

Clearly, there must be some benefit to mutual funds or there would not have been such an explosion in their growth across Canada and around the world. What do you gain by investing in mutual funds? Several things, including:

Management Talent

Once you have decided which mutual funds you want to invest in, you are, in effect, relying on the decisions made by an investment professional. It is their full-time job to make the right choices in managing the investments in the fund—they continually decide what investments should be bought and sold by the fund in their efforts to meet the objectives of the fund.

Flexible Risk

There are all kinds of different mutual funds to match different risk objectives. In Canada, there are in excess of 1,600 mutual funds that you can choose from. This means that you can pick and choose the types of mutual funds that best match your particular risk factors, and diversify your portfolio so that it carries both low-risk and high-risk funds, or a mixture of low-growth and high-growth funds.

Low Cost

One reason for the explosive growth of mutual funds is that they permit more Canadians, who might not otherwise be able to invest in anything much more sophisticated than bank term deposits, to invest in any number of different funds for a relatively low entry cost. You can invest in some mutual funds with investments starting as low as $500 or less, allowing you to diversify your investments beyond savings accounts or Canada Savings Bonds.

Yet, in spite of all the positive aspects of mutual funds, there are also some potential downsides.

We should repeat that when you invest in mutual funds, you are relying on the decisions made by an investment professional. You certainly hope that these people are good at what they do. But remember that professional investors make mistakes just like amateurs do. The fact

---

A couple of years ago, the U.S. Securities and Exchange Commission proposed the idea of having mutual fund companies develop and disclose a single numerical measure of risk. The idea was dropped after fund companies protested. Self-interest on the part of the fund companies? Maybe. Yet the fact remains that there is no single tell-all measure for fund risk.

ROB CARRICK, "MEASURING UP A RISKY BUSINESS," *THE GLOBE AND MAIL*, SEPTEMBER 20, 1997

---

that they are professionals does not mean they are perfect. Here in Canada, we have seen some of the highest profile and most successful mutual fund managers fall from grace, as the performance of their particular fund goes from fabulous to terrible in the space of just a few years.

You should also be aware that, in one way or another, you are going to have to pay for the services of those investment professionals! You can end up paying in several ways:

- Management fees are deducted from the fund assets. Since your return comes from the growth in the value of the fund, and also depends on the income it earns, the management fee, in essence, comes out of the value of your investment. Management fees range from $1/2\%$ up to $2^{1}/2\%$ or more, and are charged on an annual or monthly basis against the total assets of the fund.

- "Front end load" funds charge a commission on the sale when the person or firm sells you the fund. This means that some of your money goes to the salesperson rather than to your investment. This is in addition to the management fees charged annually to the fund.

- "Back end load" funds assess a sales commission if you redeem (i.e., sell) the fund within a certain time period, often within several years. So, while you might not pay a sales commission up front, you still end up paying one when you want to get out of the fund! (You don't pay the commission if you hold on to the fund for the prescribed period of time.)

- Some fund firms charge other expenses related to the fund (such as printing, administration, and other fees) directly to the fund, while others take this money from the management fee that has been charged. You should always check a fund description when looking at the management fees, to see if other additional expenses are charged to the fund.

Before you invest in a particular fund, you should determine the type of fee and commission (load) that you might pay and compare this to other similar funds. Many newspaper reports, books, and certainly Web sites report on the management fees and other charges within a mutual fund.

Choosing a Mutual Fund

Look at a newspaper during mutual fund season, and you will see a mutual fund company boasting about their "historical rate of return," which is an indication of how well the fund has done in the past. If it shows a big number, many investors think it's a good investment, and plunge ahead and purchase the fund.

You will often see a particular mutual fund company advertise these rates of return, often listing one-, three-, and five-year rates. This issue warrants special attention. "Historical returns" should not be the basis for an investment decision. If a fund has done well in the past, it does not mean that it will necessarily do well in the future. Past performance is not an indicator of the future performance of the fund, but it is not the only indicator. More important are the objectives of the fund and the types of assets in which it invests.

Assessing the Fund's Portfolio and Its Risk Factor

In the previous chapter, we discussed how your decision to invest in CSBs, GICs, stocks, and/or bonds should depend on the appropriateness of each to your current financial situation and risk objectives.

Investing in mutual funds is no different. Purchasing a mutual fund that invests in government bonds is far less risky than one that buys a lot of gold stock out of penny mining companies! Therefore, you must learn to assess the underlying type of assets held in a particular mutual fund and determine if they match your desired risk profile.

Management Fees

You should also assess the fund's management fees. Are they low, high, or average compared to industry norms? Are you paying too much compared to other fund investments? A normal fee is considered by most to be about 2%.

Sales Commissions

Find out if there are front-end or back-end fees. If it is a no-load fund, are there other fees that might be charged that could reduce your investment? Also, make sure you examine back-end charges or penalties that might be placed on you should you seek to withdraw your money from the fund.

The seemingly negligible annual fees that funds charge do far more damage to your return than previously imagined. According to new studies conducted separately by the Securities and Exchange Commission and Princeton University, investors lose roughly two percentage points in return for every one percentage point they pay in annual expenses.

RUTH SIMON, "HOW FUNDS GET RICH AT YOUR EXPENSE MONEY. THINK 1% OR 2% A YEAR ISN'T MUCH TO PAY FOR YOUR FUND? WAIT UNTIL YOU SEE WHAT THOSE NASTY ANNUAL FEES DO TO YOU," *MONEY*, FEBRUARY 1, 1995

Reputation of the Organization

Consider the reputation and background of the organization as part of your evaluation of the fund.

Obviously, mutual funds from such financial institutions as banks and the larger mutual fund companies have more of a track record than some of the smaller, newer mutual fund companies on the block. But that's not to say that you are necessarily safer with a larger organization—keep in mind the comments we made earlier about the Canadian Investor Protection Fund.

Reputation of the Fund Management Team

Remember that once you have chosen a particular mutual fund, you are relying on someone else to make investment decisions for you. When analyzing different funds, it's important to factor in the reputation, background, and history of the fund management team—how well have they performed managing their funds and others they may have been involved in? Organizations that sell mutual funds usually include this information on their Internet sites.

Performance

Finally, after you have analyzed the fundamentals of the fund, you can return to the issue of performance. You might assume that if the fund has done well in the past, it might do well in the future, or conversely, that the past is no indication of what is to come. Whatever the case may be, past performance is one factor to consider when you weigh the future possibilities of any particular fund.

What It Comes Down To

When it comes right down to it, mutual funds can be a pretty good investment. There are a lot of individuals who are seeing some pretty good returns on their mutual fund investments.

Yet at the same time, there are others who aren't doing so well, simply because they have selected a mutual fund that is not performing well.

Mutual funds are not a panacea—they are like any other investment, in that some do well and others do not. The real key for you is to figure out which ones are appropriate for you, and which have a good likelihood of success. That's an issue we'll explore in the next chapter.

Web Sites Mentioned in This Chapter

AGF Group of Funds	www.agf.ca
Altamira Investment Services	www.altamira.com
Canada Trust	www.canadatrust.com
Canadian Investor Protection Fund	www.cipf.ca
Dynamic Mutual Funds	www.dynamic.ca
E*Trade Canada	www.canada.etrade.com
Investors Group	www.investorsgroup.com
Mackenzie Financial	www.mackenziefinancial.com
Phillips, Hager & North	www.phn.ca
Royal Bank of Canada	www.royalbank.com
Saxon Funds	www.saxonfunds.com/~saxon
Scudder Funds of Canada	www.scudder.ca
Talvest Mutual Funds	www.talvest.com
Trimark Mutual Funds	www.trimark.com

Determining What to Invest In

No great discovery was ever made without a bold guess. ISAAC NEWTON

HIGHLIGHTS

- When it comes to investing, everyone has a theory. It is important that you learn that no theory is definitive and there are no absolutely right answers.

- The best way to determine what to invest in is to educate yourself about the different categories and types of investments and think about how these investments relate to the characteristics of risk, growth, and income.

- You will encounter a number of "asset mix" questionnaires on the Internet which purport to give you guidance on the types of investments you should be considering. Use these tools as a guide, but be aware of their limitations. Focus on those Web sites that provide useful educational information about the concept of asset allocation.

- The Internet can assist you in preparing your investment objective statement and determining an appropriate asset mix whether you use a financial planner or advisor or not.

In chapters 8 and 9 we reviewed some of the basics of investing, and examined the types of investments that are available to you. We observed that different types of investments have different characteristics—some are riskier than others but have a good potential to grow in value, while others might have very little risk and a solid stream of income, but no potential for growth in overall value. As we indicated, every investment has a certain combination of risk, income, and growth characteristics. We also discussed the need for you to determine the type of investor you are. Are you risk adverse? Are you looking for long-term growth in the value of your investments—and are you willing to subject yourself to a little more risk to help accomplish that? Or do you need a solid stream of income from your investments right now, and therefore can accept little risk?

All of these things need to be considered when trying to answer the next two questions:

- What are my investment objectives; what is the goal I am trying to reach?

- What specific investments will I need in my investment portfolio to help meet my investment objectives?

When determining your investment objectives you should spend some time learning about some basic concepts. They are diversification and asset mix.

- Diversification means that you should put your money into a range of different types of investments. It is extremely important that you diversify your portfolio.

- Developing your own asset mix means determining what assets (investments) to hold and how much of each type. To do this you need to spend some time educating yourself as to the risk, income, and growth characteristics of different types of investments.

Combining these concepts is how you determine what to invest in. There is one caution that we have for you, however—everyone has a theory!

Everyone Has a Theory

As you plunge further and further into the world of investing, you will quickly realize that everyone has a theory about the best way to decide what you should invest in. Here are three examples:

- Some financial experts live and die by the statistical formulas they to rank various investments. In the mutual fund industry, many experts go to great lengths to assign a numerical ranking to each and every mutual fund, based upon a series of elaborate calculations involving the various characteristics of the fund. They believe that this scientific approach to investing will help investors make the best decisions.

- Other people research the past performance of investments, and use numeric ranking methods to figure out the best investments. With mutual funds, this is done through an exhaustive examination of mutual fund tables in order to highlight the best performers. With stocks, these analysts chart all kinds of aspects of past performance. Some people who ascribe to this theory believe that the best recent performer is likely a good target for investment, while others believe that longer-term performance is a better indicator of potential future performance.

- In the mutual fund industry, some people make their investment decisions based on the track record of the fund managers. In other words, they place their investments with fund managers who have successful track records, and they avoid fund managers whose track records aren't so stellar.

> **...investment advisers have this bit of advice: be prudent. Past returns are no indication of future performance. And everyone should be prepared for lower returns, or even a drop after three years of high returns on equities.**
>
> SUSAN NOAKES, "MUTUAL STAMPEDE—DOUBLE-DIGIT RETURNS ON EQUITY FUNDS LOOK ENTICING, BUT EXPERTS ADVISE PRUDENCE," *FINANCIAL POST*, FEBRUARY 1, 1997

There is probably a degree of merit to each of these theories. Yet regardless of what types of investments you're considering, there's no one best solution and no quick route to success.

We think this is an important point to raise, because as you travel through the Internet you will encounter an often overwhelming number of investment theories. You'll read all kinds of information and discover a number of people who indicate that they have the "definitive" or "best" answer when it comes to learning how to invest.

We think you should keep in mind this basic fact—a theory is just a theory, and when it comes to investing, everyone has a theory. No theory is foolproof.

The Need for Diversification!

Even though there are all kinds of theories about how to go about deciding what to invest in, most financial experts agree on one simple, basic principle. When investing, whether for your retirement or otherwise, you should spread your investment money across a variety of different types of investment.

This is another way of saying that you shouldn't place all of your eggs in one basket.

Any investment professional will tell you that you shouldn't place all of your investment money in one type of investment—instead, you should be prepared to place your money in a number of different types of investments. This lets you have a range of investments with different risk, growth, and income characteristics in your overall investment plan.

At the same time, they will also advise you not to invest in too many things—don't carry too many eggs in your basket! Most professionals would say that a well-diversified portfolio may consist of anywhere from five to ten different types of investments, but not more—otherwise, you are making things far too complex.

This is called diversification—a basic but significant investment strategy.

Examples of diversification

Now, you might say "Why would you want to do that?" Let's explain the reasons for diversification using three examples.

First, let's say that you are the type of investor who is willing to live with quite a bit of risk in the types of investments that you are going to make because you really want to see some growth in the value of your overall investment. You decide to place all of your investment money in the stock market—whether directly or by way of mutual funds that invest in stocks. If the stock market suffers a major upheaval, you will probably lose a good chunk of money. On the other hand, if you had invested at least some of your investment money in cash-based securities, as well as some in stock based investments, you would be safer, since the cash-based investments won't fall in price when the stock market falls.

Second, let's say that you are the type of investor who does not feel comfortable with any sort of risk and therefore have placed all of your investment money in cash-based securities. You'll have a very secure investment portfolio, but you will not see much of an increase in the value of your investment over time, as cash-based securities generally have no growth element attached to them. If you had put at least some of your investment money into stock-based investments, you could share in some of the growth that can come from an increase in the value of such investments.

Third, let's say that income is your most important investment objective. You place all of your money in blue chip stocks, and certainly earn a regular stream of income in the form of dividends. Yet, over time, you don't share in any of the spectacular growth that is occurring with the share values of small companies—so while you've got steady income, the overall value of your investments isn't increasing. Instead, if you place a small percentage—say, 10% or 20%—of your overall investment in the stock of such small companies, you'll still get the regular income from the balance of your investments that are held in blue chip stocks, while obtaining some investment growth from those smaller stocks.

Diversification means that you want to have a mix of assets in your investment portfolio. You should invest in a mix of investments, each of which is different in terms of their income, risk, and growth profile.

Educate Yourself

We think that your first step to figuring out your asset mix should be to use the Internet to do some *basic* research as to the risk, growth, and income characteristics of different investments.

You really need to understand clearly that different types of investments will serve different purposes for you—and with the need for diversification, you'll have a need to have multiple different investment types.

What should you do? We think you should examine various mutual fund descriptions online, to see how they describe themselves in terms of risk, growth, and income. Spend some time reviewing online information about cash-based investments so as to understand their characteristics. Read about and understand how stocks and bonds fluctuate in value—which you can often do simply by reading many financial reports online. You do not need to review every investment or mutual fund that exists, only enough to give you a good understanding of the characteristics of each type of investment.

> **With something like 1,600 funds on the market, and virtually all of them available through any number of channels, mutual funds have long since become a commodity. Frankly, there's not a lot that anyone can tell you about individual funds that you couldn't eventually dig out of the library or from the back issues of this paper...providing you had the time to sift through it all.**
>
> GORDON POWERS, "MAKE SURE YOU AND YOUR ADVISER ARE IN SYNCH," *THE GLOBE AND MAIL*, SEPTEMBER 27, 1997

When it comes to mutual funds, remember that you want to learn about the following:

- First, use the Internet to learn more about the basic categories of mutual funds—equity, bond/income, money market, mortgage, dividend, resource, specialty, and balanced funds. Re-examine the types of investments held in such funds, where the return comes from, and the risk profile associated with each investment. In light of your own circumstances, what seems most appropriate for you? Which ones interest you, and which ones make you too nervous? Jot down a preliminary list of the various fund categories that are most appropriate for you, keeping in mind you are trying to figure out where particular types of funds fit in with your investment objectives.

- Second, take some time to learn more about the funds available within these particular fund categories by using the Internet. Visit the Web sites for particular mutual funds as we describe in chapter 12, and seek out several examples of each fund category. For example, examine the descriptions and objectives for a few equity funds, and look at the descriptions for a few mortgage funds, and the same for every other fund category in the list from chapter 9. What are the characteristics of the various categories and types in terms of risk, income, and growth? Which particular types within a category meet your objectives?

- Third, take some time to learn how particular funds might fluctuate in light of the investments held in the fund. When reading the online descriptions, take a look at the investments that a particular company has placed its money in. You will find that most Web sites offer details about the major investments held in a fund. For example, if you look at an equity fund, you will see that you can obtain a list of the largest holdings in the fund. Think about how the value of the fund might change in the future in light of this information.

- Fourth, work with some of the online analysis tools such as GLOBEfund that we describe in chapter 12. These tools will help you to understand how a particular type of fund fluctuates in value compared to other types of funds or in comparison to other factors such as the performance of the stock market.

- Fifth, use these same tools to help you identify funds which have particularly good or particularly poor histories over the long term, to understand more about their growth potential. You will find that services like GLOBEfund and PALTrak, which we discuss in chapter 12, permit you to analyze the performance of funds. They also allow you to highlight particularly good performers, which is useful when you actually begin to decide which funds to invest in.

By doing this type of background research before it is time to figure out a specific asset mix for you, you'll have learned more about what is involved, and have a better understanding of what types of investments make sense for you.

Asset Mix

You will continually encounter the concept of diversification as you deal with the investment world. You will hear words such as "diversification strategy," "investment mix," "asset mix," "asset allocation," and many other similar phrases.

All of these phrases have to do with the basic investment premise that you should invest your money so that it is in a variety of investments that have different levels of risk, income potential, and growth potential.

> **The asset allocation approach is a long-term strategy that has been proven to be effective to reduce overall risk and increase one's overall rate of return.**
>
> DEB MACPHERSON, "ASSET ALLOCATION BEST WAY TO START INVESTING," *THE HAMILTON SPECTATOR*, DECEMBER 2, 1996

Your "asset mix," or the different types of investments you will have, is directly determined by your investment objectives.

By determining your investment objectives you can figure out what your "asset mix" should be. Your asset mix is usually expressed in the form of a percentage of your total investment that you will place in various investment types.

Here's one example of a well-balanced investment objective: you might want an investment portfolio that has a good opportunity for growth in the value of your stocks, yet pays a consistent income and leaves at least some money in very low risk investments.

To meet these objectives, you might establish an asset mix as follows: you decide to place 25% of your investment money into some blue chip stocks that pay a consistent income in the form of dividends, another 50% into medium risk, medium growth-potential investments; and the remaining 25% in low risk, low growth, cash-based investments. That's a good way of describing your asset mix.

Online Questionnaires

Next, spend a little bit of time with several of the online asset mix questionnaires that you can find on the Internet—while recognizing the clear limitations of these tools.

Throughout the Internet, particularly at the sites of mutual fund companies, you will come across many online questionnaires that appear to simplify your investment decisions. These are called "asset mix" or "asset allocation" questionnaires, since they help you determine the mix of mutual fund assets that you should purchase—and hence, purport to help you figure out an asset mix that is just right for you.

Answer the questions, and you will receive a suggested asset mix. Thus, you can use these tools as a useful step to help to understand your investment objectives and asset mix.

Try Out a Few Mutual Fund Asset Mix Tools

First, try out some of the mutual fund asset questionnaires to be found online.

Take a look at how it works. You answer some simple questions about your attitude towards mutual funds, investing, risk, and other factors.

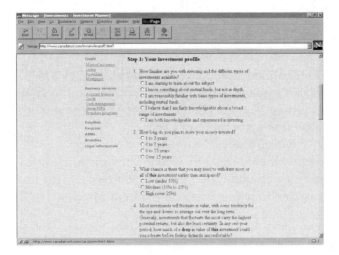

Then, a few seconds later, the site recommends a mix of diversified investments that is "appropriate" for you based on the information you supplied.

Tools such as these are found on many investment Web sites in Canada—you won't have to look far to find a number of them.

But don't make a mistake—you have to be very cautious of such tools.

Take this Canada Trust site as an example. The planner's opening screen says that "in a few seconds, you'll see our recommendations for the right combination of Canada Trust investments designed to meet your goals." You should be suspicious as soon as you see a statement like that—especially once you realize that the suggested asset mix consists mostly of specific mutual funds from Canada Trust.

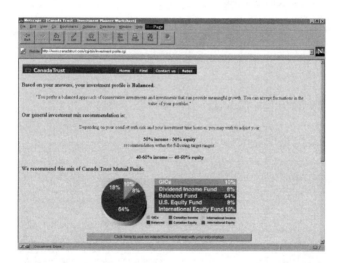

The thing about these investment questionnaires is this—while the solutions they present certainly seem to make life simple, they are often too biased to suggest anything other than a rough form of guidance.

After all, it would be wonderful if our complex investment decisions could be simplified by answering a few questions. Unfortunately, investment decisions aren't that easy. We'll discuss this issue in greater depth below.

Try Out a Few General Asset Mix Tools

We find that the mutual fund questionnaires, such as the one seen above, are very biased. Having said that, there are some financial Web sites that provide asset mix information in a manner that is far more even-handed.

Rather than telling you which specific funds or investments to buy, they offer guidance on the types of mutual fund investments you should be considering.

For example, definitely spend some time on the Financial Pipeline Web site. It promotes itself as an independent source of investment information, where "all articles are screened and edited for accuracy and impartiality." Sponsored by such companies as C.T. Private Investment Counsel and the Canadian Bond Rating Service, the site features an extensive selection of useful background information on a wide variety of mutual fund topics, including a number of articles about asset mix decisions.

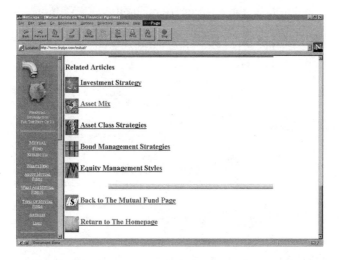

At The Fund Library Web site, you can fill out an "Investor Profile Questionnaire" that will help you assess what type of investor you are, and what your primary investment objectives should be.

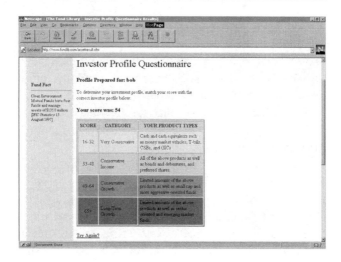

Fidelity Investments, one of the largest mutual fund companies in the world, has a software program called ThinkWare to help you with your asset mix decisions. You can download the program from Fidelity's U.S. Web site.

Since the program doesn't suggest specific Fidelity investments, it is more unbiased than some of the other tools we've seen.

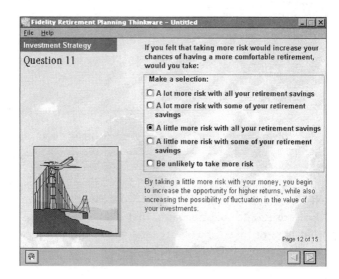

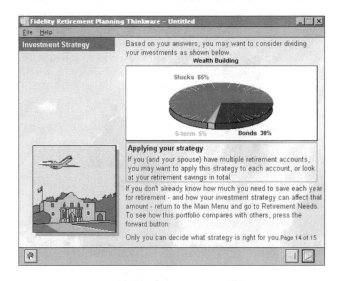

For some good background information on how to make an asset allocation decision, we recommend the Merrill Lynch OnLine Web site. There, in the "Investor Learning Centre," you'll find a document called the "Investor's Handbook." It features some good, general guidance about the types of investments you should consider.

Also visit the investment section of the *Vancouver Sun*'s Web site. You'll find it under the Business category. They have an excellent investment area that includes information on how to decide what to invest in.

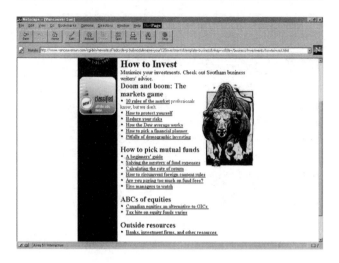

Recognize the Limitations of These Tools

What's the bottom line? We suggest that you experiment with the asset mix questionnaires you find on the Internet, but use them with caution. We would also suggest that you use a number of them, to see how the answers that they suggest might differ.

While mutual fund asset mix questionnaires can provide you with general guidance on the types of funds you should consider—such as equity, bond, or mortgage funds—they should not and can not serve as a definitive answer to your investment needs.

We think playing around with these tools can be useful—but we also think that you shouldn't fall into the trap of thinking that they provide a definitive answer to what is essentially a very complicated question. While asset mix questionnaires are a tremendously powerful marketing tool, they really can't give you a good, accurate indication of where you should be investing your money. First of all, they often simplify what are really complex financial deci-

> **When you move from being a saver to an investor, the world suddenly gets a lot more complicated. The issue of where to get proper advice becomes critical, and there's a battle among stockbrokers, fund dealers and financial planners to provide that advice.**
>
> JONATHAN CHEVREAU, "GIC REFUGEE FLOOD DRIES UP,"
> *FINANCIAL POST*, AUGUST 14, 1997

sions. In addition, they are often biased toward the financial institution administering the questionnaire.

We find that asset mix questionnaires fall prey to the "we'll-suggest-what-we-sell" syndrome. For example, after you answer the questions, the final recommendation is usually that you buy the investments offered by the financial institution that prepared the questionnaire. But this should come as no great surprise because the firm obviously isn't going to refer you to any of its competitors. Naturally, they are going to recommend their own funds.

Your Investment Objectives

Now that you've spent time learning more about the characteristics of different investments, and have considered some of the online asset mix tools that are available to get some guidance on your own investment needs, it's time to bite the bullet and write down your investment objectives. Establishing your investment objectives in the form of a single paragraph is perhaps the most difficult thing for you to do—but is an absolute necessity.

> **All you have to do is say the magic words: "I am a financial planner." The words imply clinical objectivity and expertise, but the truth of the matter is that most people using the title are mutual fund sales people whose interests lie in convincing you that a good financial plan involves buying what they are selling.**
>
> BARRY NELSON, "SETTING STANDARDS IN THE FINANCIAL PLANNING BUSINESS," *CALGARY HERALD*, NOVEMBER 17, 1996

Many financial planners and investment advisors can help you figure out your investment objectives and assist you in coming up with an asset mix based on these objectives.

Often, their advice can be well worth the fee that they will charge you—they have the expertise, background, and historical track record to help you figure out what you want to accomplish with your investments, and can translate that into an easily understood investment objective. From that, they can assist you in establishing a good, diversified mix of different types of assets that will help you achieve those objectives.

Yet many people decide to figure out their investment objectives and therefore their "asset mix" on their own.

There is no simpler way to go through this than to write out your objectives. Carefully balance what you think you need in terms of growth in your investment portfolio, your attitudes towards risk, and what you might need in terms of income.

Here is an example of what we mean.

"I am investing for my retirement for the long term. I'll therefore place the majority of my investments in assets that have a good long-term potential for growth. I'm willing to take some risk with those long term investments, but not a great deal. I'll also ensure that I have a ready source of cash available, so I'll place some of my investments in cash-based investments so that I can access it if needed. Since I'm investing for my retirement, I don't really need to focus on investments that provide a regular stream of income in the short term."

You've got to prepare the same type of statement—and you can only do this by sitting back and thinking about what you really want to accomplish. There isn't much the Internet can do here to help you—you can only do this through some long, careful thinking on your part.

Figuring Out Your Asset Mix

Finally, you will need to translate this investment objective statement into a definitive asset mix.

Keep in mind that the percentages we use below are examples—what is right for you depends on your own investment objectives.

First, figure out what percentage of your overall investment holdings should be in cash-based holdings, recognizing that you always want to have some percentage of your investments in this low risk category. This might include GICs, CSB's, or term deposits; mutual funds that invest in these types of cash-based investments; or a combination of both. You might decide, for example, to ensure that 20%–25% of your total investment portfolio includes cash-based investments.

Second, diversification means that you should have a mix of different types of investments for the remaining 75%–80%. So you have to figure out, in terms of percentages, how the rest of your investment portfolio should be allocated among different types of investments. What percentage should go into investments that have a good opportunity for growth but are high risk? Medium risk and medium growth? Low risk and low growth?

You might decide to place 20%–25% of your money in high-risk investments, another 30%–35% in medium-risk investments, and the remaining 20%–25% in investments that provide a consistent income with low risk.

Your asset mix percentages would then look something like this:

- 20%–25% cash-based investments

- 20%–25% high risk

- 30%–35% medium risk

- 20%–25% income investments

Now you have to figure out what investments to place in each of these categories.

There is no magic answer to figuring out your investment asset mix in terms of percentages as expressed above. Nor is there an easy way to figure out what investments are appropriate in each of these categories. What it really comes down to is some basic and hard thinking as to what your investment objectives are, and what asset mix is appropriate to help you meet those objectives.

Always remember this—there is no definitive, absolutely right, correct answer—it is all a matter of judgment.

The Role of the Internet with Your Investments

Can the Internet help you to determine what investments are appropriate for you so that you meet you investment objectives?

Certainly you can use it to research possible investments and obtain guidance on the types of investments you should consider. But in the final analysis, the Internet is only a tool. Your judgment and analysis of your investment objectives and of particular investments is the key to discerning what best suits you, in light of the risk, growth, and income specifics that you are willing to accept.

In the next several chapters we will show you how you can use the Internet as a tool to learn more about cash-based investments, mutual funds, and other investments.

Web Sites Mentioned in This Chapter

Canada Trust	www.canadatrust.com
Fidelity Investments Canada	www.fidelity.ca
Financial Pipeline	www.finpipe.com
GLOBEfund	www.globefund.com
Merrill Lynch OnLine	www.plan.ml.com/index.html
PALTrak	www.pal.com
The Fund Library	www.fundlibrary.com
Vancouver Sun	www.vancouversun.com

Cash and Cash-Equivalent Investments on the Internet

Retirement kills more people than hard work ever did. MALCOLM S. FORBES

HIGHLIGHTS

- You can use the Internet to understand more about cash-based and cash-equivalent offerings from various financial institutions.

- Web sites such as CANNEX and CANOE can help you compare interest rates from different banks and trust companies.

- Financial institutions often introduce new variations of existing cash-based investments. You should learn how to do research online to find independent news articles that assess these new cash-based offerings.

- On the Internet, you can research whether your cash-based investments are covered by federal deposit insurance or some other form of deposit insurance.

If you have determined that you don't want to have a self-directed RRSP because you consider yourself to be a passive investor, then you will be making your contributions into a "non-directed" RRSP. As you will recall from chapter 5, non-directed RRSPs are investments offered by banks, trust companies, full-service brokerage firms, insurance companies, and credit unions. You can choose to invest your money in a variety of "eligible investments," including savings accounts, Canada Savings Bonds (CSBs), Guaranteed Investment Certificates (GICs), term deposits, and mutual funds. A non-directed RRSP is managed for you by the financial institution.

There are about 7 million holders of Canada Savings Bonds.

Since mutual funds will likely be one of your primary investment vehicles we devoted all of chapter 12 to them. But mutual funds aside, for the purposes of this discussion we'll lump all of the other investments mentioned above into the category of "cash-based or cash-equivalent investments," since they act very much like cash.

We'll start by looking at how to find out more about these investments. Given the massive number of Canadian financial institutions that have established Web sites, it is no surprise that you can find a lot of information about their cash-based and cash-equivalent offerings online.

Researching Cash-Based Investments on the Internet

As you put together your investment strategy, you will find that most financial experts will recommend that you diversify your RRSP portfolio. This means that some portion of your overall savings should be in cash-based or cash-equivalent investments. You should therefore understand the options that exist for these investments, and learn how to determine the income and risk associated with them.

The first thing to keep in mind is that many financial institutions have two categories of cash-based invest-

Canadians hold approximately $30 billion in outstanding Canadian Savings Bonds.

ments: those that are only available through an RRSP and those that are not eligible to be held in an RRSP. When using the Internet to research cash-based investments, look for RRSP/retirement sections on the Web sites of financial organizations. This will help you to identify those cash-based investments that qualify for your RRSP.

Savings Accounts

Most banks, credit unions, and trust companies provide online details about the types of savings accounts that they offer, and the current rates that are available.

For example, Scotiabank offers a useful section on their Web site that includes descriptions of their "deposit accounts" as well as the current rates that are offered.

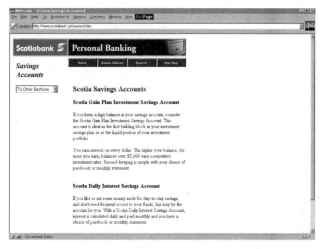

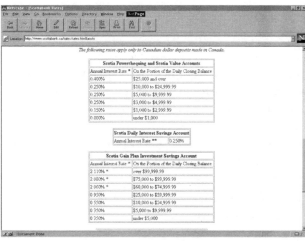

One thing you should do if you are going to place some of your money into such an account is to check whether the account is insured. Most banks and credit unions are insured through insurance corporations such as the Canada Deposit Insurance Corporation (CDIC) for banks, and various provincial corporations for credit unions. If you are dealing with a smaller financial institution, however, be sure to find out if your deposits are covered by some type of insurance. Often this information will be included on the organization's Web site, if one exists. This information should be factored into your overall assessment of the risk of your investment. We discuss this issue further toward the end of the chapter.

Canada Savings Bonds

You can learn a lot about Canada Savings Bonds at the Federal Government Web site for CSBs.

The Web site will give you the current rates for CSBs as well as an FAQ (frequently asked question summary) about using CSBs in your RRSP.

> **Approximately 20% of cash buyers of Canada Savings Bonds account for 87% of the value of the bonds issued.**

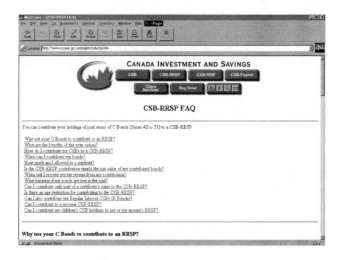

GICs/Term Deposits

If you are thinking of placing part of your RRSP investment in a GIC or term deposit, there are several things you should do. First, recognize that most bank, trust company, and credit union Web sites offer good descriptions of these particular investments, including any restrictions on withdrawal of the funds, RRSP eligibility, and other issues. For example, at the Web site for Vancouver City Savings Credit Union (VanCity), they have descriptions of their term deposits:

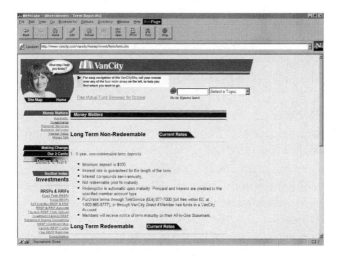

You can also learn about their rates:

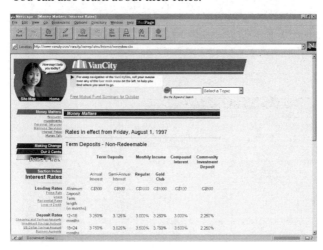

Using the Internet to Compare Savings Rates

The Web sites of most financial institutions offer a concise overview of GICs and term deposits, as well as current interest rates. Yet, what if you want to compare the savings rates offered by several institutions? You might do this in order to determine where you might get the best deal on a term deposit or GIC for your RRSP.

There are two good Web sites that you can turn to. First, check out CANNEX, an organization that has supplied interest rate surveys to the financial world for many years. On their site you can get an extensive list of comparative rates for GICs, term deposits, and deposit accounts.

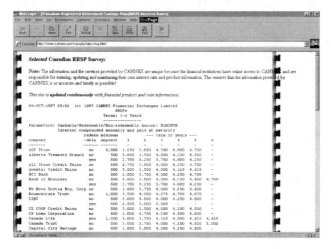

Similarly, CANOE (Canadian Online Explorer) offers a listing of comparative savings account and term deposit/GIC rates.

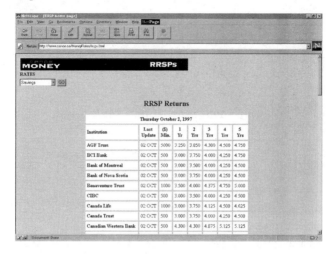

Remember the general rule concerning risk that we discussed in chapter 8? The rule went as follows: the higher the rate of return (in this case interest), the higher the risk of the investment.

Why is this important? If every financial institution is offering a rate of $3^1/2$% to 4%, and another financial institution is offering 6% or 7%, there's probably a higher element of risk associated with the latter investment. For example, it may not be insured. If you see a dramatic difference in the interest rates offered by two financial institutions for similar cash-based investments, check to see if the institution offering the higher rate is insured. Be vigilant and question why they would be offering such a dramatically higher rate.

Understanding Innovative Product Offerings

Financial institutions often introduce new variations of basic cash-equivalent accounts in order to make them more attractive to RRSP holders. They often provide details of these new product offerings on their Web sites, such as the example on the next page from the CIBC site.

You will see many advertisements in newspapers and magazines during RRSP season. You should take the time

to use the Internet to learn more about the income, growth, and risk characteristics of the investments being advertised. If the Web site doesn't answer all your questions, you can usually contact the financial organization by email to ask specific questions.

> **When asked what types of investments they would place in their RRSPs for the 1997 taxation year, 56% of Canadians said mutual funds, 27% said GICs or term deposits , 23% said stocks or bonds, and 22% said savings accounts.**
>
> SOURCE: ROYAL TRUST SURVEY, **www.royalbank.com**

You should also learn to use the Internet to find independent news articles that assess new financial products. Consider the following situation. We received a brochure from the Royal Bank of Canada that promoted a host of new financial products. These new products had names such as:

- Market Rate Increase GIC

- Medical Access GIC

- Canadian Market-Linked GIC

- Global Market-Linked GIC

- Five-in-One GIC

- Building Block GIC

- One-Year Cashable GIC

When you visit the Royal Bank Web site you can certainly learn more about these products. For example, they provide a full page of information about the "Market-Linked GIC", and they describe the benefits associated with this type of investment.

On the surface, it sounds like a great, no-lose investment. But what *isn't* clear is the potential risk associated with the product.

> **Interested in finding out what you might earn on your savings account, GIC, or term deposit? Visit the Hypertechmedia compound interest calculator at http://hypertechmedia.com/Interest.html—it lets you do a lot of quick calculations.**

To get an independent, unbiased view of these products, you could use the Internet to locate stories in the financial press related to "market-linked GIC products." How might you do this? In our case, we went to the CANOE Web site, which includes online features from the *Financial Post* newspaper, and we did a search for the terms "market-linked" and "GICs".

After a few seconds of searching its database, CANOE found numerous articles for us.

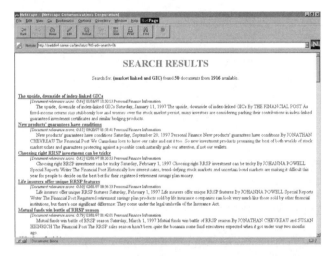

The first one contained a very concise overview of the benefits and risks of market-linked GICs.

The article helped us understand that while the basic investment is guaranteed there is no guarantee of any *income* on the initial investment should the stock market take a significant downturn. That is an important risk to understand, yet it wasn't clearly identified on the Royal Bank Web site. This example illustrates the importance of balancing the information you obtain online from a financial institution with independent advice from another source such as CANOE.

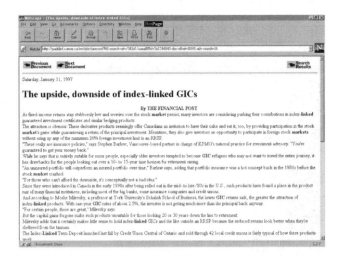

Many financial institutions aren't as up-front as they should be when it comes to the risk of the financial investments they promote. In some cases, this attitude has carried through to their Web sites.

But any investment carries risk—and the Internet can be a powerful ally to help you learn more about the risk associated with financial products you may be considering. The Internet's usefulness as an investment tool extends far beyond the Web sites of financial organizations. It's important to go beyond the online promotional material and research the pros and cons of investments like we have done in the example above. Only then will you be able to make a fully-informed decision.

The lesson to be learned? Whatever you do, don't plunge into an investment without fully understanding what you are getting into. Learn to use the Internet to uncover information that the Web site of a financial institution might not tell you.

Learning About the Security of Your Investment

Once again, we want to stress the importance of finding out whether the financial institution you are dealing with is covered by some type of deposit insurance. This isn't necessarily an easy question to answer online. Many financial institutions don't provide this information on their Web sites.

But some do. For example, here is a page from the Hy-Line Credit Union in Manitoba.

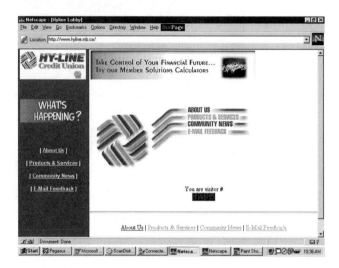

Browse through the site, and you'll come across the following section that explains how the credit union protects the deposits of its members.

To learn more about the topic of deposit insurance, we recommend you visit the Web site for the Canada Deposit Insurance Corporation (CDIC), which features a concise overview of how the CDIC deposit insurance system works and a list of banks and trust companies that are members of CDIC. You'll also find a test that you can take to assess your familiarity with the topic.

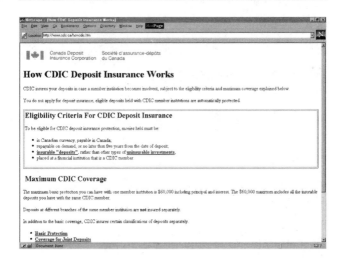

The site also provides helpful information on insurance coverage for deposits held in RRSPs.

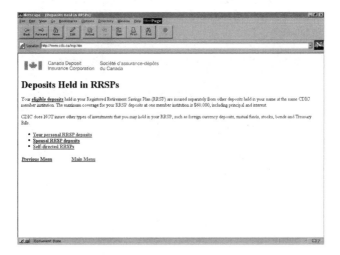

In chapter 8, we pointed out that money held in a credit union is not covered by the Canada Deposit Insurance Corporation. Instead, it is usually covered by a provincial corporation. Some provincial deposit insurance corporations, such as the Deposit Insurance Corporation of Ontario, have a Web site where you can learn more about the coverage they offer (see page 176).

The Web site for Credit Union Central of Canada, the umbrella organization for all the provincial credit union associations, provides links to most of the provincial credit union Web sites. Visit these sites, and you can usually

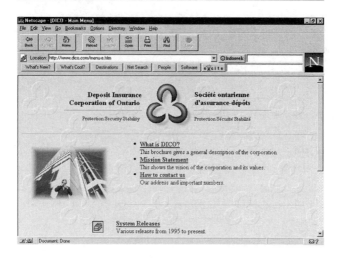

find out more about the deposit insurance system for credit unions in that province. For example, if you visit the Web site belonging to Credit Union Central Alberta, you will learn that deposits in Alberta credit unions are guaranteed 100%.

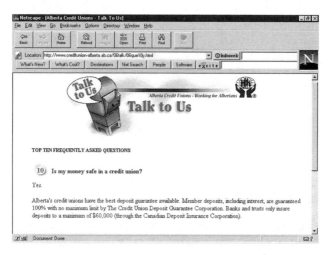

If you decide to place your money in an organization that is not a bank or credit union you will need to check with them directly to see if they are insured by another organization.

There are other ways to find out about the provincial deposit insurance system. Every province in Canada has an organization that represents credit unions in that province. Look for the article "RRSP planning should address risk concerns" from the February 8, 1997 edition of the *Financial Post*. You can find it on the CANOE Web site using the search command. The article features a good overview of the coverage with respect to your cash-based RRSP investments.

Conclusion

Right now, investing in cash-based investments doesn't carry the same appeal as investing in mutual funds or the stock markets, given that interest rates are so low. Yet this might not always be the case. Certainly, if we see another downturn in the stock market as we did in the late 1980s, with a related rise in interest rates, these investments will vastly increase in importance to investors.

That is where the Internet can play such a powerful role, by helping you to quickly compare cash-based investments for the best rates and offerings. Certainly if you invest part of your money in cash-based investments such as those covered in this chapter, you'll find the Internet to be a powerful and useful ally in finding the best deal.

Web Sites Mentioned in This Chapter

Canada Deposit Insurance Corporation	www.cdic.ca
Canada Savings Bonds	www.cis-pec.gc.ca
CANNEX	www.cannex.com
CANOE	www.canoe.ca
CIBC	www.cibc.com
Credit Union Central Alberta	www.creditunion-alberta. ab.ca/
Credit Union Central of Canada	www.cucentral.ca/

Deposit Insurance Corporation of Ontario	www.dico.com
Hy-Line Credit Union	www.hyline.mb.ca
Royal Bank of Canada	www.royalbank.com
Scotiabank	www.scotiabank.ca
Vancouver City Savings Credit Union	www.vancity.com

Mutual Funds on the Internet

Perplexity is the beginning of knowledge. KAHLIL GIBRAN

HIGHLIGHTS

- The Internet is an extremely useful place to learn about the fundamentals of mutual funds. In order to take full advantage of its potential, you will need to distinguish between those sites that want to educate you, and those sites that simply want to sell you something.

- Most mutual fund companies have Web sites that allow you to obtain descriptions, prices, and other background information about their funds. You can also use the services of sophisticated fund resources such as GLOBEfund, E*Trade Canada (a subscription service), and The Fund Library.

- You can access various tools on the Web that allow you to analyze the performance of various funds, or to find the best performers in a particular class of funds. When using these tools, recognize that past performance is not indicative of future performance.

- Online discussion groups can be used to debate and discuss particular funds or investment strategies with other Internet users. Keep in mind that these discussion groups are often used to spread rumours and other misinformation.

If you determine that you want to place part of your retirement investment into a variety of mutual funds, you'll quickly discover that the Internet can be a very powerful ally as you try to determine which funds you should invest in.

How can the Internet help you as you wrestle with the issue of mutual funds? In this chapter, we describe some of the ways you might use this technology to help you with your mutual fund decisions.

Learning About Mutual Funds

Survey after survey indicates that there is a pressing need for Canadians to know more about the basics of mutual funds. There is no doubt that many of us rush into such investments without really thinking about what we are doing.

It is important that you take the time to understand the fundamentals of mutual funds before you invest in them. This book will help you. If you want to learn more, you will discover that there is a lot of good educational material available online.

> The phenomenal growth in mutual fund business has created some confusion for consumers because of the profusion of funds and companies offering funds. Most people don't have sufficient basic knowledge to allow them to reduce their risk through proper assessment of funds, and to evaluate other factors such as fees....
>
> VICKI BARNETT, "BOOM TIMES FOR MUTUAL FUNDS," *CALGARY HERALD*, JUNE 17, 1997

Many of the retirement sites we outlined in chapter 6 are good starting points, since they often provide basic background information on mutual funds and how they work. Yet, as we pointed out in chapter 6, you have to learn to distinguish between the sites that are simply sales-oriented, and those which provide truly useful background and educational information.

As you tour the Internet to learn more about mutual funds, keep the following caveat in mind: your goal is to find the sites which provide good, concise information—not those that simply want to sell you something. We think that you will quickly develop an ability to know the difference between useful, non-biased information and the down-and-dirty sales pitch. What should you look for? Focus on the Web sites that describe the fundamentals of mutual funds and that make it easy for you to find the answers to the questions you have.

Some of the more useful sites that fit this category are the following:

- As a starting point, visit the *Globe and Mail* GLOBEfund site, which features a comprehensive learning section. It includes a glossary, a "Getting Started" section, and "The Wise Investor" section. The latter contains a variety of mutual fund articles from some of Canada's best known financial authors, including Duff Young.

- Several other Canadian newspaper sites include mutual funds sections. For example, The "Money" section on the CANOE Web site (see page 182) includes the article "Mutual Funds 101" by Jonathon Chevreau, a well-known writer for the *Financial Post*.

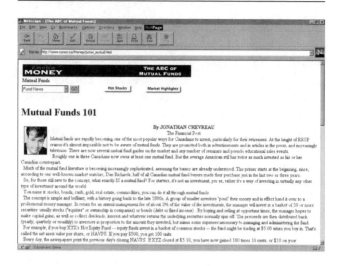

PERSONAL PAGES

What are some likely features to be found on mutual fund companies' Web sites in the near future? Most fund companies will probably soon offer a "Personal Page," which will allow you to automatically create your own personal Web page. Your page will contain details about the mutual funds that you have with that particular company. The trend is already well underway in the U.S.

- Take a look at documents such as "What Is a Mutual Fund?" and "The 10 Most Frequently Asked Questions About Mutual Funds" at the Investment Funds Institute of Canada site. The Institute represents the Canadian mutual funds industry. Its site also features an online glossary of mutual fund terms, which can be helpful when you encounter jargon you are not sure of.

- Check out "Invest Wisely—Learning About Mutual Funds" at the U.S. Securities and Exchange Commission Web site. Even though some of the specifics in that document are not appropriate for most Canadian investors, it is still a good introduction to the fundamentals of mutual funds.

- The Financial Concept Group, a Canadian Financial Planning organization, deserves plaudits for focussing less on the hard-sell and more on education on its Web site. Its "Complete Guide to Mutual Funds" is a very good overview that is well worth a read.

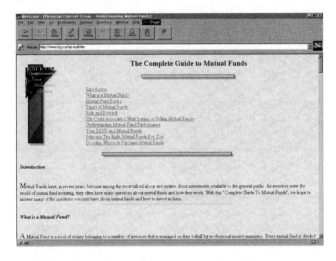

- Many financial authors and advisors are creating Web sites where they post articles and other information they have written. For example, well-known author and columnist Duff Young publishes articles about mutual funds on his TopFunds Web site. Visit it, and you can find many useful articles such as "Quick answers to the 7 most common mutual fund questions."

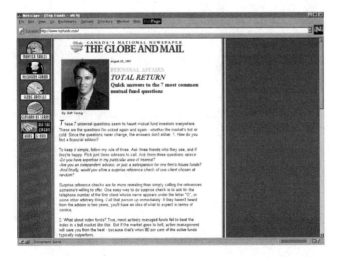

- Check out the Mutual Funds Switchboard, an excellent and comprehensive resource that lists various Canadian mutual fund information sites. It's one of the most comprehensive indices available on the Web.

- Spend some time in the Financial Pipeline, a site we mentioned in chapter 10. It includes some very useful educational material about mutual funds.

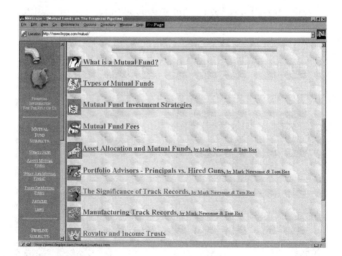

- Sometimes an Internet search can be very helpful. For example, simply typing *"what is a mutual fund"* into a popular Web search engine such as AltaVista returns a lengthy list of useful sites that you might research.

> Canada's $170-billion mutual-fund industry is booming
> but rapid growth has brought its own set of problems.
> With over 1,100 funds to choose from, investors are
> getting bombarded by sales pitches from all quar-
> ters…the mutual-fund consumer is confused, badly
> informed and often badly served by the industry.
>
> PETER HADEKEL, "FUND INVESTORS STILL DON'T UNDERSTAND THE
> RISKS," *THE MONTREAL GAZETTE*, SEPTEMBER 30, 1996

Researching Specific Mutual Funds on the Internet

In chapter 10 we outlined the process you should go through to determine what you want to invest in. Our methodology involved using the Internet to understand the various mutual fund asset classes and which specific mutual funds are appropriate for you.

It is no small undertaking to figure out exactly which mutual funds you should purchase. With over 1,600 mutual funds available in Canada, this is not an easy thing to do.

The Internet can both help and hinder you in this regard. The Internet helps, since it makes it very easy for you to obtain individual fund descriptions from most fund companies in Canada. However, the Internet can also be a hindrance because it exposes you to so much information and such a wide array of choices and options. It can be quite overwhelming.

Once you have identified the asset classes that are appropriate for you, we suggest that you do the following:

- **Compare individual funds in an asset class**
  For example, if you think that at least one third of your retirement portfolio should be from the equity asset class, and that at least half of that should be in aggressive growth funds within that class, examine the various growth funds that are available.

  You can do this by examining mutual fund descriptions at the Web sites of various companies, as well as by reviewing descriptions at all-encompassing mutual fund sites such as The Fund Library, GLOBEfund and E*Trade Canada.

- **Do a performance analysis**

  Use some of the analysis tools discussed below to identify and analyze the performance of funds in particular
  categories. This will help you to learn more about the
  track record of particular funds.

  These two steps will help you determine which funds
  you might want to invest in. Let's look at each step in a
  bit more detail.

Step #1: Compare Individual Funds in an Asset Class—Obtaining Descriptions, Prices, and Objectives of Various Funds

It is easy to access online descriptions of individual funds
from the many mutual fund organizations that have Web
sites in Canada.

You can obtain a list of the Web sites for most major
mutual fund companies in Canada at several of the sites
that we have already mentioned, such as the Investment
Funds Institute of Canada, at The Fund Library, and at
the Mutual Fund Switchboard. Or simply visit a Web
directory such as Yahoo! Canada and type in the name of
the mutual fund company you are looking for.

Keep in mind that while the vast majority of mutual
fund companies have Web sites, some companies have
been slower than others in learning to market online. As
a result, there are still some mutual fund companies without any online presence. Also, among those companies
that do have Web sites, some of those sites are more
sophisticated than others.

What should you be looking for in a mutual fund site?
Several things:

- **An overview or description of the fund**

  This would include information about the assets that
  make up the fund, the risk profile of those assets, an
  overview of the objectives of the fund, as well as an up-

EXCELLENT INTERNET REAL ESTATE

The U.S. company, New England Funds, was smart
enough to grab the Web address mutualfunds.com.
They estimate that a large number of investors who
might never have heard of them do so now simply by
typing in www.mutualfunds.com.

to-date fund management report. Look for details, not marketing fluff. For example, if it is a stock fund, does it actually list the names of the stocks that are held in the fund, or does it just list the types of stocks in the fund?

- **Loads**
  The loads are the commissions that are charged on the fund on purchase (at the front-end) or on sale (at the back-end).

- **Historical performance**
  This information indicates the fund's returns.

- **The management expense ratio (MER) and other expenses charged to the fund**
  The management fee (as an annual percentage of total assets in the fund) and other expenses charged against the fund can be a very important factor in the overall return you get on your fund. Take a look at the article "Three things savvy investors are likely to demand," by financial expert Duff Young in the GLOBEfund site or on his own TopFunds site. It describes the impact of management fees on your overall return.

- **The background of the investment team**
  What experience does the team involved in managing the fund have?

- **Background information concerning the fund**
  Look for detailed information such as the fund's most recent results, expected outlook, major changes in the fund, and other commentary.

- **The prospectus for the fund**
  Details of the prospectus should be available online, and the site should allow you to request a paper copy.

A LIBRARY OF FUNDS

At The Fund Library site (www.fundlibrary.com), you can quickly obtain detailed brochures on a wide variety of Canadian mutual funds in Adobe Acrobat format. This lets you see and print the brochure, exactly as it would have appeared in print. These brochures offer a good synopsis of various mutual funds in a simple, one page format.

Every fund must have a formal prospectus, which describes the fund in a great degree of detail. Some fund companies place the full prospectus online, while others permit you to easily request a paper copy.

As we mentioned earlier, you can get information about particular mutual funds from several sources. First, most major mutual fund companies in Canada provide Web sites that contain detailed background information about their particular funds.

For example, Altamira's Web site provides an overview of each of its funds, including background information on the objectives of its funds as well as a listing of the major investments held in each fund.

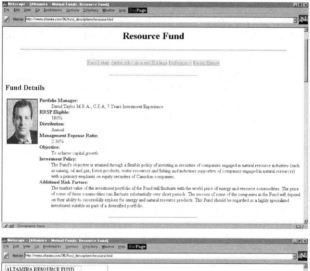

You can also access several sophisticated fund resources that are appearing on the Web. GLOBEfund, an initiative of the *Globe and Mail*, provides you with access to good, concise overviews of most Canadian funds. For example, you can access a profile of a mutual fund company:

or review details of a particular fund:

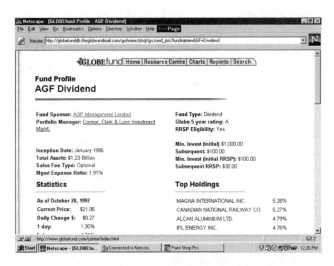

The latter includes statistics on the historical performance of the fund, a listing of the major holdings or investments held in the fund, and other information. While looking at a specific fund's Web page on GLOBEfund, you can quickly access news articles that have appeared about the fund, link to the Web site for the fund, or generate a chart that examines the performance of the fund from a variety of different perspectives.

Similarly, if you are a paying customer of the E*Trade Canada online stock trading service, you can access a variety of fund descriptions, such as this graph of the investments held in a particular health care mutual fund:

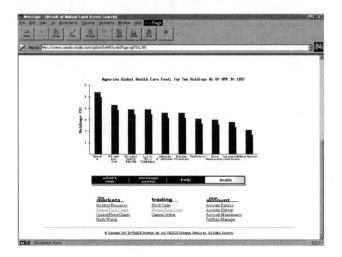

You can also use The Fund Library Web site to research Canadian mutual funds. It gives you access to background information on a wide variety of funds, although we found that The Fund Library was somewhat more sales-oriented than the GLOBEfund site.

UP AND UP

Canadian mutual fund assets pushed through the $200 billion level for the first time in November 1996—an amount equal to one quarter of the economic output of Canada. The total just one year previous was $142.8 billion, while six years ago the total was about $50 billion.

Step #2: Performance Analysis

The physicist Niehls Bohr once observed that making a prediction is very difficult, especially when it concerns the future. He might have been talking about mutual funds—particularly when you are trying to use the past performance of a fund to predict its performance in the future.

When looking at various mutual funds, many people look at historical performance information to help them figure out which mutual fund to purchase. Some people believe that the past performance of a fund is a good indication of how the fund will perform in the future. In this line of thinking, identifying the top performers in a class of funds, such as the best performer in Canadian equity funds, can be a useful exercise in getting started, or to back up your findings.

Yet don't forget about our comments from chapter 9. Historical performance should not be used as an indicator of expected future performance.

ONLINE FUND RANKING

To get an up-to-date ranking of mutual fund companies in Canada, visit the Web site for the Investment Funds Institute of Canada (www.mutfunds.com/ific**). In its Statistics section, you can find a monthly report that features a regularly updated ranking of mutual fund companies.**

If you do want to use performance data to help you decide which funds to invest in, this is one area where you definitely want to take advantage of the Internet. The Internet is full of tools and information that help you examine the performance of a single fund, or compare one fund's performance against another.

A good place to start is Fundata Canada, a company that supplies daily fund information to the Canadian financial industry. It features a page with the best and

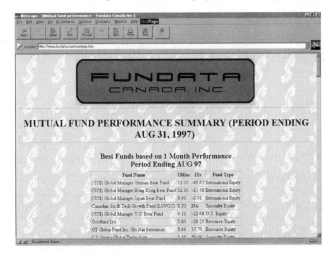

worst Canadian mutual funds for the last month; last three months; and the previous one, three, and five years. It's a good place to go to learn about the winners and losers.

Such rankings of the "best" and "worst" are found throughout the Internet. In particular, check out the mutual fund/investment sections on the Web sites of CANOE, the *Vancouver Sun*, and BellCharts.

As mentioned earlier, you can use the Web to discover the best performers within a specific category. For example, at E*Trade Canada, a subscription service, you can specify that you want a list of all Canadian equity funds that have exceeded a 2% return in the last month.

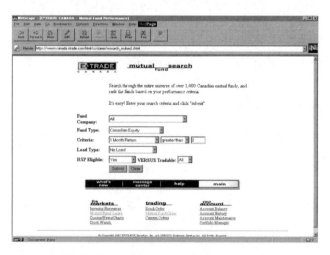

E*Trade Canada then displays the funds that meet the criteria you specified.

This type of tool can be extremely powerful. For example, if you decide that you want 30% of your portfolio to be equity funds, you can use a Web site such as this one to find the best performers in this category. You can then research the funds on the list, to find out which ones are best suited to your needs. To find other performance listings and analysis tools, start out at the Mutual Fund Switchboard site that we mentioned earlier in the chapter.

Finally, GLOBEfund, the *Globe and Mail*'s mutual fund service on the Web, lets you quickly prepare charts examining the performance of a fund against a variety of criteria. For example, on the screen below we've charted the performance of a fund that invests in Latin American securities against the performance of major companies on the Toronto Stock Exchange (TSE). The resulting graph tells us whether this investment has performed well compared to other potential funds, such as a fund that consists of investments in companies on the TSE.

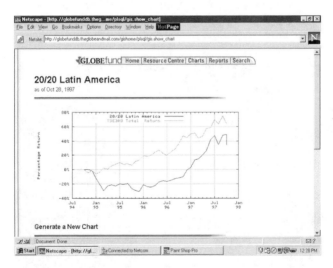

Tools such as these are useful to help you identify potential candidates for your money, but we must stress again that they should not be the only criteria that you use to select your funds. Remember—past performance is not always indicative of future performance!

Online Discussion Forums

Finally, if you are brave, and have the time, fortitude, and wherewithal, you might consider visiting a couple of the many mutual fund forums that exist on the Internet, to examine what others are saying about particular fund investments.

ONLINE BRAVERY

Some mutual fund companies are being brave enough to set up discussion forums on their own Web sites. Altamira did this some time ago, and uses the site to encourage feedback from clients. Such a forum can be a double-edged sword—take a look at the Altamira forum(www.altamira.ca), and you'll see that criticism as well as congratulatory back-slapping is found in the online discussions.

For example, at Duff Young's TopFunds site, you can join a number of different online discussions about particular mutual funds:

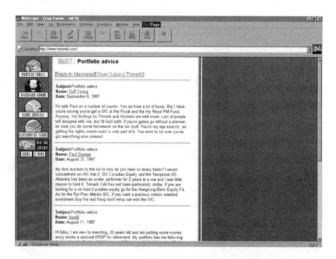

And over at The Fund Library, you can browse through a number of discussions about fund investing.

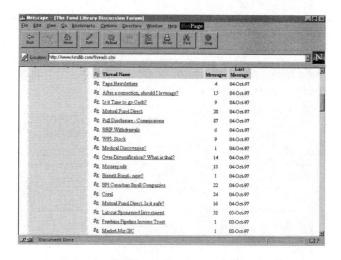

Thread Name	Messages	Last Message
Faps Newsletters	4	04-Oct-97
After a correction, should I leverage?	15	04-Oct-97
Is it Time to go Cash?	9	04-Oct-97
Mutual Fund Direct	28	04-Oct-97
Full Disclosure - Commissions	87	04-Oct-97
RRIF Withdrawals	6	04-Oct-97
WFI- Stock	9	04-Oct-97
Medical Discoveries?	1	04-Oct-97
Over-Diversification? What is that?	14	04-Oct-97
Mousepads	18	04-Oct-97
Bissett Bond - now?	1	04-Oct-97
BPI Canadian Small Companies	22	04-Oct-97
Corel	24	04-Oct-97
Mutual Fund Direct. Is it safe?	16	04-Oct-97
Labour Sponsored Investment	32	03-Oct-97
Pembina Pipeline Income Trust	1	03-Oct-97
Market Mix GIC	1	03-Oct-97

You can find additional discussion forums through the Mutual Fund Switchboard.

As you use these discussion forums, keep in mind that the information they contain can be wrong, false, misleading, incorrect, or even downright fraudulent. Some investors use discussion groups to plant false rumours and illegally manipulate the price of stocks.

Nicholas Negroponte, founder and director of the Media Lab at the Massachusetts Institute of Technology, predicted that the Internet will take over delivery of investment management vehicles like mutual funds, rendering the intermediary, such as a broker or financial planner, obsolete.

CHRISTINE WILLIAMSON, "ICI TALKS UP EDUCATION, EXPECTATIONS," *PENSIONS & INVESTMENTS*, JUNE 9, 1997, V25 N12 PP: 35

Making a Decision

We certainly think that there is a lot of useful information online to help guide you in your decisions. Yet, keep in mind that as useful as the Internet might be, your foray into the world of mutual funds comes down to one simple basic rule. To succeed, you must select the fund or funds which best match your investment objectives.

The Internet can provide you some information and guidance to help you with your decisions, but at the end of the day, it will be your judgement, opinion, and perhaps even your gut feelings, or the guidance/expertise of your investment advisor that will guide you in what you decide to do.

Web Sites Mentioned in This Chapter

Altamira Investment Services	www.altamira.com
AltaVista	www.altavista.digital.com
BellCharts	www.bellcharts.com
CANOE	www.canoe.ca
E*Trade Canada	www.canada.etrade.com
Financial Concept Group	www.fcg.ca
Financial Pipeline	www.finpipe.com
Fundata Canada	www.fundata.com
GLOBEfund	www.globefund.com
Investment Funds Institute of Canada	www.mutfunds.com/ific
Mutual Funds Switchboard	web.onramp.ca/cadd/723mut.htm
The Fund Library	www.fundlibrary.com
TopFunds	www.topfunds.com
U.S. Securities & Exchange Commission	www.sec.gov
Vancouver Sun	www.vancouversun.com
Yahoo! Canada	www.yahoo.ca

CHAPTER 13

Stocks and Bonds on the Internet

Money is better than poverty, if only for financial reasons. WOODY ALLEN

HIGHLIGHTS

- The Internet makes it possible for investors to access a wide range of information about the stock and bond markets. The sheer volume of information can often be overwhelming.

- There are numerous Web sites that will help you learn about the fundamentals of investing in stocks and bonds. Examples include the sites of securities regulators as well as comprehensive investor resources such as invest-o-rama.

- Online resources such as Carlson On-line Services, the Wall Street Research Net, DailyStocks, and StockHouse provide investors with access to news releases, media coverage, stock data, and other financial information on publicly traded companies.

- It's important to balance the information you receive from a company's Web site with independent information from other sources on the Internet.

If you wish to invest your RRSP in something other than mutual funds and cash-based securities, you can turn to the stock market and other investments.

To use these investments as a tax deduction, however, you must set up a *self-directed* RRSP. This is usually as easy as filling out a few forms at your bank, or setting up a self-directed RRSP on one of the online trading services we discuss in chapter 15.

The Impact of the Internet on Investing

For the millions of Canadians who have never invested in anything more sophisticated than a savings account or Canada Savings Bonds, the Internet represents an opportunity to educate themselves about—and participate in—other investment alternatives.

Many Canadians restrict themselves to simple investments in cash-equivalent investments or mutual funds due to a lack of expertise with the stock and bond markets. People generally believe that they won't be able to comprehend what stocks, bonds, and other financial instruments are all about.

Certainly, the complexity of these investments is one reason why many Canadians stay away from them. The investment industry also has its own unique terminology, which usually manages to confuse the average investor. Even once an investor learns about the instruments and understands the jargon, the process of figuring out what to invest in is quite challenging.

Lack of access to information has also hampered the amateur or individual investor. The individual investor has long been restricted to the financial news in the business and financial press, and traditionally it has not been easy for people to access other corporate and industry information. And it's not just company background information that is hard to find—the individual investor has traditionally not had easy access to the up-to-date news reports and rate/price information that are the standard tools of the investment professional.

All this has changed with the arrival of the Internet.

As we cautioned in chapter 2, the Internet doesn't replace the professional expertise of an investment professional. However, individual investors can use the Internet to become more involved in their financial decisions. For those Canadians who use financial advisors, how many *really* comprehend the decisions that their financial advisors are making on their behalf? We encourage you to use the Internet to become more knowledgeable about investment matters, so that when your financial advisor talks to you, you'll understand the terminology and be able to ask intelligent questions.

There are a number of useful guides on the Internet that you can read to enhance your understanding of the stock and bond markets. You can also find many useful investment glossaries online which will help you understand the terminology used throughout the investment industry.

Mixed Feelings

The Internet is both a boon and a challenge to the average investor.

On the one hand, it is beneficial because the Internet provides investors with access to a wealth of information from companies themselves, their competitors, and the industries in which they operate. Not only that, but investors can access comprehensive news and rate/price information from all over the world.

Yet on the other hand, if you plunge into the world of stocks, bonds, and esoteric investments such as commodities and options online, you may feel completely and utterly overwhelmed.

The sheer volume of online financial information about the stock and bond markets is so stunning that we think that once you begin to look around, you might feel rather ill at ease, unsure of where to start, where to go, and what to look for.

That's why we suggest that one of the first Web sites that you should visit is the site of the British Columbia Securities Commission (BCSC). The BCSC has created a useful publication called "Be an Informed Investor."

The document raises two key questions that you should think about before plunging into the world of stock market information on the Internet. *Is the investment right for you?* and *Do you understand the investment?* These two questions should always be at the forefront of your mind as you explore these types of investments.

Having said that, in this chapter we give you a short and concise outline of how you can use the Internet to assist you with your exploration of the world of stocks, bonds, and other financial investments.

Learning More About the Stock Market and Other Investments

It's easy to invest in a Canada Savings Bond and earn a safe return, but it's quite another thing to venture into the stock or bond market and expect solid, low-risk growth. There is a world of difference between the expertise required to invest in Canada Savings Bonds and that required to manage any kind of stock or bond investment. This is because the risk is higher in the stock market and the complexity of what you become involved in can be much greater.

You should not expect the Internet to make you a financial expert; indeed, it might even have the opposite effect. Some people have found that the Internet is simply too big, and too overwhelming to use as an investment tool. The data that you will find on the Internet is just that—data. It is not information. It takes knowledge and expertise to turn it into a usable resource.

If you decide that you want to explore the world of the stock market and other financial investments, then your first task is to use the Internet to gain insight into some basic investment concepts. Fortunately, there is some good stuff out there.

The best places to start are the Web sites of independent organizations such as regulatory authorities or associations for individual investors.

The Investor Learning Centre of Canada has some excellent information that you can access on Canada Trust's CT Securities Web site. Featured on the site are investor "briefings" that describe how the stock, bond, and securities markets operate in Canada.

Also check out the publication called "What Every Investor Should Know—A Handbook from the U.S. Securities and Exchange Commission" at the Securities and Exchange Commission Web site—look under the "consumer" section. While written from a U.S. perspective, the document is a good introduction to the fundamentals of the stock market.

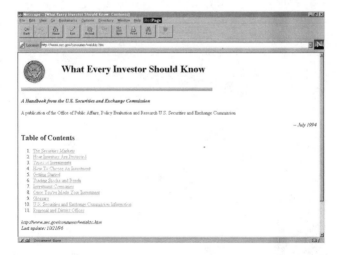

It offers pointers on how securities markets work, how to choose an investment, what is involved in trading stocks and bonds, and other related issues.

There are many other useful documents on the SEC Web site. For example, you should also take a look at "Invest Wisely: Advice from Your Securities Industry

Regulators," which is a good overview of many things you should consider before plunging into the stock market.

You can learn how specific stock exchanges work by accessing their Web sites. The Vancouver Stock Exchange's Web site provides a good overview of its role, as does the Web site belonging to the Montreal Stock Exchange and the Toronto Stock Exchange.

What about bonds? Check out Bonds Online—although American, it does include "The Bond Professor," which can be a good source of information about the fundamentals of these investments:

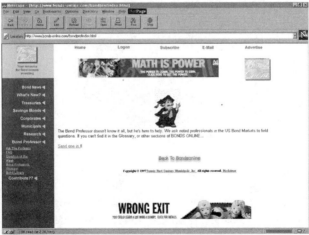

As for associations, check out the American Association of Independent Investors (AAII). Although the site has a U.S.-focus, they provide a lot of good investment information at both the basic and advanced level. While some of the information they provide is free, to get access to the full range of information they make available you must pay a fee.

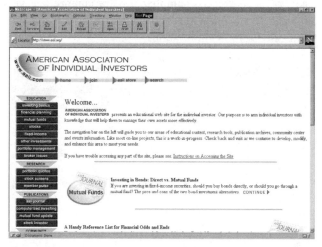

There are many other similar associations online, but you need to use caution. While there are associations like the AAII that have long track records, there are also those that are rather new or which are scams, and simply want your money.

The next document you should look at is the "Investment FAQ." Compiled on the Internet over a period of several years, it is a multi-part document that deals with many different aspects of investments, including stocks, bonds, options, and other investments.

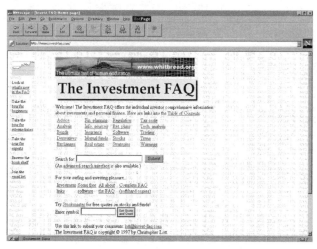

This document provides additional background information to help you understand the stock market or other financial topics, including links to other sites. Specifically, consult the "Information Sources—Internet" section. That will lead you to a number of very comprehensive information sites where you can often find useful investor-education information.

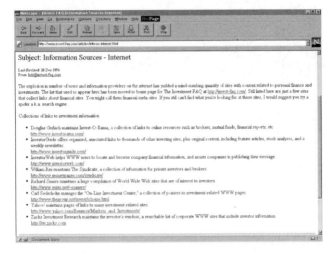

For example, from the FAQ we traveled to a site called "invest-o-rama," which featured a fairly complex investor education area:

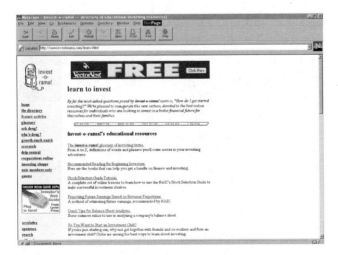

Using the Internet to learn about investing is a challenge in and of itself. The Investment FAQ notes that "the explosion in number of users and information providers on the Internet has yielded a mind-numbing quantity of sites with content related to personal finance and investments."

We couldn't have said it better.

Using the Internet for Company Research

As an investor in stocks, bonds, or other investments, it is important that you understand how to locate online information about companies, their competitors, and their industries. You need this information to help you decide whether to invest in the stocks or bonds they have issued, or if you wish to judge the safety or future performance of a stock or bond that you already own.

For example, you might want to obtain background information on a company or industry, as well as up-to-date reports on a company's financial activities.

Of course, as we point out throughout this book, obtaining the information is one thing, but the most important step is analyzing it. In this section, we offer our advice on where to find online information about companies and industries, but we do not provide guidance on how to analyze that information, a topic that is obviously far beyond the scope of this book.

Finding the Company Online

Suppose that you want to investigate a public company's financial and operating history; understand its markets, competitive challenges, outlook, and opportunities; or update yourself on their recent activities. You will want this information in order to weigh their opportunities for success and income against the risks of failure and loss.

Fortunately, both publicly traded and private companies are quickly moving to establish Web sites for a variety of business purposes, one of which is to provide information to existing and potential investors. Organizations will often include their annual reports, press releases, stock information, and other data on their Web sites, making this a useful starting point in your research.

Therefore, your first step should be to determine if the particular company has a Web site. There are several ways to do this:

- If you have the company's annual report, see if it lists their Web site address—many organizations are now including this information in all their investment materials.

- Try searching for the company's Web site in an Internet directory such as Yahoo! Canada or on a search engine such as AltaVista, Excite, or Lycos.

- Call the company's investor relations department and ask them if they have a Web site.

It's important to recognize that a company's Web site—if one exists—is not likely to have answers for all your questions. The only information you will find there is the information that the company has chosen to make available online. Also, keep in mind that the Internet is, for all intents and purposes, a relatively new system. Since many businesses are still actively exploring its role, they might not yet have established a Web site for the company, or the site they do have may not have a lot of useful information on it.

Using the information found on a company's Web site is a good starting point, but it's important that you also seek out independent sources from outside the company. You never want to rely solely on official corporate information as the basis for making an investment decision.

Researching a Company

In order to broaden your research, you should use the Internet to examine:

- news reports
- industry analyses
- market histories
- comments from analysts, and
- other independent sources of information.

How else can you obtain information about a company or its industry? There is no shortage of online sources. Check out the Web sites of competitors, if they exist. In particular, search Yahoo! Canada for information on the industry you are researching.

Special Investor Sites

There are a large number of special investor sites online that are designed to help you find information about public companies.

If you are researching a publicly traded Canadian company, visit Carlson On-line Services, which bills itself as "the source for Canadian public company investor information and research." Carlson provides you with quick access to news releases, stock information, and industry data on hundreds of Canadian companies.

For example, suppose you are looking for information about the Canadian mining company Inco. If you do a search for "Inco" on Carlson's Web site, you can access a page of information which includes the latest Inco press releases, contact information for the company, a link to Inco's Web site, research reports, stock charts, and information on the mining industry from Industry Canada. You can also connect to an online discussion group about the company!

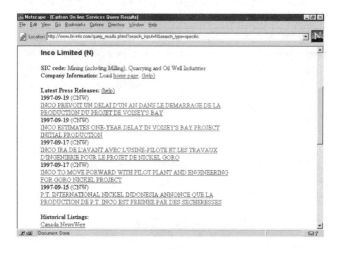

To do the same type of thing with American companies, start out at a site such as invest-o-rama (see page 208).

Despite the odd-sounding name, invest-o-rama is an extremely useful site. You can use it to access company information from hundreds of different sources on the Internet.

For example, in the screen below, we've asked for information about a company named Wolverine World Wide. Invest-o-rama has prepared a comprehensive summary of Web sites that include information about the company. Using invest-o-rama, we can retrieve online profiles about the company, stock prices and charts, the filings the company has made with the Securities and Exchange Commission, as well as recent news and press releases.

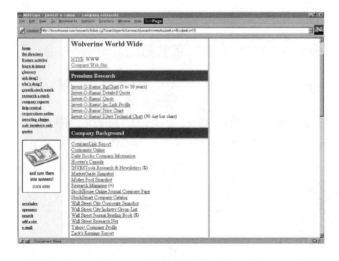

If you're researching publicly traded U.S. companies, an excellent starting point is the Wall Street Research Net.

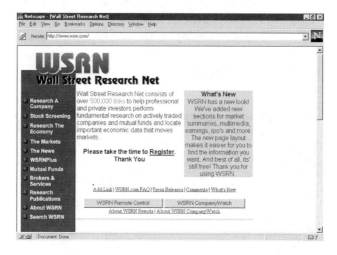

On this site, you can access information about over 17,000 companies, including SEC filings, company home pages, annual reports, news releases, stock quotes, graphs, and more. Wall Street Research Net also provides users with access to economic databases, market news, research publications, as well as links to online brokerage firms, online quote services, and other financial resources on the Web.

Also check out the DailyStocks Web site, where you can access an incredible array of information about Canadian or American public companies. Here's the page for Inco:

Other popular sites include INVESTools, researchmag. com, and StockHouse.

On StockHouse, you can retrieve press releases for companies as well as link to news stories that have appeared in major newspapers. For example, in the screen below, StockHouse is displaying news items about Suncor Energy that have appeared in the *Calgary Herald* and the *Financial Post*.

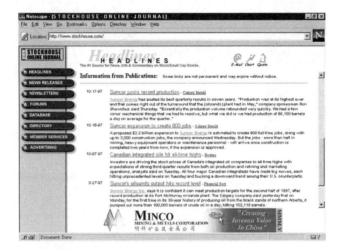

You should also consult online press release services such as Canada NewsWire, Canadian Corporate News, PR Newswire, and Business Wire. Many of these services permit a limited search for past press releases by using a keyword or company name.

Online News Sources

Web sites belonging to newspapers, magazines, and wire services are also a good starting points for online research.

Check out sites such as CANOE (which includes archives from the *Financial Post*), the Wall Street Journal Interactive Edition (a subscription service, but well worth the money), SmartMoney Interactive (information on over 8,000 U.S. companies), CNNfn (CNN's financial news network), and Reuters' MoneyNet.com.

With the exception of CANOE, all of these news services have a U.S. focus, but that doesn't diminish the usefulness of their market and company information. Having said that, when you are visiting investment sites on the

Internet, it's important that you *always* check to see whether the service is Canadian or American.

Government Organizations

Various government securities bodies are requiring publicly traded companies to electronically file their regular financial statements and other regulatory filings.

In some cases, this information is then made available to the public through the Internet. A good example is the EDGAR Database (Electronic Data Gathering, Analysis, and Retrieval system), a U.S. Securities and Exchange Commission project. You can search for information provided by various companies on the EDGAR Web site as well as SEDAR, the System for Electronic Document Analysis and Retrieval from the Canadian Depository for Securities.

Online Trading Services

Finally, many of the online stock trading services we discuss in chapter 15 give you access to background information about publicly traded companies.

Online Research

If you are serious about using the Internet as a research tool, then you have to invest the time to learn how to do effective research online.

There are many different search tools on the Internet. We mentioned several of the major ones (Yahoo! Canada, AltaVista, Excite, and Lycos) earlier in the chapter.

The difficulty with doing research on the Internet is that each of these major search tools operates somewhat differently. Commands that work on one search tool may not work on another. It is beyond the scope of this book to teach you the fundamentals of online research. If you're interested in developing this skill further, and we recommend that you do, you might want to consult one of our other books—*The 1998 Canadian Internet Directory and Research Guide*. The book provides tips and techniques to help you become an expert at searching for information on the Internet.

Web Sites Mentioned in This Chapter

AltaVista	www.altavista.digital.com
American Association of Independent Investors (AAII)	www.aaii.org
Bonds Online	www.bondsonline.com
British Columbia Securities Commission	www.bcsc.bc.ca
Business Wire	www.businesswire.com
Canada NewsWire	www.newswire.ca
Canadian Corporate News	www.cdn-news.com
CANOE	www.canoe.ca
Carlson On-line Services	www.fin-info.com
CNNfn	www.cnnfn.com
Daily Stocks	www.dailystocks.com
EDGAR Database	www.sec.gov/edgarhp.htm
Excite	www.excite.com
Inco	www.incoltd.com
Investment FAQ	www.invest-faq.com
invest-o-rama	www.ctsecurities.com/ilc/index.htm
INVESTools	www.investools.com
Investor Learning Centre of Canada	www.investorama.com
Lycos	www.lycos.com
Montreal Stock Exchange	www.me.org
PR Newswire	www.prnewswire.com
researchmag.com	www.researchmag.com
Reuters MoneyNet.com	www.moneynet.com
SEDAR	www.sedar.com
SmartMoney Interactive	www.smartmoney.com
StockHouse	www.stockhouse.com
Toronto Stock Exchange	www.tse.com
U.S. Securities and Exchange Commission (SEC)	www.sec.gov
Vancouver Stock Exchange	www.vse.ca
Wall Street Journal Interactive Edition	www.wsj.com
Wall Street Research Net	www.wsrn.com
Yahoo! Canada	www.yahoo.ca

CHAPTER 14

Monitoring Your Performance

The chief value of money lies in the fact that one lives in a world in which it is overestimated.
H. L. MENCKEN

HIGHLIGHTS

- There are many online calculators that you can use to determine the maturity value of a GIC or term deposit.

- You can track the value of your mutual fund holdings on the Internet in four basic ways: by looking up the daily Net Asset Value of your funds, by generating simple reports and graphs, by using sophisticated "portfolio trackers" such as those offered by The Fund Library and GLOBEfund, and by using portfolio management software such as PALTrak.

- You can obtain delayed stock quotes on the Internet using Web sites such as CANOE, the Canadian Stock Market Reporter, and the CT Market Partner, run by CT Securities/Canada Trust. Web sites such as InvestorsEdge allow you to manage a portfolio of stocks, while organizations such as Telenium allow you to manage all your investments with a single piece of software.

- Using Quicken, a sophisticated personal financial management program, you can manage all your investment needs and link to the Internet for current Canadian mutual fund, stock, and other investment data.

After you've made your way through the complexities of figuring out what you want to invest your money in, it becomes time to monitor the performance of your investments.

Take a deep breath. As you venture further into the world of online finance, you will discover that there are all kinds of methods you can use to track how you are doing.

This chapter examines how you can use the Internet to monitor the performance of your cash-based investments, mutual funds, and stocks.

Cash-Based Investments

There is not much you can do to monitor the value of your cash-based investments, other than checking the balance of your savings account online or figuring out what a GIC or term deposit might be worth upon maturity.

Most major financial institutions in Canada offer Internet banking services that will allow you to check the balance of your savings account online.

When it comes to GICs and term deposits, keep in mind that these are investments that are taken out for a fixed period of time—anywhere from 30 days to five years or more. In most cases, you are earning a fixed rate of interest on the investment, and when the time period for the investment is up, it is said to *mature*. Hence, the key piece of information you might like to know is its *maturity value*, or how much money you will get from the investment at the end of its term.

Usually you are given this information when you take out a GIC or term deposit at a financial institution. However, if you don't have that information readily available, and would still like to know what your GIC or term deposit will be worth upon maturity, there are a few calculators on the Internet that will let you figure out the future value of your investment.

A useful starting point is the Web site belonging to Munica, a company that develops software for use by companies with Web sites. On their site, they feature two GIC calculators.

The first one lets you do a basic calculation to find out how much you will get for a particular GIC investment upon maturity. In our example below, we wanted to know the maturity value of investing $3,257.78 in a GIC for two years at the rate of 8.25%.

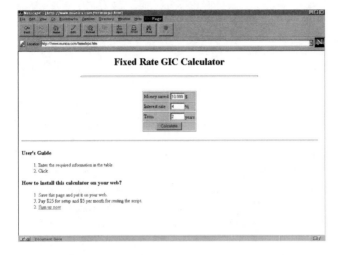

Munica's calculator instantly provided the details:

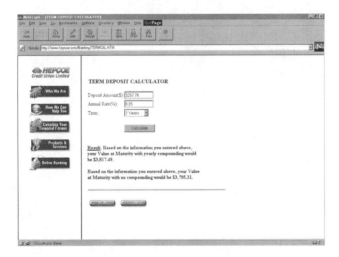

The second calculator lets you figure out how much your GIC/term deposit will be worth if there is a different rate of interest each year (as there are with many such products in the marketplace today):

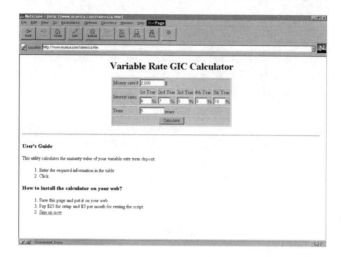

If you're looking for a calculator that does this calculation for GIC/term deposit investments of less than a year, turn to Hepcoe Credit Union, which lets you do the same thing for GICs/term deposits of 30, 60, 90, 120, 180, or 270 days, in addition to various annual calculations:

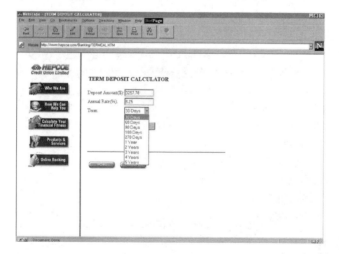

Finally, Altamira's Web site has an online calculator called the "Capital Builder Calculator." You will find it under the "Tool Kit" section of their "Resource Centre." You can use this calculator for a variety of different purposes in order to figure out how much an investment might be worth in the future.

When using this calculator, if you simply ignore the tax rate box, and leave the payment box blank, you can use it

for the same purpose as the calculators we described above.

In addition to using these online calculators, you should be aware that some financial organizations, such as Canada Trust, will let you examine the maturity value of your GIC or term deposit as part of their online banking services, particularly when the investment is included in your RRSP.

If you hold Canada Savings Bonds, you can figure out their value at maturity by visiting the federal government's Canada Savings Bond Web site. Simply indicate the particular CSB that you own and a "valuation date", i.e., today's date if you would like to know what it is worth now:

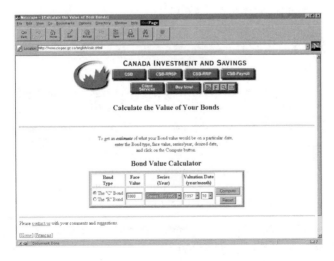

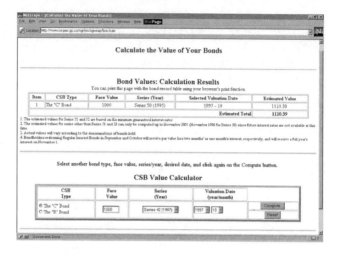

Within a few seconds you will be provided with the value of your bonds.

What's the bottom line? There is no shortage of useful calculators on the Web that will help you figure out how much you might earn on your cash-based investments.

Mutual Funds

What about your mutual funds? Is there anything you can do online to monitor how they are performing?

Of course there is! Lots! You can:

- look up the daily Net Asset Values (NAV) of any particular mutual fund in order to determine how the value compares to the previous day

- obtain simple reports and graphs to see how you are doing with a particular fund, or to see how your fund has performed historically

- sign up with sophisticated "portfolio trackers" that let you see the overall value of your mutual fund holdings on a day-by-day basis, as well as analyze their performance through tables and graphs

- use individual "portfolio manager" software programs that allow you to do even more sophisticated tracking and analysis of your mutual fund holdings.

Over the next several pages, we will provide examples of each of these applications.

Daily Net Asset Values

Most Canadian mutual fund Web sites include a section where daily Net Asset Values (NAVs.) are posted, usually within a few hours of the close of the previous business day. Consider, for example, this report from AGF Group of Funds:

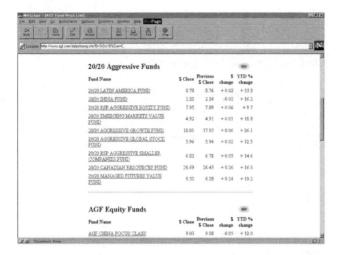

You can also get comprehensive listings of daily fund NAVs at such sites as The Fund Library, GLOBEfund, and CANOE. Each site lets you examine NAVs in a variety of different ways.

You can use these sites to see how your fund is performing by comparing the daily NAV to the NAV on the date you purchased each mutual fund.

However, the use of such information can be deceiving. In many cases, income earned on various types of mutual funds is often added back into the fund, with a resultant increase in the number of units that you own.

Why is this so? When you purchase certain types of funds, you are asked if you want any income on the fund to be reinvested, or if you would like it to be paid out to you. If reinvested, it is used to "purchase" a few more units for you. This additional "purchase" complicates the calculation so much that these simple calculators do not give a completely accurate picture of an investment. Many investors use the NAV as but one indicator of the overall performance of a fund.

Simple Performance Reports and Graphs

A few Canadian mutual fund Web sites include tools that let you calculate or graphically view how your funds have performed over time.

At the Phillips, Hager & North Web site, for example, you can find out how much an investment in their funds will have grown over time—they call this their "what-if" analysis.

On the following screen, we've asked to see how an investment in their Money Market fund would have increased in value from January 1993 to August 1997:

We were advised that every $1,000 invested in this fund at the start of 1993 would have grown in value to $1,235.72, for an effective annual rate of return of 4.73%.

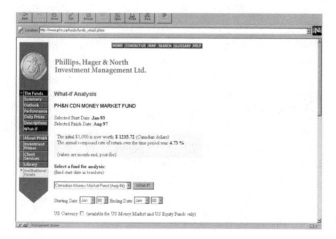

The Royal Bank Web site lets you do the same thing, but also allows you to view the results in a simple graph that charts the performance of a particular fund. You provide details on the date that you invested in the fund, as well as the amount that you invested.

Within a few seconds, you are provided with a graph that shows you the fluctuations in the value of your fund investment over time, as well as the estimated value of the investment and the average annual rate of return on the fund during that time period.

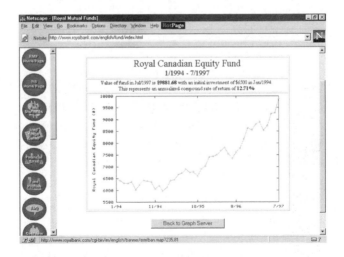

Finally, AGF lets you prepare similar graphs for up to three investments at once:

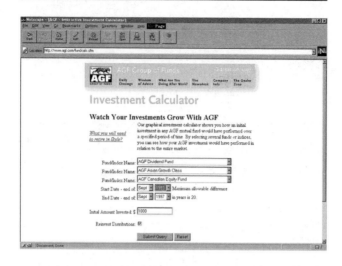

These are but a few examples of the tools provided directly by the organizations that offer mutual funds. Be sure to check the company Web sites of the funds you own, since they also might offer tools to help you to assess your portfolio's performance.

However, there are a few downsides to these simple performance reports and graphs:

- Your analysis cannot take into account multiple investments in the same fund over a period of time. The calculations and graphs described above simply recognize the change in the value of your investment over a period of time. If you invested in the fund again in the subsequent year, and again the following year, the graphing that you do will not show that fact—you must run a separate graph for each investment you made.

- The Web sites described above only let you do an analysis with the funds they sell. For obvious competitive reasons, the Royal Bank doesn't let you chart or view performance for AGF funds, and vice versa.

- These tools do not allow you to save your graph under your own name or some other identifying factor, meaning that you must enter in your investment data each time you visit.

Even with these limitations, however, these simple tools are an effective and straightforward means of graphically viewing the performance of your mutual fund investments.

Portfolio Trackers

A more sophisticated way to monitor the performance of your mutual fund investments involves the use of "portfolio trackers."

A number of independent financial sites—in particular, The Fund Library and GLOBEfund—provide you with the capability to track the overall performance and value of all of your mutual fund holdings on a day-to-day basis.

You can, for example, set up an account at The Fund Library to use their Personal Fund Monitor. After you create a "library card" to obtain a user ID and password, you simply add the funds that you own to your personal list. You can then go back to The Fund Library at any

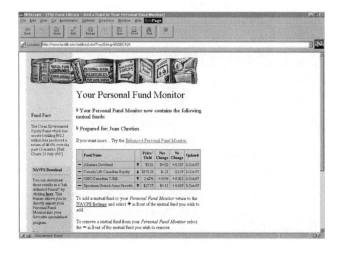

time and view a simple listing of the NAV of your various mutual fund holdings, as well as the change in those values from the previous day.

You can increase your understanding of the performance of your funds by taking advantage of the Enhanced Personal Fund Monitor at the same Web site. Compared to the Personal Fund Monitor, which merely gives you a list of the increase or decrease in unit values of your mutual funds compared to the previous day, the Enhanced Personal Fund Monitor provides you with the ability to view the actual increase and decrease in the value of your mutual fund holdings. The value is based upon the actual number of fund units that you own, with reference to the date that you purchased the funds. You can thus use this service to obtain, on a regular basis, the exact values of your own mutual fund holdings.

To set yourself up on the Enhanced Personal Fund Monitor, you fill out a form to obtain, in this case, a "Premium Library Card" to get a user ID and password. After doing that, you need to set up your portfolio. You do this by first selecting the fund company that manages the fund.

You then select the mutual fund that you purchased from that company.

Next, you provide further details about your fund, such as
the date that you purchased that particular fund, the
number of mutual fund units that you purchased, and the
cost per unit. If you made multiple purchases over time in
the fund, you have to enter each of these transactions
separately.

The information about your exact mutual fund purchases is necessary, as The Fund Library will use it to provide you with the exact value of your mutual fund
holdings at any time. You will also have the ability to
track the performance of your funds from the date you
purchased them to the current point in time.

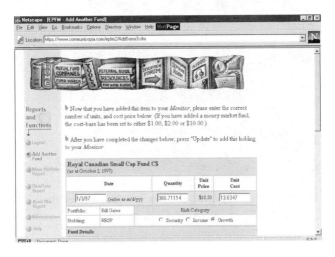

The information you provide for each fund transaction is summarized in a table so that you can correct it if necessary, or enter another transaction:

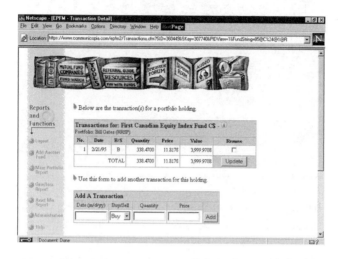

Once you do this for all your mutual fund purchases, you can return to The Fund Library daily to view the value of your holdings, based on the previous day's Net Asset Values for each fund.

There are two reports that you can produce at this site. The first is a report on the gain or loss on your mutual fund holdings since the date of purchase.

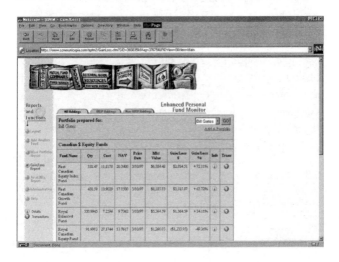

And the second is a basic set of graphs with information about the makeup of your fund portfolio.

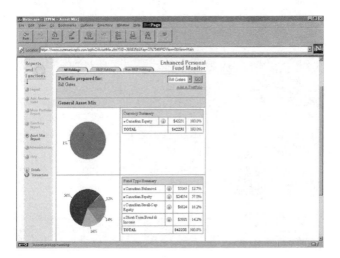

The *Globe and Mail*'s GLOBEfund site also provides you with the ability to prepare some very useful reports on your fund holdings using your "Fundlist."

Once you have set up the listing of funds that you own, creating what is then referred to as your "Fundlist", you can quickly obtain a report on the value and performance of your funds. One of the key benefits of GLOBEfund is that you can sort the report in different ways. For example, you can choose to see which funds are performing best in the short term; over one, three or five years; or by the most recent percentage change in fund values.

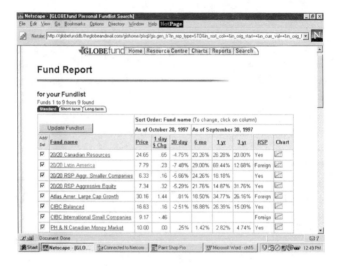

In addition, you can chart the performance of any particular fund against other funds that you own, and compare it against other factors such as the overall performance of funds on the TSE.

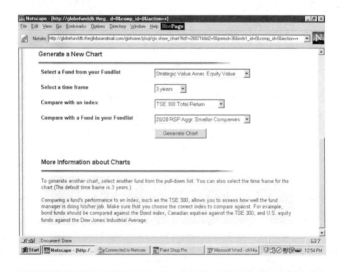

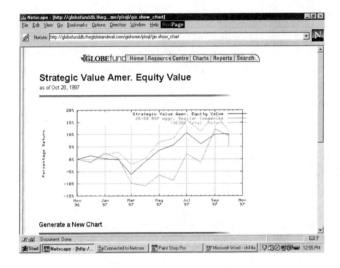

Finally, check out many of the Southam newspaper Web sites such as those of the *Vancouver Sun* or the *Hamilton Spectator*. They include a portfolio manager that you can use to track your mutual funds:

You can get a full list of Southam newspapers at the Southam Web site.

Portfolio Management Software

The last method of monitoring mutual fund performance on the Web is to use portfolio management software, which runs as a separate program, not in your Web browser.

Such programs let you examine mutual fund data faster than through a Web browser, often feature extensive historical information, offer accounting capabilities that easily let you track each and every mutual fund sale and purchase, and generally offer a wealth of other features not offered by the tools we've looked at so far.

One of the best examples of this type of software is PALTrak from Portfolio Analytics. On their Web site they describe the product as "Canada's most comprehensive mutual fund sales, analysis and research software," and that claim isn't stretching it.

You can download a fully functional version of the software from the Portfolio Analytics Web site. The program is fully usable, but contains outdated data. If you want the most recent data, you can purchase the most recent month's fund information for $39, or buy an annual subscription for $399.

What can you do with this program? First and foremost, the program contains comprehensive information on all available Canadian mutual funds, including details on performance over time, most recent NAVs, and other useful information.

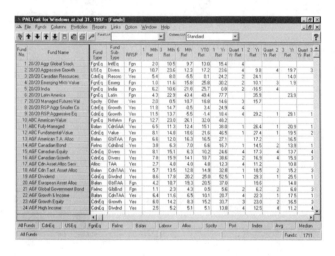

To create your own portfolio, you merely highlight the particular funds that you own:

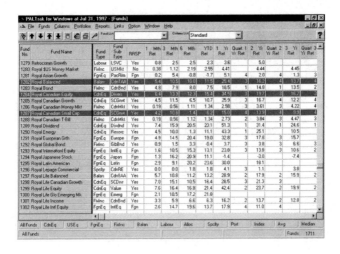

You then need to provide the transaction details for each fund that you own, much like you need to do at The Fund Library site.

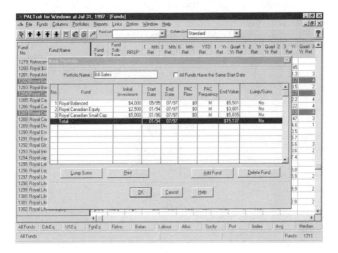

Once you have done this, you can use PALTrak to analyze your portfolio from a wide variety of different perspectives. For example, on the following screen, the performance of funds held by an investor is being compared to the returns that would have been earned had the money been invested in a Canada Savings Bond or five-year GIC.

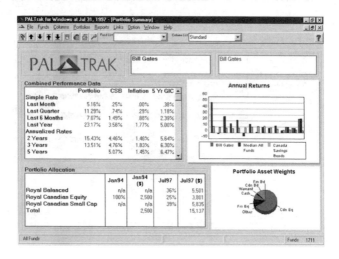

On the following screen, we've asked for a breakdown of the fund investments by fund type. The results will tell you whether your fund investments match the investment objectives that you established earlier.

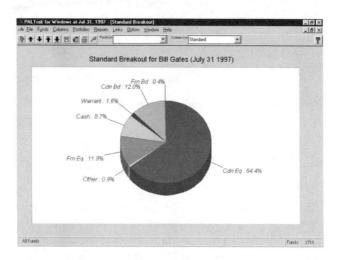

On the next screen, we've asked PALTrak to give us an overview of the types of holdings found in our equity mutual fund investments:

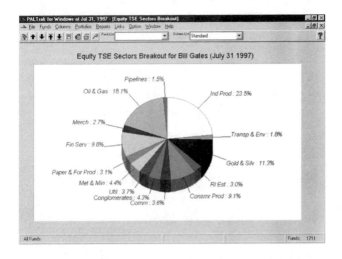

Through the use of increasingly sophisticated programs such as PALTrak, you will not only have a better understanding of how your funds are doing, you will also find out if they match the investment objectives that you had previously set for yourself.

Stocks

In addition to cash-based investments and mutual funds, you may have placed some of your money in stocks. There are a large number of possibilities for tracking the performance of your shares on the Internet.

Online Stock Quotes

There is no shortage of Web sites that you can use to obtain recent stock quotes. Most of the services that we describe in this section offer "15- or 20-minute delayed" quotes for free. This means that the most current stock price that you can see is from 15 or 20 minutes ago.

If you want to get "real-time" quotes—i.e., up-to-the-second quotes—you will have to pay for them. Often the price for such a service is $50 or more a month. One of the most popular services on the Web for obtaining real-time stock quotes is Quote.com. For most investors who simply want to track how their stocks are doing, 20-minute delayed quotes are more than sufficient. More serious investors who need up-to-the-second stock prices may want to consider the real-time information services provided by sites such as Quote.com. As you can see in the table below, some of the quote services on the Web offer only stock quotes from Canadian exchanges, some only offer quotes from U.S. exchanges, and some offer quotes from both Canadian and American exchanges.

Examples of Web Sites That Provide Free Stock Quotes

Service	Address	Canadian Quotes	U.S. Quotes
Canada Stockwatch	chart.canada-stockwatch.com	Yes	No
Canada Trust	www.canadatrust.com	Yes	No
CANOE	www.canoe.ca/Investment	Yes	Yes
Canadian Stock Market Reporter	www.canstock.com	Yes	No
Carlson Online Services	www.fin-info.com	Yes	Yes
CheckFree Quote Server	www.secapl.com/cgi-bin/qs	Yes	Yes
E*Trade Canada	www.canada.etrade.com	Yes	Yes
InvestorsEdge	www.investorsedge.com	No	Yes
Quote.com	www.quote.com	Yes	Yes
Charles Schwab	www.schwab.com	Yes	Yes
Telenium	www.telenium.ca	Yes	No

CANOE (Canadian Online Explorer) is one of the dozens of Web sites that provides free access to delayed stock prices:

An increasing number of sites are setting up services that allow you to quickly obtain prices for stocks that you own, without you having to manually type in the stock symbols each time you visit.

For example, CT Securities, a Canada Trust company, lets you set up a personal portfolio so that you can track the most recent quotes for up to 20 different stocks. Using the CT Market Partner Web site to set up your own portfolio is easy, and it's free.

If you don't know the symbol of a stock you want to monitor, the site provides a simple way to look it up.

Once you have established your portfolio, you can return at any time to obtain the most recent (15-minute delayed) value of your shares.

You can also obtain additional details for any stock in your portfolio, including a list of the most recent trades, and the year's high and low price on the stock.

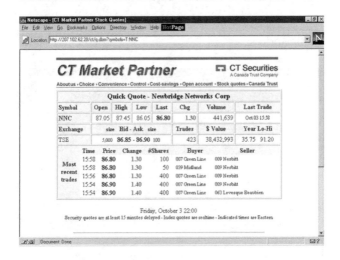

You can do the same thing at the CANOE site:

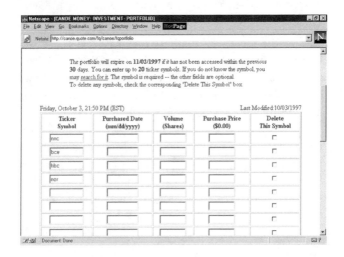

You can also return at any time to see the most recent trading prices:

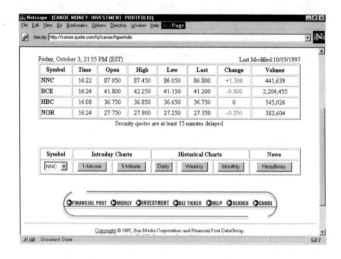

One of the most useful stock-tracking services on the Internet is the Web site run by Carlson Online Services. Carlson allows you to quickly find stock prices, news information, news releases, and other information for publicly-traded Canadian companies.

Type in the stock symbol (a lookup capability is provided if you don't know it), and you are given a page that provides access to information on the Internet about the company. This site is extremely useful when you want to research a specific publicly-traded Canadian company.

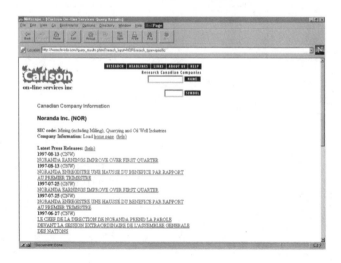

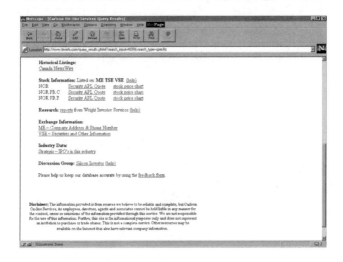

If you want to get a current stock price for a Canadian company, Carlson's Web site provides a link from its site to an Internet stock quote service called the CheckFree Quote Server, seen in the screen below.

Online Stock Portfolio Managers

When we looked at mutual funds earlier in the chapter, we saw that there were a number of Web sites which let you set up detailed information about your portfolio, such as the number of units purchased of each fund. This lets you examine the total value of your mutual fund holdings at any time.

It should come as no surprise that a number of increasingly sophisticated "stock portfolio manager" programs

are becoming available on investment Web sites throughout the Internet.

A Web site called InvestorsEdge, for example, lets you
create a number of different portfolios. Simply enter the
stocks you want to monitor, including the quantities you
own and the commission you paid:

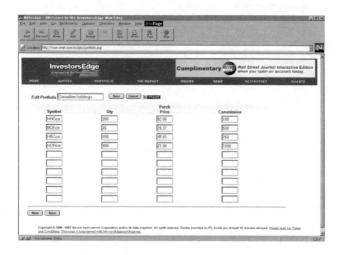

You can then examine, at any time, a report summarizing
how well you are doing with these stocks:

Similarly, E*Trade Canada offers a commercial portfolio
manager service, seen on the next screen. If you sign up
with E*Trade in order to sell or purchase mutual funds or
stocks, you can take advantage of their service.

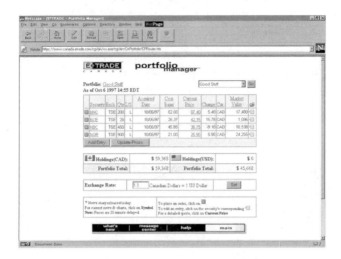

The features available on these online stock portfolio managers are constantly changing. For example, StockSmart lets you set up an "alert" so that you are notified via email (or pager, if you prefer) if a certain stock price falls above or below a certain amount.

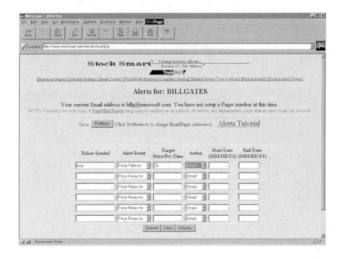

StockSmart will also allow you to "download" your portfolio information so that you can use the data in a spreadsheet or other program on your computer.

Integrated Software Programs

What if you want to use only one piece of software to track all of your investments?

Telenium, a Canadian software company, provides the Personal Portfolio program which allows you to obtain an up-to-date valuation of your investment portfolio, including your stocks *and* mutual funds.

Simply key in the stocks and mutual funds that you own and then press a button to get an up-to-date report. Current information is then retrieved through your Internet connection.

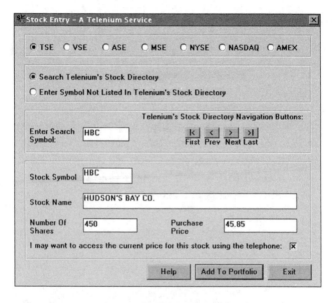

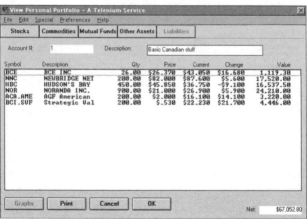

The Future of Investment Tracking Online

Finally, it's useful to look at a software program called Quicken for a glimpse of how sophisticated things are becoming.

Quicken is a computer program used for personal financial management or for business accounting. It is one of the most popular personal computer programs in the world.

Quicken also includes tools for investment management. Quicken 98, which became available in the fall of 1997, features the ability to retrieve, via the Internet, up-to-date Canadian mutual fund, stock, and other investment values, thus making it an extremely useful investment portfolio manager.

The program provides users with many different options for managing their investments. For example, you can enter any number of investments into any number of portfolios.

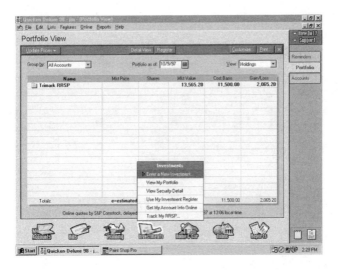

Each of your investments can be placed into categories that you define, thus helping you to keep things organized. For example, in our hypothetical case on page 244, we'll list our Royal Bank RRSPs in one "folder", and Trimark RRSPs in another.

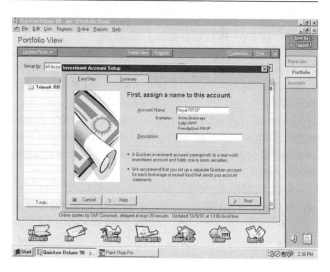

The program allows you to assign investments to an RRSP category. Alternatively, you can indicate that they are for general investment purposes only. This will help you to keep different investments separate for purposes of your income tax return.

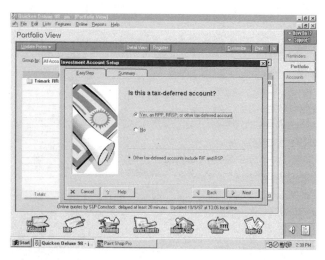

When you set up your investments on Quicken, you can input the "ticker symbol" for a stock, mutual fund, or other financial investment. These are symbols used throughout the investment industry. The program includes a "lookup" feature to help you if you do not know what the symbol is for a particular investment. These symbols are used to look up the market value of your investments through the Internet.

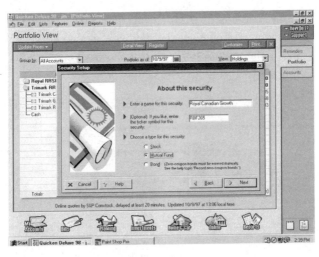

You can also use Quicken to keep track of how diversi-fied your portfolio is. For example, you can identify whether a particular investment was for purposes of growth or income, or whether you would classify it as a high risk or low risk investment. This can become very useful later, when running the reports the program allows you to generate, for it can help you understand if your investment profile in terms of risk matches your risk objectives, or whether you have a mix of growth and income investments that matches the objectives that you set out earlier.

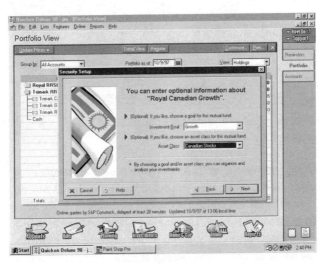

Not only that, but the Quicken software is a full-fledged portfolio manager, in that it lets you build an exact record of your investment transactions. For each and every investment, you enter in the date you purchased it, the cost, and the commission paid. This allows you to view the performance of your investment later on.

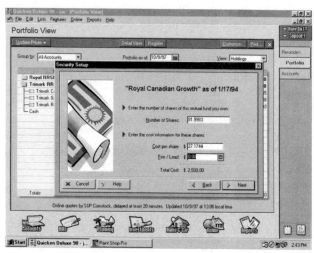

Once you have done this, you have a concise summary of your investments. Want updated market values? Simply press "Update", and the Quicken software will use your Internet connection to get them. This will generate a report that tells you how your investments are performing based on their current market value.

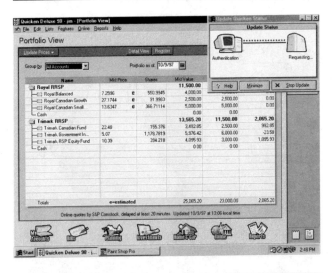

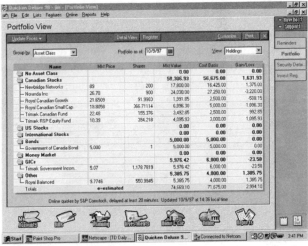

One of the great benefits of the program is that you can
generate reports to examine the performance of your
investments from a variety of perspectives. You can indicate, for example, what types of information you would
like to have appear in your reports (see page 248).

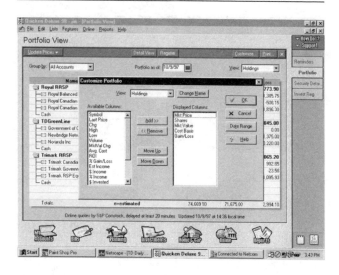

You can choose to view reports about the value of your portfolio, the performance of your investments, how much you have lost or gained once you have sold your investments, or how much income you have made.

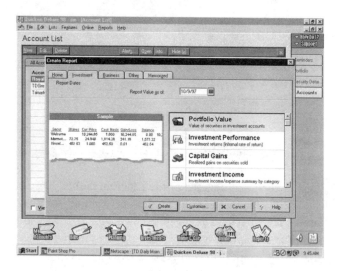

The level of detail and the number of report options are extensive. For example, in the next screen, we are examining our performance for the current year, and the report is organized by type of investment. You can also examine this report for any other time period, as seen in the drop-down menu:

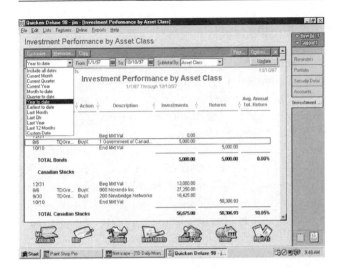

Below, we've asked for a report on our investments, based upon our investment objectives. As seen in the drop-down menu, we could view this report in any number of other ways.

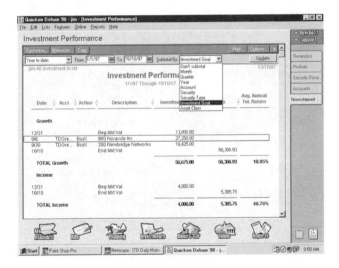

Finally, Quicken has also released a program called Investor Insight, which specializes in helping you to analyze the performance of your investments, and keep yourself up-to-date on news affecting those investments. A trial version is available on their Web site. It is worth checking out.

The Bottom Line

It used to be that as an individual investor, unless you had an accounting designation and knew what you were doing, there was very little opportunity for you to easily track the performance of your investments.

This is no longer the case. As we have seen in this chapter there are many simple but sophisticated and effective tools that you can use to track your investment portfolio. By doing so, you will have a better sense of how you are doing with your investments, and a better idea as to whether you need to change your approach or objectives.

Web Sites Mentioned in This Chapter

AGF Group of Funds	www.agf.com
Altamira Investment Services	www.altamira.com
Canada Savings Bonds Web Site	www.cis-pec.gc.ca
Canada Stockwatch	www.canada-stockwatch.com
Canada Trust	www.canadatrust.com
CANOE	www.canoe.ca
Canadian Stock Market Reporter	www.canstock.com
Carlson Online Services	www.fin-info.com
Charles Schwab	www.schwab.com
CheckFree Quote Server	www.secapl.com/cgi-bin/qs
CT Securities	www.ctsecurities.com
E*Trade Canada	www.canada.etrade.com
GLOBEfund	www.globefund.com
Hamilton Spectator	www.southam.com/ hamiltonspectator
Hepco Credit Union	www.hepcoe.com
InvestorsEdge	www.investorsedge.com
Munica	www.munica.com
PALTrak	www.pal.com
Phillips, Hager & North	www.phn.ca

Quote.com	www.quote.com
Quicken	www.intuit.com
Royal Bank of Canada	www.royalbank.com
Southam Newspapers	www.southam.com
StockSmart	www.stocksmart.com
Telenium	www.telenium.ca
The Fund Library	www.fundlibrary.com
Vancouver Sun	www.vancouversun.com

Online
Investing

Anybody with money to burn will easily find some-one to tend the fire. ANONYMOUS

HIGHLIGHTS

- Many discount brokerages and other firms such as E*Trade Canada offer online trading of stocks, mutual funds, and other investments over the Internet.

- When choosing an online trading service there are many factors that you should consider, including the firm's fee structure and security policy, account features, insurance coverage, and availability of service and support.

- A major benefit of online trading services is that they allow you to trade securities at lower commissions than those charged by full-service brokerages. To compensate for these reduced fees, however, most online trading services do not dispense investment advice.

- The Internet has placed downward pressure on the commissions charged by brokers to execute the sale and purchase of securities. This trend is expected to be especially dramatic within the mutual fund industry.

- To keep yourself up-to-date on developments within the online trading field, you can access the Web sites of online brokers, visit independent news sites, and browse specialized financial sites such as SmartMoney Interactive.

Now that you've made your way through the complexities of figuring out what you want to invest your money in, the time has come for you to do the actual financial transaction.

If you are investing money in an RRSP and choose not to go the self-directed RRSP route, or if you want to invest some money but you don't want to get involved with the stock market directly, you will be limiting yourself to cash-based investments and the purchase of mutual funds. In this case, you will likely make your investment by visiting a financial institution, calling up your broker, calling a 1-800 number, or you might even purchase an RRSP on a financial institution's Web site.

However, if you opt for a self-directed RRSP, you might consider some of the online investing services that have become available. Similarly, if you are investing money outside of your RRSP, you want to be more involved with your investment decisions, or you wish to buy stocks and bonds, you might consider doing the same.

In Canada today you can sign up with a number of online trading services and buy and sell all kinds of investments through the Internet, including stocks, bonds, mutual funds, and other financial securities.

Discount Brokers on the Internet

Traditionally, if you wanted to buy stocks or bonds, you had to deal with a broker or investment advisor. You would often end up paying them a rather hefty commission to buy or sell the investment for you.

The thinking behind the commission fee was similar to the thinking that exists with load-based mutual funds today—the broker works hard at providing valuable advice and guidance on your investment decisions, and hence, should be compensated for his or her efforts.

As investors began to take on more responsibility for their own investment decisions (for example, by doing their own research), they sought cheaper methods of buying and selling stocks.

The result? The emergence of the "discount broker," organizations that will buy investments on behalf of their clients for a very small fee. In comparison to full-service brokers, discount brokers do not dispense financial advice, and as a result, their commission fees are lower. Discount brokers are popular with sophisticated investors who know what they want and don't require the advice of an investment advisor.

Once the Internet exploded onto the scene, the stage was set for these discount brokers to migrate to the Internet.

> **The U.S.-based Charles Schwab & Co., one of the largest financial brokerages in the U.S., had no one working on Internet projects in 1994. By the end of 1997, 100 people were dedicated to Internet activities including an online trading business and Web site. The company's online brokerage business has 700,000 customers, and $50 billion in customer assets. The company indicates that 28% of all its trades are being done through personal computers.**

Today discount brokerages allow you to buy and sell stocks, bonds, mutual funds, and other investments online, either through a Web site or by using a private data network that you can access with your computer.

Researching Internet-Based Online Trading Services

If you begin to explore the field of online investing, there are a number of questions you might have.

Who Offers Online Trading Services?
It is becoming a rather busy marketplace.

All of the major banks in Canada either provide or have stated their intention to make available, online trading/brokerage services through the Internet. In addition, trust companies such as Canada Trust have become involved, as have other Canadian banks such as the Hongkong Bank of Canada.

If you visit the Web sites of Canadian banks and trust companies, you will find information about their online investment services, which usually have their own distinct brand names (e.g. *netTRADER* from the Hongkong Bank of Canada and *StockLine* from Scotiabank). Toward the end of the chapter, we provide a table that summarizes the Web addresses for many of the major online trading services in Canada.

> **Two U.S.-based research firms, FIND/SVP and Jupiter Communications, indicate that online trading should grow from a current 2% of all transactions to 8% by 2001.**

For extremely security-conscious individuals, many of these same institutions offer proprietary software programs that allow you to conduct your transactions through a private data network without going through the Internet. However, the industry seems to have concluded that Internet security concerns are minimal, and we expect these proprietary software programs to become only marginal players in the future.

In addition to the banks and trust companies, other firms have entered the online discount trading market. For example, VERSUS, a private Canadian company that has long served the financial investment community in Canada, teamed up with the U.S.-based E*Trade service to offer E*Trade Canada. E*Trade Canada allows to you to trade securities such as stocks and mutual funds over the Internet.

> **E*Trade gained notice with the launch of its electronic trading service in 1996, which featured a rather in-your-face advertising campaign. The campaign featured headlines such as "Your broker is now obsolete," "Don't let high commissions bite your assets," and in one ad that featured a kid sticking out his tongue, "Boot your broker."**

What Can You Buy and Sell?

Some online trading services allow you to trade only stocks and bonds, while others have added mutual funds into the mix. Those that don't sell mutual funds now will likely do so in the future, simply because of competitive pressure in the marketplace.

Even if an online trading service *does* allow you to trade mutual funds, they might not offer the particular funds you want. Check their Web sites for a catalogue or listing of the funds they allow you to buy and sell.

Interestingly, the field of discount trading often provides some fascinating results. For example, at the TD Bank Greenline discount brokerage, you can buy over 600 mutual funds, including those available from the mutual fund subsidiary of the Royal Bank. And at Canada Trust, you can buy funds from the mutual funds subsidiary of the Bank of Montreal.

What About Security?

We don't think that financial institutions would be offering online banking and online stock trading if they didn't believe that their services were secure.

That being said, security should be one of the factors you take into consideration when choosing an online trading service. Most online trading firms provide information about their security measures and policies on their Web sites.

Perhaps the bigger concern is the reliability of the service—there have been reports of people being frustrated by technical problems and challenges with particular online trading services, particularly in the U.S.

Worried about online trading? Take a look at the article, "Online trading's travails," as reported in *InformationWeek* on August 25, 1997. In it, noted technologist Cheryl Currid indicated that "It can be done, but doing it right takes more than a little effort. Proceed cautiously, and beware the buggy brokerage." You can find the article online at the Information Week Web site—www.informationweek.com. Simply do a search for the title of the article.

Is My Investment Insured?

Yes, in the same way that it might be if you had bought it from a broker, agent, or directly from a mutual fund company.

You will find that most online brokers are members of the Canadian Investor Protection Fund, and as a result your investment is covered to a certain maximum amount if the organization where you do your trading collapses.

That being said, you should always keep in mind that you aren't covered for any decrease in the value of your investment due to normal fluctuations in the market.

What Services Are Offered?

Beyond offering the basic capability to buy and sell securities online, some firms provide lots of bells and whistles with their online trading accounts. These services include personalized home pages, email notification if a stock falls below a certain level, access to research reports and company information, 1-800 support lines, real-time stock quotes and news bulletins, and more.

If these "extras" are important to you, make sure that you shop around and compare account features and options. Most online trading services provide this type of information on their Web sites.

What Can I Expect in Terms of Service?

This depends on who you sign up with. Some discount brokers are just that—they will undertake the purchase and sale of securities on your behalf, with no additional assistance offered or provided.

No longer associated with techno-geeks, online trading is experiencing a boom in popularity as a growing number of brokerage firms offer it to their customers.

RUTH PRINS, "ONLINE TRADING TAKES OFF," *US BANKER*, MAY 1997

Other discount brokers, such as the Hongkong Bank of Canada netTRADER service, indicate that while they do not provide advice or guidance on which investments to purchase, they do offer a 1-800 number that you can call at any time with other questions that you might have.

Make sure you find out what level of support you can expect before signing up with an online trading service.

What Is Involved in Setting Up an Account?

From the Web site of the Internet brokerage you can either sign up online or you can request that an information package and sign up form be sent to you.

You will have to deposit sufficient funds with the brokerage to cover your anticipated investment purchases. You usually do this by sending a cheque in the mail to the online brokerage. In most cases, your account will not be activated until your funds are received. Visit the various online trading Web sites to find out what is involved. At E*Trade Canada, for example, you must deposit a minimum of $1,000.

When you set up your online trading account, you will be asked if the account is to be used for a self-directed RRSP. Some people have several online trading accounts. For example, you might have one for a self-directed RRSP at one online brokerage, and another account at the same brokerage or at another brokerage for other general, non-RRSP investments. Both accounts might hold a mix of mutual funds, cash investments, stocks, bonds, and other financial investments.

What Are the Benefits and Risks of Doing Your Trading Online?

Most organizations that offer online trading services have commission structures that are far less than the commissions charged by full-service brokerage companies. And if you use a discount broker to execute your online trades, the discount broker will usually charge commissions that are even lower than their regular rates because it's cheaper for them to process your orders over the Internet. This means that you're getting a discount on the discount broker's already discounted rates.

Clearly, the primary benefit of using an online trading service is that you can save a lot of money.

In addition, as you get accustomed to doing more of your investment research on the Internet, you'll find that the Internet is a more convenient trading medium.

Why? Suppose you are doing stock research on the Internet and you decide to purchase some shares in a company. Instead of picking up the phone or using a proprietary software program, you simply move from the Web site you are looking at to the Web site for your online trading service, and you can place your order on the spot.

If you are buying or selling a stock that is fluctuating rapidly, the extra few seconds you gain by doing your trading over the Internet could save you a lot of money—but keep in mind that as we pointed out in chapter 3, it is also possible that the Internet will experience a slowdown or technical glitch at the very moment that you are trying to complete your trade. If this happens, the time that you lose could end up costing you a lot of money!

Of course, the cheaper commissions offered by the online trading services come at a price. The tradeoff is this: while you will certainly save money by using an online trading service instead of a full-service brokerage, most online trading services don't offer financial advice, and you are responsible for doing your own research.

In other words, you're on your own when it comes to making decisions about which stocks to buy and sell. It's not for everyone.

Commissions and Fees

When it comes to selecting and using an online brokerage, you should research the fees.

The field of Internet-based investing is causing dramatic change in the investment industry, as increased competition places downward pressure on the commissions charged by brokers for the purchase or sale of securities.

Today, many online brokerages offer a flat fee for stock purchases up to a certain dollar amount. E*Trade Canada, for example, charges a flat rate of $28.88 for trades of less than $3,500, and $38.88 for trades in excess of that amount. In the United States, price wars have already broken out among competing brokers. Other brokers have fees that are higher and some have indicated that they refuse to be drawn into a price war.

Of course, all of this makes for a rather interesting marketplace, with constant change in the rates that are charged. The only way to keep up is through news reports, and by visiting the Web sites of various online brokers.

Many online brokerage services provide a commission calculator on their Web sites that you can use to determine what commission fee you will have to pay. And as we will see below, you are usually told what the commission will be when you buy or sell your stocks or bonds.

Browse through the fee schedules offered by major discount brokerages in Canada, and take the time to understand the way their fee structures work. You will find that all of them have a page of information where they describe their fee structure. For example, E*Trade Canada's Web site describes how their transaction fee changes depending on how many shares you are trading:

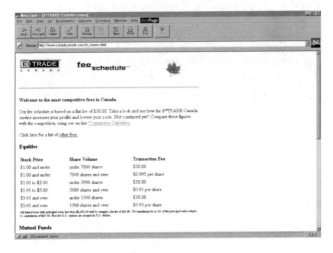

Similarly, at the Toronto Dominion Bank's Green Line Brokerage Web site, you can access a page that describes their fee structure:

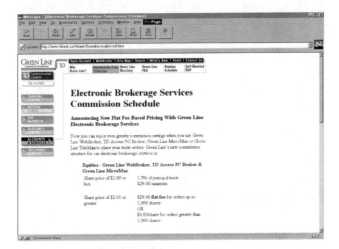

Mutual Fund Commissions

The issue of mutual fund commissions bears special attention since it can be a very confusing situation. We'd suggest that you shop around carefully to understand what your options are when it comes to mutual fund commissions. Keep in mind these two facts:

- Some organizations don't charge any basic trading commission on mutual funds. Others do, based on the type of mutual fund.

- If you are told there is no commission on execution of a mutual fund trade, there isn't—at least, not the $30 or so trading commission described above. Yet the online trading company is still keeping the "load" or commission on the sale of a loaded mutual fund. In effect it is earning that money as a commission for conducting the sale. Similarly, it might be earning a "trailer fee" once you sell the fund.

Let's have a look at how the situation can vary from company to company.

At the CT Securities Web site, the online home of the investment arm of Canada Trust, you might find that the commission rates on mutual funds vary depending on whether it is a no-load, load, or back load fund (we explain these concepts in chapter 9):

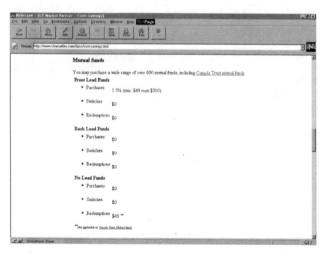

Yet at E*Trade Canada, you might find that the commission they charge on most mutual funds is "free," but that there are a few fine print items:

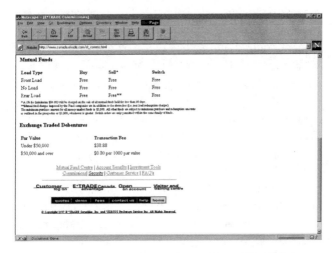

And at the Hongkong Bank of Canada netTRADER service you can expect commission rates of a few percentage points based on the type of fund that you are purchasing.

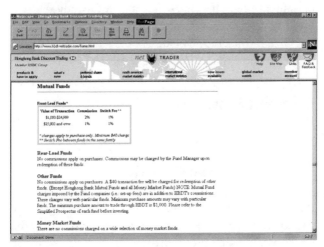

How can some companies buy and sell mutual funds for you and not charge for it? Why do others charge a fee? This is part of the turmoil that exists in the newly emerging field of online mutual fund sales.

To understand why things are so different—and why they will, no doubt, keep evolving, you should keep in mind several factors:

- some online brokers will argue that they charge a fee because they are still providing you with some investment counsel and advice that would previously have been supplied by the financial planner, broker, or agent.

- in many cases, even though you might not be charged a commission, the broker will still be receiving a fee from the mutual fund company. This will come either as a commission up front (for load funds), on your sale of the fund (as a back-end load), or in the form of a "trailer fee" just as a financial planner or agent would if you bought the funds direct from them. Trailer fees are paid to whomever has sold you the fund for investment advice on an on-going basis in addition to front or back end loads. All mutual funds charge trailer fees.

Given the current turmoil, it is likely that the entire issue of online mutual fund fees will change with dramatic speed. We discuss this issue further at the end of this chapter.

One other word of advice. When researching the fees on mutual funds, it is important that you study the fine print. For example, you will find that many brokerages will charge you a fee if you don't hold a fund for a certain period of time, and sometimes a fee is charged if you move your money from one fund to another.

Online Calculators

Finally, while you're researching commissions, keep your eye out for one very useful feature—the online commission calculator.

Many discount brokerages have calculators on their Web sites that you can use to calculate the commission that you will be charged on a certain trade. This can be useful if the fee is an important factor for you when choosing an online broker. The calculators can help you understand how the commission structures work.

Often a discount broker will compare their fees to those charged by their competitors. For example, at E*Trade Canada you can calculate the commission E*Trade Canada would charge on a stock trade. Simply enter the share price and the number of shares you want to purchase:

Based on the information you supply, E*Trade Canada will calculate its commission and show you what other discount brokers would charge.

While these calculators are useful, you should be wary of the comparison. Be sure to check that any comparative calculations like this are based on the most recent fee schedules of other discount brokers. If the Web site doesn't tell you which company its fees are being compared to, ask!

If in doubt, check the math yourself, or ask the discount broker for confirmation that the calculator reflects the current commission structures of their competitors.

An Example of Online Trading

Once you've signed up with a particular online broker, you will find that the process of buying and selling stocks, bonds or mutual funds is remarkably straightforward.

> **When it comes to tapping the Internet investment crowd, Christos Cotsakos, the president of online brokerage E*Trade, thinks Wall Street hasn't a clue. Commissions are too high, brokers are overpaid, and the technology stinks. Even their ads are boring.**
>
> HAL LUX, "ON THE NET WITH E*TRADE: NOT YOUR FATHER'S BROKER," *INSTITUTIONAL INVESTOR*, JANUARY 23 1997

In the hypothetical example below, we'll examine how E*Trade Canada works, and operate under the assumption that you already have an E*Trade Canada account.

Let's say you want to purchase shares in Noranda. First, you fill out the stock purchase form on the E*Trade Canada Web site, indicating the number of shares you would like to purchase. You must indicate whether you are willing to buy at the current market price, whatever it might be, or whether there is a limit on the price you are willing to pay:

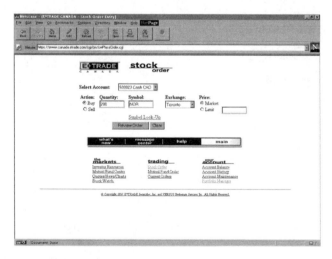

Once you have entered the details of your order, you'll receive a screen confirming them, which also indicates the commission that will be charged on the order. Obviously, you should review the information on this screen very carefully.

If you want to go ahead with the trade, you provide your "trading password," which is a special password that you will have created strictly for the purpose of confirming your online orders.

Once your order has been placed, it will be executed by VERSUS Brokerage according to your instructions. After the order has been placed, you can check on its status and modify it if necessary. If it has been executed, you'll be notified.

Of course, if you don't have sufficient funds in your account when you attempt to execute an order, you'll be told:

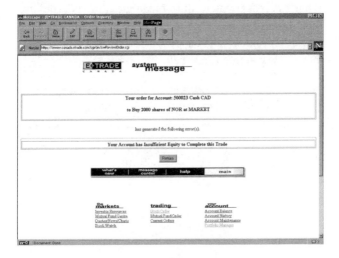

You can review a listing of the cash and securities you
have in your E*Trade Canada account at any time:

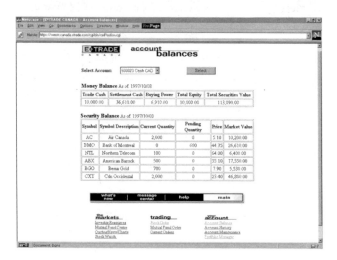

What happens if you want to buy mutual funds? The first
thing to keep in mind is that like all other online brokers,
E*Trade Canada lets you view a listing of the funds that
they allow you to buy and sell:

Placing a mutual fund order is no more complicated than
buying shares in a stock:

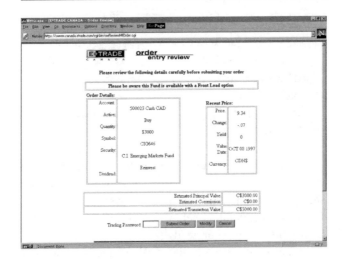

You go through a similar series of steps if you want to sell stocks, bonds, or mutual funds.

Continuing to Learn About Online Trading

Since this industry is changing so rapidly, it's important to keep up with the changes. The Internet will be very useful to you as you continually assess the features, costs, benefits, and value-added services associated with the various online trading firms.

Web Sites

The most obvious way of gathering information about online trading is to visit the Web sites of the online brokers themselves. In the table below, we've summarized the addresses of many of the major online trading services in Canada. Keep in mind that many other financial institutions will be setting up online services in the months and years to come, so the list is not all-inclusive.

Web Addresses for Online Trading Services in Canada

Bank of Montreal: InvestorLine	www.investorline.com
CIBC: Investor's Edge Discount Brokerage	www.investorsedge.cibc.com
CT Securities (Canada Trust): Market Partner	www.ctsecurities.com

E*Trade Canada	www.canada.etrade.com
Hongkong Bank of Canada Discount Trading: netTRADER	nettrader.hkbc.ca
Scotia Discount Brokerage (Scotiabank): StockLine	www.sdbi.com
Toronto Dominion Bank: Green Line WebBroker	www.greenline.ca

By visiting these sites you can obtain information on each firm's commission structure, security policy, range of services, account types, insurance coverage, and more. Use this information to help you decide which online brokerage best meets your needs.

Some online brokers, like Green Line, the discount brokerage arm of the Toronto Dominion Bank, have news sections on their Web sites with information about recent enhancements to their offerings:

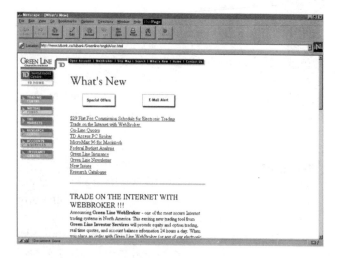

Online News Archives

It's important that you balance any information you receive from the discount brokers with information from an independent source such as a newspaper. On some news sites, you can look at archived news stories and do a search for articles that have referred to online trading in the past few months. This is a very useful way to keep on top of the changes which might have occurred within the industry.

Two notable places to visit to obtain this independent verification are:

- **CANOE**

  At this site you can quickly and easily retrieve articles that have appeared in the *Financial Post* during the last several months. From the main CANOE home page, select "Search", and then choose "Business Information."

  In the example below, we're looking for any articles that contain the words "Internet" and "stock" and "trading."

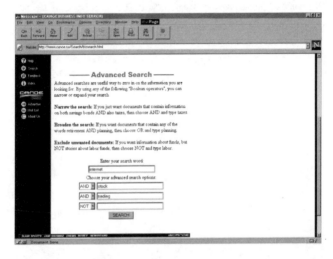

CANOE searches its database and displays a lengthy list of candidate articles. From here, you can access any of the articles shown on the screen without charge.

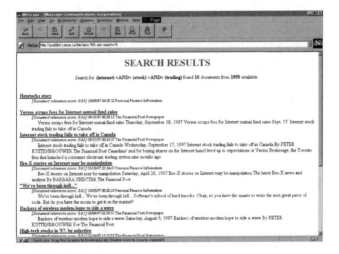

- **GLOBEfund**

  At this site, you can search the full text of articles from the *Globe and Mail*'s special mutual fund reports. Sometimes you can find useful articles about online trading here. Simply key in the phrase you are looking for:

Next, GLOBEfund will display a list of matching articles:

To access the full text of any of the articles, just click on the headline of the article you want to view.

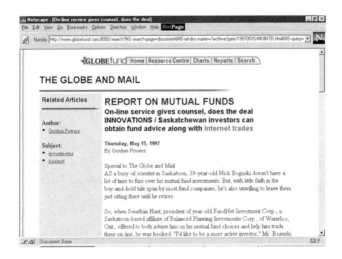

There are also specialized financial news sites such as CNNfn and SmartMoney Interactive (shown below). Although most of them are U.S.-centric, they can still help you to keep up with recent developments in the industry.

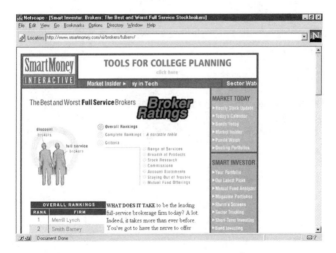

The Future?

What can we expect in the future?

There is no doubt that the entire field of online trading promises to be one that is constantly evolving and rapidly changing.

We have no doubt that more of the major American online stock trading services will enter the marketplace, either through their Canadian subsidiaries or by partnering with an existing Canadian financial institution. For example, American Express is a major player in the U.S. market, as is Charles Schwab with their e.Schwab online trading service.

According to Forrester Research, the number of brokerage accounts on the Internet will rise from three million in late 1997 to 14.4 million in 2002.

You might want to have a look at BrokerLinks, a site which tracks developments in the online brokerage field. Although it only covers American brokerages at this point, it might cover Canadian services in the future, and does provide some insightful information about the way in which the industry is evolving.

Similarly, visit Gomez Advisors, an organization that also tracks developments in the industry, and that includes a ranking of the major American online services on their Web site.

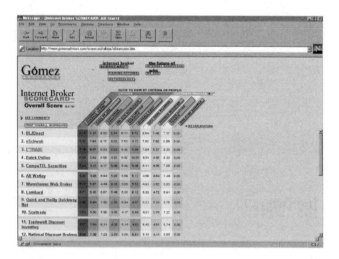

The second significant change that online trading will lead to is a dramatic change in the load that is charged on various mutual funds in Canada, as more and more sales

> **Only 30% of investment companies say that their online offerings are making money, according to a new report from Forrester Research. That's nothing to crow about of course, but it's still a substantial improvement over a year ago, Forrester says, when respondents had no expectation of short-term profits. About 30% of online trading firms are now making money**
>
> KIMBERLY WEISUL, *INVESTMENT DEALERS DIGEST*, SEPTEMBER 8, 1997

occur through online brokers. This in itself will lead to significant change in the overall structure of the mutual funds industry in Canada.

Why will the industry change so significantly? The emergence of Internet-based mutual fund sales means that you can now buy "load" (commission-based) mutual funds from a number of online systems. Previously, the companies that sold these mutual funds would have directed you to a financial planner, broker, or agent to complete the sale. In essence, the commission was built into the fund so as to provide a return to this third party.

But, with the emergence of the Internet, sales of load funds are now occurring through a third party—the online broker—who in most cases is not acting as an investment advisor, and often does little to facilitate the sale of the load fund, other than shuffle a few electronic bits. Yet that discount broker is still earning the full "load" on the sale of the load fund to you, in addition to earning a "trailer fee."

Hence, while the online discount brokers might state on their Web sites that there is no straight trading commission on the fund, such as the commission of $30 or so that we described above, they are still keeping the load provided to them directly from the mutual fund company. This can often be a substantial sum of money.

We expect that over time, the Internet will drive down the load provided on these types of mutual funds—a significant change for an industry that has been built around the concept of commission-based mutual funds.

Web Sites Mentioned in This Chapter

American Express	www.americanexpress.com/canada/index.html
Bank of Montreal	www.bmo.com
BrokerLinks	www.brokerlinks.com
Canadian Investor Protection Fund	www.cipf.ca
CANOE	www.canoe.ca
CNNfn	www.cnnfn.com
e.Schwab (Charles Schwab)	www.eschwab.com
E*Trade Canada	www.canada.etrade.com
GLOBEfund	www.globefund.com
Gomez Advisors	www.gomezadvisors.com
Hongkong Bank of Canada	www.hkbc.ca
Royal Bank of Canada	www.royalbank.com
Scotiabank	www.scotiabank.ca
SmartMoney Interactive	www.smartmoney.com
Toronto Dominion Bank	www.tdbank.ca

The Future of Finance on the Internet

Everybody gets so much information all day long that they lose their common sense. GERTRUDE STEIN

HIGHLIGHTS

- The Internet is altering the relationship that individual investors have with the financial community.

- Financial institutions will have to recognize several key trends in order to adapt in this new marketplace: customer research capabilities have been enhanced, customers are becoming more demanding, there is a fight for "mind-share", and generational marketing will become important.

- The Internet is causing massive structural change in the financial services industry by reducing the need for financial intermediaries, by placing downward pressure on industry commissions, and by heightening competition.

- Canadian securities regulators are far behind the United States when it comes to educating consumers about investment fraud on the Internet.

The Internet is causing businesses and consumers to evolve together in ways that will forever change the nature of finance.

From our perspective, one of the most important things about the Internet is that it is helping to turn the tables in favour of the ordinary consumer/investor—you! Consumers are being empowered because of "disintermediation" (which we explain below), reduced fees, and heightened competition.

Another very significant change has to do with the very nature of financial information. In what we might call the "good old days," the financial information that was made available to investors was subject to very stringent forms of quality control. Financial statements were audited, news releases were vetted, and news came from established media organizations.

The free-flowing and unrestricted nature of the Internet has altered that information stream in a dramatic way. Today, investors no longer make decisions based solely on information that has undergone strict quality control procedures. In addition, investors are exposed to lots of information that has escaped the examination of a securities regulator.

Instead, investors are making decisions using information they find on the Internet. While this reality puts a lot of power in the hands of the individual investor, it creates a lot of potential problems as well. While some of the information that an investor might come across on the Internet has been screened for quality control purposes, much of it has not. And as we have seen, there are unscrupulous people online who take advantage of this fact.

In light of the potential for online fraud that we discussed in chapters 3 and 4, there is an urgent need for Canadian regulatory authorities to help guide individual investors in this new and wild world of finance on the Internet.

Changing Relationships

For a long time, individual investors—whether they were simply placing money in an RRSP or investing in the stock market—felt ill-at-ease with the complex world of investments and finance. All too often, they had to rely upon the financial community to guide them with their financial decisions.

The Internet alters the very nature of that relationship, providing more power to the individual investor. Used wisely, the Internet can be a very potent tool.

The Internet is changing the way that financial organizations reach and deal with their customers. At the same time, consumers are expecting better service and support from their financial institutions. Think about how the Internet is changing how consumers deal with their finances:

- **Customer research capabilities are enhanced**

  What the Internet really represents in the world of finance is an absolutely massive change in the way that people obtain the information used for their RRSP, retirement, and investment decisions. This is happening both from an individual and business perspective.

  The "electronic investor" is an individual whose investment decisions and activities are influenced by the information they find online.

  The impact of this trend for any financial organization is clear. As the Internet becomes the dominant means by which Canadians shop for financial products and services, financial organizations will have to adapt to a world in which consumers are self-educating themselves about their financial alternatives. In short, financial consumers are becoming more sophisticated than they used to be.

- **Customers are becoming more demanding**

  In addition to seeking out knowledge on the Internet, the electronic investor is coming to expect—and even demand—a heightened degree of support, assistance, and guidance from their banks, trust companies, brokers, and other financial organizations. Not only are investors demanding more support, they are demanding that this support be provided online.

  They have come to expect a prompt response if they leave a detailed investment question on a financial institution's Web site, and they are ready to take their business elsewhere if their electronic queries aren't given the same degree of attention and respect as other forms of correspondence. They expect to find answers to their questions online, and they are increasingly unforgiving if the information they are seeking cannot be found. Many of today's investors don't want the hassle of dealing with people over the telephone—they would rather use the Web to quickly and easily locate information.

Organizations will find that such meticulous and demanding customers can be a significant challenge as well as a drain on existing support systems.

- **There is a fight for "mindshare"—a battle to seek the attention of the Internet user**
The electronic investor seeks out knowledge and information and doesn't respond well to a sales pitch. They thirst for the knowledge that might help them to make the right decision—and are willing to search for it.

That is why we suggest that as you use the Internet to educate yourself, you seek out those sites that are education oriented, and stay away from the ones that are nothing more than a down and dirty sales pitch.

Marketers who want to reach these investors will have to refocus their efforts and move away from the glitzy promotions of the past.

Legal comfort is in short supply on the Net these days. As marketing managers and Internet gurus dream up new ways of delivering financial services on the World Wide Web, securities lawyers, compliance directors and regulators are struggling to come up with rules that protect firms and investors.

HAL LUX, "COMPLIANCE FOLLIES," *INSTITUTIONAL INVESTOR,* JULY 24, 1997

- **Generational marketing will become important**
Some people discount the impact that the Internet investor will play in the future. After all, they argue, the demographics and studies show that there aren't a lot of people who use the Internet today.

Yet consider the following. Today, we have an entire generation growing up with computers and the Internet. These kids do not suffer from a fear of computers. For them, the Internet is a source of wonder, entertainment, and perhaps most importantly, it is a useful information-gathering tool. For kids, media consists of television, radio, newspapers, magazines, and the Internet—not necessarily in that order.

The financial world is set to change as the younger generation—fully schooled in use of the tools of the Internet—comes to expect a world of finance where competing companies meet their needs online, and on their own terms.

These changing expectations—primarily, a desire by the customer for more information—are inevitable.

Changes Will Come to Financial Organizations

If the customer—the investor—changes dramatically, and the Internet continues its relentless march forward, what is the real impact on the world of finance?

No one can be quite sure, but it will be dramatic. We think, for example, that there are several certainties:

- **Massive structural change**

  One certain impact of the Internet will be a pronounced and dramatic change in the structure of the financial services industry.

  Consider, for example, what is set to happen in the mutual funds industry. Many mutual fund companies have organized themselves around "load" or commission-based mutual funds. They have structured themselves so that the sales of these funds can only occur through their agents, brokers, or personal financial planners, who earn a commission with each sale.

  If you read the business press, you'll see a lot of talk about the potential impact of "disintermediation." Disintermediation means that the middleman is beginning to lose value in the relationship between a business and its customers. In the mutual funds industry, the middleman is the broker, agent, or personal financial planner.

  Disintermediation is already occurring. Visit an online service such as E*Trade Canada, or any number of other online trading initiatives, and you can buy load funds online. You still pay the commission, but you don't have to deal with a third party broker or agent if you don't want to. Disintermediation is leading to a significant change in the structure of the financial services industry.

- **Reduced fees**

We suspect that disintermediation will result in reduced fees on the sale of investment products. The commission charged on "load" funds will drop dramatically, as more people take on responsibility for their own investment decisions.

The Internet has already had a dramatic impact on the commissions charged for the trading of stocks. As discussed in the previous chapter, online trading services allow you to buy and sell stocks on the Internet and save on the commission.

> **Sure, individual investors can always hunt around online for stock quotes and hot research prospects, and through discount brokerage firms such as Fidelity and Charles Schwab customers can use their PCs to place trades electronically. But though the PC is the ideal tool for monitoring the ebb and flow of Wall Street, the real savings for PC investors comes from cutting out the broker and trading directly.**
>
> CHRIS SHIPLEY, "MAXIMIZE YOUR INVESTMENT DIVIDENDS THE PC WAY," *PC MAGAZINE*, OCTOBER 25, 1994, V13 N18 P37(2)

- **Heightened competition**

The Internet also increases competition dramatically in the field of financial services. This is because it introduces a level of competition not previously seen by the world of finance.

The competition comes from several different fronts. Certainly geography becomes irrelevant with the Internet. Wells Fargo Bank, for example, is providing financial services in Canada by using the telephone, Internet, and other technologies, and doesn't have a physical branch in the country.

It isn't just geography—it is the fact that the Internet permits a form of time-compressed competition that has never been possible before. It also levels the playing field. For example, two relatively small players in the field—E*Trade Canada and Hongkong Bank of Canada—outflanked most of Canada's big brokerages and banks by being among the first to offer online stock trading services in Canada. With the Internet, everything is speeded up. In the scenario described above, all of the large banks had to quickly move ahead with their plans to provide online trading in order to stay competitive.

Competition can be a wild and wonderful thing. For example, travel to the Toronto Dominion Bank Web site on the Internet, and you can buy Royal Bank mutual funds. You could do this before the Internet, but inevitably, as more people use the Internet, it will increase the trend toward greater choice for the consumer.

For you, the consumer, all of this means more choice, lower fees, and better service. It's a heck of a deal!

Government Online

Certainly there is an upside to the Internet, as seen above, that generally works in favour of the consumer. Yet, every silver lining has a cloud—and when it comes to finance on the Internet, there certainly are some very significant downsides.

First and foremost, it might not make sense for you to try to make all of your retirement, RRSP, and investment decisions on your own. It might not be a smart thing for you to operate in a vacuum. Remember our comments from chapter 2 that you should not lose sight of the role of the investment professional. While financial professionals do charge to advise you on your financial affairs, the advice they provide is often well worth the money you spend. Even though the Internet provides you with a lot of information, that fact alone doesn't help you to make better investment decisions.

Then there is the issue of "cyberfraud." The wild, unregulated atmosphere of the Internet, coupled with the large numbers of amateur investors who venture online without thinking about the quality or accuracy of the information they are accessing, is leading to a number of problems, which we discussed in chapters 3 and 4.

It is time that the investment community in Canada—companies, regulatory authorities, and industry associations—becomes prepared to help the electronic investor deal with the complex world that is emerging on the Internet, particularly issues such as scams and fraud.

At the time we were finishing this book, there was very little online guidance being offered by Canada's securities regulators.

A Lack of Regulatory Action

When we released our book *Canadian Money Management Online—Personal Finance on the Net* in the fall of 1996, we expressed concern that Canadian financial institutions hadn't kept up-to-date with their U.S. counterparts.

In rather anguished frustration, we commented:

> **You will notice a lot of *American* content in this *Canadian* book.**
>
> **It was a bit shocking to us too.**
>
> **As we toured the Internet preparing this book, we quickly came to the conclusion that American-based financial organizations are far ahead of their Canadian counterparts in understanding the strategic potential of the Internet. Quite simply, we believe that many Canadian financial institutions deserve a failing grade with respect to their recognition and use of the Internet as a customer service and support tool.**
>
> JIM CARROLL, RICK BROADHEAD, *CANADIAN MONEY MANAGEMENT ONLINE—PERSONAL FINANCE ON THE NET*, (PRENTICE HALL, 1996) P. 289

Since that time, of course, many Canadian financial organizations have become aggressively involved in the Internet and have established many sophisticated and information-rich Web sites. They have finally come to realize that Internet-savvy customers are seeking electronic relationships with their financial institutions.

Yet sadly, government and regulatory authorities have not kept up-to-date in the same way. It's an appalling situation.

> We are adding a new section to our Web site which lists
> all the institutions that we regulate, and explains what
> it means to be regulated and supervised by OSFI. The
> purpose of this initiative is to help consumers under-
> stand the protection afforded them in dealing with
> Canadian regulated institutions, and some of the risks
> they face in dealing with unregulated institutions. In
> this new section of our Web site, we will offer guidance
> to consumers in making inquiries about financial insti-
> tutions they might be considering dealing with,
> whether those institutions are regulated or unregulat-
> ed. In a world in which it will be increasingly easy for
> foreign and unregulated institutions to offer services to
> Canadians without having a legal presence in Canada,
> we think that consumer education may be the best
> protection.
>
> REMARKS BY J.R.V. PALMER, SUPERINTENDENT OF FINANCIAL
> INSTITUTIONS CANADA TO THE CANADIAN INSURANCE
> ACCOUNTANTS ASSOCIATION CONFERENCE, MONTEBELLO, QUEBEC,
> SEPTEMBER 24, 1997

Comparing Two Countries

To understand the situation, let's take a look at who is
involved in regulating the securities industry in Canada
and the United States.

In Canada, provincial securities commissions such as
the Ontario Securities Commission and the British
Columbia Securities Commission regulate securities trading in their respective provinces. In addition, federal bodies such as the Office of the Superintendent of Financial
Institutions regulate federal financial institutions and
pension plans. Individual stock exchanges such as the
Toronto Stock Exchange and the Montreal Exchange
facilitate trading in equities and other securities; and
industry associations such as the Investment Dealers
Association of Canada, and the Investment Funds
Institute of Canada set standards for the Canadian investment community.

In the U.S., there are many similar organizations
involved in the regulation of financial activities. At the
top level, the SEC (Securities and Exchange

Commission) gets very involved in stock market regulation, with the assistance of various state securities regulators. Individual exchanges like the Nasdaq Stock Market and the New York Stock Exchange manage their own activities under the auspices of these regulatory bodies, and similar national associations like the National Association of Securities Dealers come up with industry-wide standards and practices.

It would make sense for any of these organizations in either country to get involved with, react to, and deal with the Internet, by providing investor education online, and by providing aggressive guidance, comments, and warnings with respect to online scams and frauds.

Indeed, given the extensive number of online frauds that are underway as discussed in chapter 4, it is critical that all of these organizations educate the many investors who are using the Internet for investment activities without a real understanding of the risks of doing so.

Certainly the many U.S. organizations we mention above are involved—but their Canadian counterparts are not. Let's look at a few examples of online investor education in the United States.

Most of the information we describe below is U.S.-centric, but a lot of it is general investment guidance, and hence is equally applicable to Canada. We suggest that you take the time to visit these sites and read the information they offer.

Securities and Exchange Commission

The Securities and Exchange Commission (SEC) enforces federal securities law in the United States. Visit the SEC Web site, and on the Investor Assistance and Complaints page you can access some extremely useful information that is designed to help you interact with the agency, learn more about investing online, find state securities regulators, and lodge a complaint or concern about what you see happening on the Internet.

The SEC site also features an Investor Alerts page with information about known scams and bulletins about investment fraud.

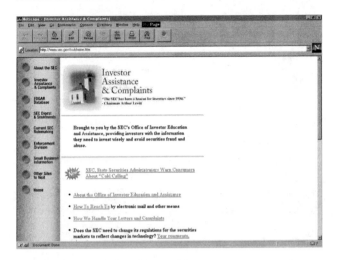

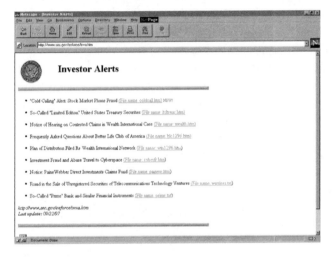

National Fraud Information Center

Another useful resource is the Web site of the National Fraud Information Center, a private initiative that works in cooperation with the National Association of Attorneys General and the U.S. Federal Trade Commission on issues such as telemarketing and Internet fraud. Its Web site (see page 288) provides general information about fraud and allows consumers to file an online incident report.

U.S. Federal Trade Commission

The U.S. Federal Trade Commission (FTC) is the U.S. government agency responsible for enforcing consumer protection and U.S. antitrust laws. The FTC has been very proactive in the fight against fraud. In the Consumer Line section of the Consumer Protection area of the site, read the publication titled "Psst...Wanna Buy a Bridge?" (you'll find it under "Education Campaigns"). It offers guidance on how to avoid investment fraud.

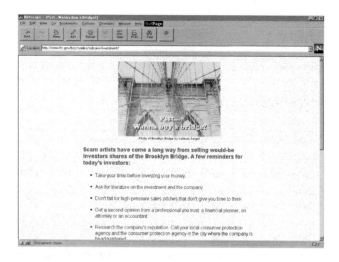

National Association of Securities Dealers

The National Association of Securities Dealers (NASD) is the self-regulatory organization for the securities indus-

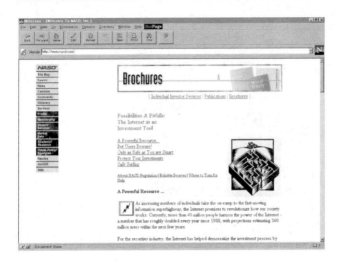

try in the United States. On its Web site it provides a variety of educational publications about safe investing.

A separate subsidiary of the NASD called NASD Regulation (NASDR) is responsible for protecting investors from securities fraud. On the NASDR Web site, under the "Investors Check Here" option, you can access a wealth of general investor education information, as well as warnings about the Internet and investing.

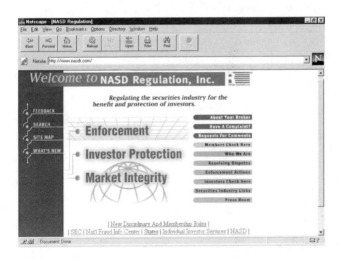

You should also take a look at the Investor Protection Trust, an organization that "provides independent, objective information needed by consumers to make informed investment decisions." The organization's Web site offers

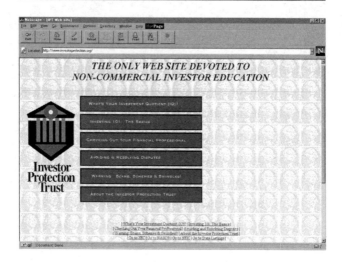

educational material designed to help investors avoid securities fraud.

Canadian Information? Hardly

Now, try to find the same type of investor education information on the Internet in Canada.

You won't—at least we weren't able to find much in late 1997. As we looked around, we were appalled at the lack of useful information from similar authorities and regulatory bodies in Canada.

Our kudos go to the British Columbia Securities Commission, which was, in late 1997, one of the few provincial securities commissions with an active—and

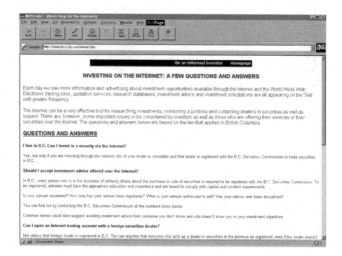

extremely useful—Web site. The section titled "Be an Informed Investor" is packed with information on how to avoid investment fraud on the Internet.

While various national investment associations in Canada have Web sites, we found their content to lack the important area of investor education.

What about the federal government? As we described in chapter 6, their site is difficult to navigate—when we went to look for information about retirement and the Canada Pension Plan, we found it terribly confusing. To get around, you seem to require an understanding of the organization chart of the federal government! We did find a consumer-oriented information site, but it had little information on the topic of the Internet and investing.

The Internet beckons to us individual investors as a level playing field that will put us on an equal footing with the institutional guys: instant access to price information, canny analysis of thousands of stocks, bonds and mutual funds at the touch of a button, bulletin boards where practically anything can be traded for, and, sooner or later, the ability to participate directly in the making of markets for all kinds of investments.

EDWARD H. BAKER, "OFF TO SEE THE WIZARD," *FINANCIAL WORLD*, JUNE 17, 1996 V165 N9 P78(2)

Our point is this—at the consumer level, Canadian regulatory authorities seem ill-prepared to deal with the Internet. They are nowhere near their U.S. counterparts in using the Internet to proactively educate and inform consumers and help them to avoid the pitfalls of using the Internet with respect to investment fraud. Given the dangers that we discussed in chapters 3 and 4, it is imperative that Canadian agencies, associations, and authorities get more involved in online investor education.

After all, isn't there something wrong when you can access the Russian Federal Commission for the Securities Market on the Internet (see page 292) quite easily—but can't access any similar major Canadian organization?

We encourage you to contact your provincial securities commission and support any efforts they may be

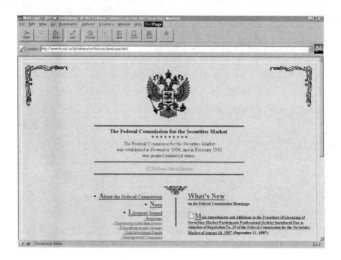

undertaking to educate Canadians about investing on the Internet (see Appendix A).

Web Sites Mentioned in This Chapter

British Columbia Securities Commission (BCSC)	www.bcsc.bc.ca
E*Trade Canada	www.canada.etrade.com
Federal Trade Commission (FTC)	www.ftc.gov
Government of Canada	www.gc.ca
Hongkong Bank of Canada	www.hkbc.ca
Investment Funds Institute of Canada	www.mutfunds.com/ific
Investor Protection Trust	www.investorprotection.org
National Association of Securities Dealers (NASD)	www.nasd.com
NASD Regulation (NASDR)	www.nasdr.com
National Fraud Information Center	www.fraud.org
Office of the Superintendent of Financial Institutions	www.osfi-bsif.gc.ca
Russian Federal Commission for the Securities Market	www.fe.msk.ru/infomarket/ fedcom/ewelcome.html
Toronto Dominion Bank	www.tdbank.ca
U.S. Securities and Exchange Commission (SEC)	www.sec.gov
Wells Fargo Bank	www.wellsfargo.com

How to Contact Your Regional Securities Regulator

This appendix provides the contact addresses and telephone numbers for the ten provincial and two territorial securities commissions in Canada. You can contact the securities regulator in your province or territory to report investment fraud on the Internet or to find out whether a specific individual is licensed to sell securities in your province/territory.

Provincial Securities Regulators

British Columbia

British Columbia Securities Commission
1100-865 Hornby Street
Vancouver, British Columbia
V6Z 2H4
Tel: (604) 660-4800
Fax: (604) 660-2688
Web site: **www.bcsc.bc.ca**
E-Mail: **inquiries@email.bcsc.bc.ca**

Alberta

Alberta Securities Commission
19th Floor, 10025 Jasper Avenue
Edmonton, Alberta
T5J 3Z5
Tel: (403) 427-5201
Fax: (403) 422-0777

Saskatchewan

Saskatchewan Securities Commission
800 1920 Broad Street
Regina, Saskatchewan
S4P 3V7
Tel: (306) 787-5645
Fax: (306) 787-5899

Manitoba

Manitoba Securities Commission
1130-405 Broadway
Winnipeg, Manitoba
R3C 3L6
Tel: (204) 945-2548
Fax: (204) 945-0330

Ontario

Ontario Securities Commission
20 Queen Street West
Suite 1800
Toronto, Ontario
M5H 3S8
Tel: (416) 597-0681
Fax: (416) 593-8241

Quebéc

Commission des valeur mobilières du Québec
800 Square Victoria, 17th Floor
P.O. Box 246
Stock Exchange Tower
Montreal, Québec
H4Z 1G3
Tel: (514) 873-5326
Fax: (514) 873-3090
Web site: **www.cvmq.gouv.qc.ca**

Nova Scotia

Nova Scotia Securities Commission
1690 Hollis Street
2nd Floor, Joseph Howe Building
P.O. Box 458
Halifax, Nova Scotia
B3J 2P8
Tel: (902) 424-7768
Fax: (902) 424-4625

New Brunswick

Office of the Administrator
Securities Branch
P.O. Box 5001
Saint John, New Brunswick
E2L 4Y9
Tel: (506) 658-3060
Fax: (506) 658-3059

Prince Edward Island

Government of Prince Edward Island
Department of Community Affairs and Attorney General
4th Floor, Shaw Building
95 Rochford Street
P.O. Box 2000
Charlottetown, Prince Edward Island
C1A 7N8
Tel: (902) 368-4552
Fax: (902) 368-5283
Web site: **www.gov.pe.ca/caag**

Newfoundland

Newfoundland Securities Division
Confederacies Building
P.O. Box 8700
St. John's, Newfoundland
A1B 4J6
Tel: (709) 729-4189
Fax: (709) 729-6187

Territorial Securities Administrators

Northwest Territories

Northwest Territories Securities Registry
Department of Justice
Government of the Northwest Territories
4903 - 49th Street
Yellowknife, Northwest Territories
X1A 2L9
Tel: (867) 873-7490
Fax: (867) 873-0243

Yukon Territory

Yukon Territory Corporate Affairs J-9
P.O. Box 2703
Whitehorse, Yukon
Y1A 2C6
Tel: (867) 667-5225
Fax: (867) 393-6251

INDEX

ALSO AVAILABLE FROM JIM CARROLL AND RICK BROADHEAD

1998 Canadian Internet New User's Handbook

Created for those with little or no familiarity with computers, the *1998 Canadian Internet New User's Handbook* is packed with up-to-date, jargon-free information that demystifies the Internet and gets you started—easily and effectively. From the basics of Net terminology and browsing to useful tips like how to make searching effective, this portable guide gives new users everything they need to make their first Internet experiences successful.

224 pages
$16.95
ISBN: 0-13-776410-3

Good Health Online: A Wellness Guide for Every Canadian

The amount of health and medical information available on the Internet is nothing less than stunning. But there are many dangers awaiting Canadians seeking health advice on the Net. To help you sort the science from the snake oil, Jim Carroll and Rick Broadhead have prepared this fascinating reference that no Canadian can afford to be without.

Good Health Online is ideal for those who want to pursue a healthy lifestyle, research a specific medical topic, or use the Internet as a tool for health communication. You will find this non-technical book to be a valuable addition to your Internet library. Produced in co-operation with Sympatico.

220 pages
$16.95
ISBN: 0-13-776428-6

1998 Canadian Internet Directory and Research Guide

The *1998 Canadian Internet Directory and Research Guide* provides details on some of the best Internet resources to be found across Canada. In addition, this year's edition features a new opening section dealing with one of the biggest challenges facing Canadian Internet users today — how to find quality information online!

This book includes a CD with an Internet tour and a FREE MONTH OF UNLIMITED INTERNET ACCESS from THE MOST™ online from Sprint Canada. Perfect for serious researchers or beginners just finding their way, the *1998 Canadian Internet Directory and Research Guide* is the ultimate guide to exploring cyberspace in Canada.

542 pages
$29.95
ISBN: 0-13-897547-7

1998 Canadian Internet Handbook

The *1998 Canadian Internet Handbook* stakes out new ground, establishing itself as the only Canadian reference work of its kind. Organized thematically, the book is divided into six sections that offer both hands-on guidance and insightful commentary on issues facing Internet users in Canada today. Themes covered include: Society and Culture, Legal and Government, Business, News and Media, Entertainment and Leisure, and Technology.

Brand new from cover to cover, the *1998 Canadian Internet Handbook* is the must-have reference work for all Canadian Internet users!

448 pages
$24.95
0-13-897554-X

The Future of Personal Finance

Presentations and Workshops by Rick Broadhead

••

Is your organization ready for the next millennium? As we approach the next century, one thing is certain—the Internet will forever change how financial markets operate. From online stock trading to cyberfraud, the Internet poses new challenges for financial advisors and individual investors alike.

Let bestselling author and management consultant Rick Broadhead guide your organization and your clients through the latest trends in online finance!

Rick has been retained as a keynote speaker, consultant, and workshop facilitator by organizations and professional associations across North America. His clients include Manulife Financial, the Financial Management Institute of Canada, Credit Union Central of Canada, Spectrum United Mutual Funds, the Canadian Institute of Actuaries, Mackenzie Financial Corporation, Microsoft Corporation, the Canadian Real Estate Association, the Municipal Electric Association, BC TEL, the Government of Alberta, and VISA International, where he was commissioned to prepare an overview of the strategic implications of the Internet for VISA's member financial institutions worldwide.

Rick's expertise has been sought by thousands of professionals in all areas of management, including marketing, advertising, human resources, corporate communications, sales, operations, and strategic planning. In addition, his consulting services have been used by many organizations seeking strategic and policy guidance with respect to the Internet and corporate Web site development/management.

Rick is also an instructor at York University's division of Executive Development in Toronto, where he has advised executives and senior managers from hundreds of leading North American firms and helped them to integrate the Internet into all facets of their businesses.

For further information about a presentation or workshop for your organization or conference, please contact Rick Broadhead using any of the methods below:

Telephone: (416) 487-5220
Fax: (416) 440-0175
E-Mail: rickb@inforamp.net

More detailed information about Rick Broadhead can be found on his World Wide Web site at
www.intervex.com

Finance in the 21st Century

Jim Carroll—Canada's leading financial visionary

∙∙

Organizations such as the Canadian Institute of Mortgage Brokers and Lenders, the Canadian Finance & Leasing Organization, the Canadian Treasury Management Association, the Investment Funds Institute of Canada, CIBC, Montreal Trust, Great-West Life, Scotia McLeod, the Royal Bank of Canada, Credit Union Central Canada, Credit Union Central Ontario, Canada Trust, Ernst & Young, and Yorkton Securities — all of them have engaged Jim Carroll to help them understand the implications of an economy in which business and customers are wired together through the Internet.

Jim Carroll, C.A., is a Chartered Accountant who excels at assisting organizations in understanding the future. He is the author of the critically acclaimed book, *Surviving the Information Age*, and he is in high demand by financial organizations seeking to position themselves for the economy of the new millenium.

He has the set the conference and meeting world on fire with his fascinating presentations that focus on the change being wrought on our social, economic, and business systems as a result of the emergence of what he calls "the wired world." Given the list of clients above, it is obvious his views on the future of finance are much sought after.

Mr. Carroll is represented by the National Speakers Bureau of Vancouver, B.C., an organization that represents Canada's leading speakers and thinkers.

Contact Jim by e-mail at jcarroll@jimcarroll.com, or by visiting his Web site at www.jimcarroll.com.

***For more information concerning personal
appearances by Jim Carroll, call:***

THE NATIONAL SPEAKERS BUREAU

IN CANADA 1-800-661-4110

INTERNATIONAL AND USA 1-604-224-2384

FAX 1-604-224-8906

INTERNET

speakers@nsb.com

To reach Mr. Carroll, call 905-855-2950

or fax 905-855-0269